The Jersey Shore

A Travel and Pleasure Guide

By Robert Santelli

THE EAST WOODS PRESS
CHARLOTTE, NORTH CAROLINA

Library of Congress Cataloging-in-Publication Data

Santelli, Robert.
    The Jersey Shore.

    Includes index.
    1. New Jersey—Description and travel—1981-   —Guide-books. 2.
Coasts—New Jersey—Guide-books.
I. Title
F132.3.S26 1986   917.49'0443   85-45695
ISBN 0-88742-066-4 (pbk.)

Cover illustration by Denise Cavalieri Fike.
Typeset by Raven Type.
Printed in the United States of America.

East Woods Press Books
Fast & McMillan Publishers, Inc.
429 East Boulevard
Charlotte, N.C. 28203

CONTENTS

For my mother and father,
Dorothy and Robert Santelli

ACKNOWLEDGEMENTS

For all their help and encouragement, I am indebted to the following: Betty Lou Applegate, Jack Aprill, Savo Balic, Pat Clarke, Wayne Hartman, Ranger Tom Hoffman, Pat Hyde, Connie Kosten, August Kraft, Jackie Kraft, Blair Learn, Sam Melton, Pauline Miller, Mary Roche, Detective Jack Santelli, Chief Ranger Pete Segge, Karen Siciliano, Charles Tomasello, Joanne Van Roden, John Wynbeek, Dora Visco and B. Michael Zuckerman, plus the Cape May County Historical Association, the Mid-Atlantic Center for the Arts, the Monmouth County Division of Tourism, the Monmouth County Historical Association, the Ocean County Historical Association, the Pinelands Cultural Society, the Renault Winery and the Southern Ocean County Chamber of Commerce.

A special thanks goes to Sally McMillan, Jennifer Mullennix, Judy Davis, Barbara Campbell and the rest of the East Woods Press crew; to Pam Kraft and Denise Fike, both of whom contributed artwork and ideas for the cover of this book; and to Jim and Janis White for their warm hospitality.

Finally, I owe an extra-special thanks to my agent and friend, Sandy Choron, for guiding me all the way; to my wife, Cindy, and my two daughters, Jaron and Jenna, for being most patient and loving down the stretch; and to my mother and father, for relocating the family to the Jersey Shore way back when.

Sandy
Hook

Highlands

Freehold ●

Long Branch

Allaire State Park ●

Asbury Park

Ocean Grove

Bay Head ●

Spring Lake

Point Pleasant
Beach

Toms River ●

Wharton State
Forest
(Pine Barrens) ●

Island Beach
State Park

Long Beach Island
Beach Haven

Atlantic City

Ocean City

Avalon
Stone Harbor
Wildwood

Cape May

New Jersey

INTRODUCTION

The ritual begins in earnest July Fourth weekend. Cars crammed with kids, coolers and suitcases; surfboards strapped on the roofs; boats on trailers pulled behind: these crowd New Jersey highways like the Garden State Parkway and the Atlantic City Expressway. Traffic thickens at the tollbooths and exits; impatience tears at the soul. The sounds of Bruce Springsteen and the E Street Band blare out of car stereos and provide the perfect soundtrack for the brewing excitement. It's summertime, and that means it's time to head to the Jersey Shore.

The annual summer migration to the Jersey Shore goes back further than the completion of the Parkway or Expressway, further even than the invention of the automobile. The original Shore vacationers, the Lenni Lenape Indians, began summering at the Shore centuries ago. Each summer many left their inland villages in June to escape the summer heat. At the Shore they fished, hunted and collected oysters, clams, berries and beach plums. Then in September they returned to their villages and made ready for the approach of winter.

Dutch and English farmers and whalers began settling at the Shore in the midseventeenth century. As word spread of the area's glorious summer climate, wealthy colonists from Philadelphia began visiting the Jersey Shore for the soothing qualities of the salt air and cooler temperatures. Eventually, guesthouses and inns were built to accommodate such visitors and their families. Thus, the Jersey Shore became the young nation's most popular summer resort, and Cape May and Long Branch, its very first resort towns.

Today, millions of people visit the Jersey Shore each summer for a variety of reasons. Most, of course, come for its sun, sand and surf. But others come for its restaurants, for its fishing and boating, for its nightlife and for its history. Tourists, for instance, from all 50 states and a number of foreign countries visit Victorian Cape May each year.

Some have more specialized interests, like gambling. Atlantic City alone annually attracts upwards of 25 million visitors to its luxurious casinos and its famous boardwalk. In just a few short years, Atlantic City has overtaken Las Vegas as the gambling and entertainment capital of America, and maybe even the world.

Some visitors spend their entire vacations at the Shore, residing in tiny bungalows or beach cottages that have been in the family for years.

Others take day or weekend trips to Sandy Hook, Seaside Heights or Sea Isle City. Mostly they come by car. Some take trains or buses. But come they do. Thanks to the Jersey Shore, tourism is now New Jersey's second largest industry.

The Jersey Shore coastline is 127 miles long. It extends from the northernmost tip of Sandy Hook, which continues to grow each year due to new sand deposits carried by swift ocean currents, to the southernmost tip of Cape May Point, a tiny beach town that sits in the shadow of the Cape May Point Lighthouse. In between these two boundaries is a rich, exciting diversity of landscape and activities that goes far beyond the standard allure of the Jersey Shore.

It is indeed true and certainly no secret that New Jersey's beaches are among the finest on the Eastern Seaboard. As already mentioned, they are the Shore's prime attraction as they well should be. But beyond the beaches and sand dunes, the boardwalks and bungalows, there is more, so much more, to see, to do and to experience that it's no exaggeration to say the Shore has something for everyone.

Here's proof. Are you a history buff? The Shore is steeped in Revolutionary War drama, Victorian memories, pirate legends and lore, and maritime adventure on the open sea. Like to shop for antiques? Try the Route 9 corridor, sometimes referred to as "Antique Alley" on the way to Cape May. Enjoy museums? The Cape May County Museum can keep you fascinated for hours. So can the Twin Lights Museum. It recalls the bygone days of the U.S. Life Saving Service and the wireless telegraphy experiments of Guglielmo Marconi. The National Broadcasters Hall of Fame brings you back to the era of Amos 'n' Andy. And you won't see a more unusual collection of seashells than what you'll find at Ocean City's Seashell Museum.

Interested in lighthouses? The Jersey Shore possesses some of the oldest in America as well as some of the most famous. Visit the Sandy Hook Lighthouse, or Old Barney or Twin Lights. Feel like camping or canoeing in a true wilderness area? Spend some time in the Pine Barrens, one of the great remaining forest areas on the Atlantic Coast. What about car racing? Set aside Saturday nights and venture to Raceway Park or Wall Stadium. Perhaps horse racing is more your style. Then it's off to Monmouth Park, Freehold Raceway or Atlantic City Raceway. Is rock 'n' roll in your soul? Asbury Park has one of America's great music halls, the Stone Pony, proving ground for Bruce Springsteen and the E Street Band, Southside Johnny and the Jukes, and many others.

I could go on, but you get the picture. With such diversity comes choice, and often too many choices result in indecision. Everything looks and sounds good. You have two days or two weeks to spend at the Jersey Shore. Where should you go? What should you see? What should you do?

Questions like these prompted the writing of *The Jersey Shore, A Travel and Pleasure Guide*. The book is not a definitive guide to the

Jersey Shore. It wasn't intended to be, however. Rather, its primary function is to serve as a companion to one's discovery of the Jersey Shore: of its beaches and boardwalks and beach towns, yes, but also of its many other wonderful traits and attractions.

During the course of researching material to include in *The Jersey Shore*, I traveled up and down the coast and visited virtually every town from Sandy Hook to Cape May Point. Having grown up on the Jersey Shore and worked there as a writer and teacher, I was aware of all its glowing attractions and a good many of the more unheralded ones, too. Yet, I still found much that I never knew existed.

Driving or bicycling or walking through towns such as Sea Bright, Bay Head, Leed's Point, Atlantic City and Stone Harbor; boating on Barnegat Bay and the Manasquan River; hiking along trails in Allaire State Park and through the marshland at the Wetlands Institute; and surfing at Sandy Hook and Seaside Heights made me realize that the Shore was truly diverse in its form, its features and its culture. But despite this, I also uncovered a subtle sense of unity, which, I hope, comes through in the book.

The chapters are arranged geographically, from north to south. Although each chapter deals with a specific section of the Shore—the North Jersey Shore, the Barnegat Peninsula, Long Beach Island, and so on—and though each possesses its own personality and highlights, it is the Atlantic Ocean and its grand influence that bonds these regions. Nearly all activities and attractions, historic sites and natural areas are somehow, some way linked with others by way of their relationship with the ocean. The only possible exception is the chapter entitled "The Inland Shore." But even there you'll find ties to the sea in one form or another.

All nine chapters contain a potpourri of information and personal observations designed first to introduce, and then help to select, places to see and things to do. Two chapters, Atlantic City and Cape May, deal almost exclusively with those two immensely popular resort towns. There was so much to write about them, that they insisted on their own chapters.

At the conclusion of each chapter you will find a list of recommended restaurants. I ate at many of the ones mentioned and many not mentioned, too. But I did not eat at all of them. To eat at and judge *every* restaurant on the Jersey Shore would have been an impossible task. There are so many—literally hundreds—that the time it would have taken to sample meals at every one of them would have curtailed research in other more important areas.

Yet dining is an essential and quite enjoyable part of any vacation or visit to the Jersey Shore. Thus, to provide some sort of guidance, I researched what restaurant critics had to say about Shore restaurants, considered readers' restaurant polls in reputable magazines such as *New Jersey Monthly*, carefully listened to word of mouth, and finally, used my own taste buds and sense of epicurean quality wherever I could to judge what restaurants should be recommended and which should not. What resulted are nine separate restaurant lists which a visitor can choose from and be reasonably assured of a fine meal anywhere on the Shore.

I also included a category concerning the price of meals, albeit, please bear in mind menus and prices can and do easily change. The price code is based on dinner prices only. Inexpensive means an *average* meal (minus drinks, remember) costs about $8 or under. Moderate means $9 to $12. Expensive means over $12.

As for lodgings, there are almost as many hotels, motels, inns and guesthouses at the Jersey Shore as there are restaurants. A large percentage of them, however, contain standard accommodations, namely, a room blandly furnished and decorated, complete with a color television and bible. Many have pools and/or beach privileges. Almost all have overly familiar nautical names and themes: Sea Drift, Seascape, Driftwood, Sunset View, Ocean View, Bay View, Captain Jack's, Ebb Tide and High Tide.

DID YOU KNOW THAT ... THERE IS A TOWN CALLED JERSEY SHORE? STRANGELY ENOUGH, IT IS LOCATED IN PENNSYLVANIA, NOT NEW JERSEY.

It would have been pointless to attempt individualized descriptions of such hotels and motels, since so many seem to have come from the same mold. Also, without actually having stayed overnight in each and every one, it would have been unfair to try to rate them. So I didn't.

There are, though, some truly special lodgings at the Jersey Shore. The grand hotels of Atlantic City, for example, and the charming bed and breakfasts of Cape May deserve special attention and get it. For those not wishing to indulge in luxury while in the Atlantic City area or experience Cape May's Victorian bed and breakfast splendor, but still requiring a place to stay for the night or week, I have provided the addresses and telephone numbers of tourist centers, chambers of commerce and accommodations agencies, which will assist you in finding the lodging that best suits your taste and budget.

Finally, I was reluctant to include admission fees to places like museums, beaches and parks simply because such information is apt to change and could date the book prematurely. In the case of meals, there is room to play with: an *average* meal costs *between* ... But with admission fees, one is dealing with precise figures. Therefore, I merely mentioned that an admission fee is required to gain entrance and left it at that.

Despite such limitations, what *is* included in the book should be more than enough for you to begin your discovery of the Jersey Shore. So set aside preconceived notions. Gas up the car. Pack your bathing trunks, hiking shoes, fishing pole, camera and suntan lotion. There's more at the Shore than you think.

Robert Santelli
October, 1985

1. THE BAYSHORE AND SANDY HOOK

Years ago, the communities nestled along the southern edge of Raritan and Sandy Hook bays were considered an integral part of the Jersey Shore. Before completion of the Garden State Parkway in 1957, visitors from North Jersey and New York would drive down Route 35 and then onto Route 36 to spend a day or a week on the Bayshore. Before that, steamships would bring passengers to Keansburg and the Highlands area from lower Manhattan.

Fishermen flocked to Keyport, Port Monmouth and Leonardo. In Keansburg, families would rent summer bungalows and enjoy the amusement rides and penny arcades when they tired of the sun and sand. During the evening, nightclubs would be alive with music. Those driving further east on Route 36 spent summer days in Atlantic Highlands and Highlands.

The opening of the Parkway registered a heavy blow to the Bayshore tourist trade, however. The new highway provided easy access to resort communities in southern Monmouth and Ocean counties. Suddenly, even Atlantic City did not seem all that far away any more. Many vacationers, therefore, began bypassing the Bayshore for the beaches and boardwalks in Shore towns such as Manasquan, Point Pleasant Beach and Seaside Heights.

But perhaps even more crippling to Bayshore tourism was the pollution that flowed out of the refineries and factories on the northern and western shores of Raritan Bay. Such unchecked discharge into the bay ultimately made it one of New Jersey's dirtiest waterways.

Sandy Hook Bay, which lay further east, was also victimized by pollution. The fish and shellfish once caught and eaten in abundance by anglers were now condemned. Swimming in Raritan Bay was prohibited. In Sandy Hook Bay it was frequently frowned upon. Without such resources, the Bayshore was all but forgotten by many Jersey Shore visitors. And with good reason.

Today, things are getting better. In 1985 the state unveiled its "Bay-shore Development Plan" to aid local Bayshore communities in improving their economies, and towns like Highlands are experiencing somewhat of a resurgence in their tourist trade. Historical sites such as Twin Lights, first-rate seafood restaurants and the superb views found atop Mt. Mitchill (also spelled Mt. Mitchell) and the bluffs overlooking Sandy Hook Bay are attracting new visitors.

Raritan Bay is somewhat less polluted than it was 15 years ago, but it is still not advisable to swim there or eat fish or shellfish caught in

DID YOU KNOW THAT ... MT. MITCHILL IS THE HIGHEST POINT,
NOT ONLY ON THE JERSEY SHORE, BUT ON THE ENTIRE ATLAN-
TIC SEABOARD? IT STANDS 266 FEET ABOVE SEA LEVEL.

it. Sandy Hook Bay is cleaner and safer; people do swim in it. But it
still suffers on occasion.

One activity, however, was not seriously affected by the Bayshore's
demise: boating. Boating is still much enjoyed on Raritan and Sandy
Hook bays as these bodies of water provide both shelter from and access
to the Atlantic Ocean to the east. A number of marinas, including a
state marina, can be found in Bayshore towns, and all remain very busy
in spring, summer and fall.

Some people still come to the Bayshore out of habit. Tradition seems
to count for something here, even though a town like Keansburg, for
example, is like a museum piece from an era long gone that simply
hasn't received the care and attention it should have received.

It's a place where dance pavilions were once filled with GIs home
on leave and girls eager for a man in uniform. It's a place where perhaps
our parents or grandparents would come for that much-deserved
week-long vacation. It's a place that had its day in the sun, so to speak,
and is now only filled with faded memories.

But if all this is true, why, one might wonder, is Route 36, that ribbon
of highway that runs parallel with the Bayshore, bumper to bumper
with cars on Saturday mornings in July and August? And why is it
even worse, or so it always seems, on Sunday afternoons and evenings
in the summer when thousands of cars inch their way west to the
entrance of the Parkway? The answer is simple: Sandy Hook.

Part of the Gateway National Recreation Area (which also includes
the Jamaica Bay Wildlife Refuge in Brooklyn and Queens, Breezy Point
in Queens and Great Kills Park and Miller Field in Staten Island),
Sandy Hook, in recent years, has become one of the most popular
recreation spots in the New York–New Jersey Metropolitan area.
Approximately 20,000 people a day converge on this sandspit at the
top of the Jersey Shore each summer day. It's not uncommon for park
rangers at Sandy Hook to close the park as early as ten o'clock in the
morning on hot summer weekends and holidays to avoid extensive
overcrowding and abuse of the facilities there.

Sandy Hook's close proximity to the metropolitan area and the vast
number of things to see and do there make it the pride of the North
Jersey Shore. Here's a sampling of activities enjoyed at Sandy Hook:
swimming, surfing, sunbathing, self-guided nature and history tours,
fishing, beachcombing, bicycling, bird-watching, girl- and boy-
watching, ship-sighting and star-gazing.

Few areas of the Jersey Shore north of Atlantic City offer so much
to visitors, not only during the summer, but throughout the year. No
longer is Sandy Hook simply a place to go when the sun is shining

and the temperature 80 degrees. Many of the activities mentioned above and detailed below are year-round activities. And those who love walking a wind-swept beach before or after summer will find Sandy Hook irresistible.

One thing a visitor to the Bayshore and Sandy Hook should keep in mind, however: this area is almost exclusively a day-visit area. Unfortunately, you'll find few quality hotels or motels in the Bayshore vicinity, and practically no inns, bed and breakfasts or guesthouses that meet minimum standards. There are no places to pitch a tent and camp, either. Those who come long distances to enjoy Sandy Hook or the Highlands should look for accommodations in such neighboring beach towns as Sea Bright, Monmouth Beach, Long Branch or even Asbury Park. Generally speaking, the farther you go south of Sandy Hook, the better your chances are of finding a variety of accommodations to pick and choose from.

During the summer, those who come for the day should plan to get to Sandy Hook and vicinity as early as possible to guarantee admission. There is much to see and do, and there are many fine restaurants to sit and sample some of New Jersey's finest seafood.

KEYPORT

Keyport lies at the crossroads of Routes 35 and 36 on the southwestern shore of Raritan Bay. It is largely a residential area with little or no facilities for tourists. Boaters, however, are fond of the town's marinas, most of which are located on Front Street. Also found there is the **Keyport Fishing Pier**, a popular spot for local and visiting anglers alike, and a good place to view the boats in Raritan Bay.

What To Do with Fish After You Catch Them

1. If you plan to take home what you catch, make sure you have a cooler full of ice on hand. Do not use garbage cans; they don't have drains to allow melted ice and water to escape. If the fish you catch lies in such water, it will quickly lose its flavor and perhaps even spoil.
2. Clean your catch as soon as possible. Cleaning a fish takes practice. And practice makes perfect. The key to cleaning a fish? A very sharp, thin-bladed fillet knife. Fishermen experienced in cleaning fish say a semiflexible blade is best. You'll also need a scaler (especially if you plan to keep the skin), a board on which to clean and scrape the fish, and plastic bags.
3. Thoroughly clean the fish of slime, innards and scales. Wash the fish clean and make sure no blood is left in the cavity. Rid fish such as tuna and bluefish of brown meat just beneath the skin; this is where the oil is found that gives improperly cleaned fish a "fishy" taste.
4. Pack your cleaned fish in plastic bags. Make sure there is plenty of ice in the cooler. Don't overstock fish in your cooler at the expense of ice.
5. Upon arriving home, remove the fish from cooler and place into freezer if you do not intend to eat immediately.

KEANSBURG

Although Keansburg caters to tourism more than Keyport, there are no recommended lodgings or restaurants in the town. Thus, the visitor should plan for an afternoon or evening outing, and little more.

The primary attraction is the **Keansburg Amusement Park**. Though often referred to as a boardwalk, there are no wooden planks to stroll on. Instead, a black asphalt walkway allows the visitor to wander through a maze of old-fashioned concession stands and amusement rides.

Compared to Jersey Shore resorts like Wildwood and Ocean City, Keansburg is in desperate need of a facelift. But therein lies its appeal to some. You'll find seemingly ancient kiddie rides, a water slide, wheels of fortune, a sausage and peppers stand here, a pizza parlor there and, believe it or not, an eatery called **Terminal Lunch**. With the right frame of mind, Keansburg can be fun. Not recommended, however, for those with high-brow intentions or the need for first-class facilities.

BELFORD

Belford is a blue-collar community of mostly commercial fishermen. It is home to one of three commercial fishing fleets on the Jersey Shore. (The other two are in Point Pleasant Beach and Cape May.) Those interested in viewing up close the rigors and hardships of commercial fishing will want to pay a visit to the docks on Main Street where the fleet is moored when not out at sea. Photographers, amateurs and professionals alike, will find the scenery especially interesting.

The **Belford Seafood Co-op**, located at the junction of Main Street and Port Monmouth Road, is where the catch of the day ends up. The Co-op distributes fish to area restaurants and to others in northern New Jersey and New York City. One can purchase fish here somewhat cheaper and fresher than at fish markets beyond those at the Jersey Shore. None of the fish, however, are cleaned or cut into fillets if you buy them right off the dock. Best bet: ling and whiting, and, when available, lobster. The Co-op is open seven days a week. Call (201) 787-6500 for more information.

LEONARDO

East of Belford is Leonardo. This and Atlantic Highlands and Highlands are the three communities that sit on the southern shore of Sandy Hook Bay. Leonardo is another important Bayshore town for boaters, since the Leonardo State Marina is located here. A popular launch area for those without permits or privileges at private basins and marinas, Leonardo, as one might expect, is quite busy during the summer.

For those wishing to launch a boat, stop first at the marina's main office and purchase a launch ticket, good for one boat for one day.

Annual permits are available at the office, too, and well worth it if you plan to launch from Leonardo on a regular basis. The marina is open year-round and 24 hours a day during the summer. Boaters wishing berths in the marina, take note. According to marina officials, there's a five-year waiting list in all three boat-size categories: 30, 40 and 50 foot.

Lighthouse buffs will want to visit **Conover Beacon**, one of three lighthouses in the Bayshore/Sandy Hook area. (The other two are Twin Lights in Highlands and the Sandy Hook Lighthouse at Fort Hancock on Sandy Hook.) Built in 1856, Conover Beacon was one of a pair of light-towers that helped guide boat captains into the Chapel Hill Channel in Sandy Hook Bay. The second light-tower in the pair is located a few miles from the coast, in Middletown. Known as the Chapel Hill Beacon, it, too, was built in 1856. However, since it now rests on private property, it is no longer possible to visit. You can, though, find photos of the light-tower as well as a keeper's log at the Twin Lights Museum.

Conover Beacon is located on Sandy Hook Bay at the end of Leonardo Road. Its red and white tower is quite simple in design. But in days gone by, its importance was great as navigation in Sandy Hook Bay would have proven hazardous without it and the Chapel Hill Beacon beaming brightly through darkness and fog.

ATLANTIC HIGHLANDS

People often confuse Atlantic Highlands as being part of Highlands or vice versa. Despite the similarity in names and the close proximity to each other—they are Bayshore neighbors—Atlantic Highlands and Highlands are separate communities.

Whereas Highlands concerns itself with the Jersey Shore tourist trade in the form of top-notch seafood restaurants, the Twin Lights Museum, and plenty of party fishing boats to choose from for a day on the ocean with rod and reel, Atlantic Highlands is primarily a residential community and does not see itself as a tourist town. Even so, the town does have a very fine municipal marina and its own fleet of party boats. It also possesses a few things to do that should not be overlooked by those visiting the area or passing through on their way to Sandy Hook.

Things to Do
Go Fishing on Sandy Hook Bay or the Atlantic Ocean. Small skiffs, rowboats and small motorboats are for rent at places like **Frank's Boats** ((201) 291-2275) on Simon Lake Drive, the road that runs parallel with the harbor. A nearby tackle shop sells bait. If ocean fishing is more your fancy, plan to fish on one of the many party boats that make daily trips to fishing holes offshore. All the boats have signs posted on their respective docks, which give essential information such as departure times, price of the trip and what kinds of fish are running.

Take a Ride on Scenic Drive. Scenic Drive is actually Ocean

Boulevard. It extends from First Avenue in downtown Atlantic Highlands, just a couple of streets south of the Atlantic Highlands Municipal Marina, to Mt. Mitchill Scenic Overlook. The drive is short (3–4 miles), but the views are excellent. Sandy Hook, Sandy Hook Bay, lower Manhattan, parts of Brooklyn, including Coney Island, and even southern Long Island can be seen. On an especially clear day, New York's Twin Towers and the Empire State Building are within sight. Be sure to stop at the vista in front of the **Hofbrauhaus Restaurant**; it has the best view on Scenic Drive, excluding the one from Mt. Mitchill.

Visit Henry Hudson's Spring. The Italian explorer Giovanni de Verrazano was the first European to explore the Sandy Hook area and Raritan Bay in 1524. Henry Hudson, nearly a century later (1609), not only further explored the area, but also sent some of his men searching for fresh water in what is today Atlantic Highlands. What they found was a spring that the Lenni Lenape Indians used for their fresh water needs.

While on Ocean Boulevard (Scenic Drive), turn left onto Lawrie Road, then left onto Hilton Road to Bay Side Drive. This will lead you to what is known as Henry Hudson's Spring or Henry Hudson's Spout. Water still trickles from the spout in the rocks, and a marker explains the historical importance of the site.

Visit Mt. Mitchill Scenic Overlook. Part of the Monmouth County Parks System, Mt. Mitchill offers a majestic view of Sandy Hook and Raritan bays and the lower part of the New York skyline. As already mentioned, Scenic Drive ends at Mt. Mitchill.

Mt. Mitchill has pay binoculars available for even better views and a small picnic area for public use, complete with barbecue pits. A plaque located under the four flagpoles is dedicated to the Americans held hostage in Iran in 1980; it was put there while they were still being held captive.

Highlands

Highlands is the seafood capital of the north Jersey Shore. It has more fine seafood restaurants and small chowder-style shanties than anywhere else in the area, and nearly all of them have nautical settings of some sort. Some even have docks on the premises, so those arriving by boat can moor there.

Most of the major restaurants in Highlands are well-known. Few serious seafood lovers have not heard about or eaten at **Bahr's**, **Longjohn's** or the **Clam Hut**, or had clam chowder at **Moby's**. And yet, a number of other not-so-known restaurants serve equally delicious seafood dishes. **Doris and Ed's**, for instance, is about as good a seafood restaurant as you're apt to find.

Highlands, however, has more to offer visitors than a belly full of fresh, tasty seafood. Take a ride along the waterfront, and you'll discover more party fishing boats than any visiting deep-sea fisherman will ever

DID YOU KNOW THAT ... JAMES FENIMORE COOPER'S NOVEL, *THE WATER WITCH*, ALTHOUGH WRITTEN IN PARIS, IS SET IN HIGHLANDS? COOPER WAS A FREQUENT VISITOR TO THE TOWN IN THE 1820s.

need. Before you select one, however, be sure to ask around as to where different boats are currently doing much of their fishing, and check this information against the fish stories you'll undoubtedly hear dockside.

Most boats fishing out of Highlands or Atlantic Highlands in the summer will be going for bluefish, fluke, weakfish or porgy. During the winter, ling, cod and whiting make up the main catch. For half-day trips and overnight trips, party boats will venture as far as 40 miles offshore in search of fish.

Highlands is also full of history. As early as 1663, the area was being considered for settlement by Dutch and British colonists. In 1678 Richard Hartshorne, for whom the woods in nearby Middletown are named, acquired use rights for Sandy Hook from the Indians for thirteen shillings. He then purchased the Highlands area from the original English settlers there.

During the Revolutionary War, the Sandy Hook/Highlands vicinity was controlled by British loyal to the Crown. When they captured a Monmouth County Continental Militia commander, Capt. Joshua Huddy, they imprisoned him and eventually took him to Highlands where he was hanged for a murder he did not commit. Visitors can view a marker set at the hanging spot in Huddy's honor. It's located in the park on Waterwitch Avenue that bears the name of the patriot.

In the mid-1800s, Twin Lights was built atop Highlands. One of the most powerful lighthouses in the world at the time, its light could be seen as far as 70 miles at sea, said sailors. It was also here that Guglielmo Marconi demonstrated the first commercial use of wireless telegraphy in 1899. Today Twin Lights is a museum and state historical site, and should be considered a "must visit" for anyone coming to Highlands. (See below for detailed information on the Twin Lights Museum.)

Tourism was a thriving business in Highlands as far back as a century ago. In the early 1900s, hotels and inns were found on almost every street, restaurants were overflowing with patrons, and Highlands's bay and river beaches were crowded with swimmers and beachwalkers. Highlands was the perfect day-trip or weekend outing for New Yorkers. There was a pier in Atlantic Highlands where steamships from Manhattan would dock and unload passengers. A seahore railroad line passed

DID YOU KNOW THAT ... GERTRUDE EDERLE, THE FIRST WOMAN TO SWIM THE ENGLISH CHANNEL, SPENT HER SUMMERS IN HIGHLANDS AND LEARNED TO SWIM THERE? SHE SWAM THE CHANNEL IN 1926. A HIGHLANDS PARK IS NAMED IN HER HONOR.

through Highlands and took visitors to other Jersey Shore resorts like Long Branch and Red Bank. It was Highlands's golden era, to be sure, and the town profited immensely from it.

Today, however, things are different. When the steamships stopped coming in the early 1930s, much of the town's tourist trade began to dry up. One by one, the hotels and guesthouses went out of business. Fortunately, Highlands held on to its reputation as a good place to fish and an even better place to eat seafood. But today, if you visit Highlands and plan to stay overnight, you'll have little luck locating decent lodging. **Conners' Hotel**, a pleasant family-run operation (326 Shore Drive, (201) 872-1500) is the only recommended accommodation in Highlands.

Despite the shabbiness of some sections of town, a sense of maritime history drifts through the streets of Highlands, which helps one recall the town's once proud seashore character. Walking or driving by the waterfront, you can easily imagine a healthy, turn-of-the-century resort filled with shops and visitors, with boats in the harbor and steamships in the bay.

Things to Do

Visit the Twin Lights Historical Site. A visit to Twin Lights is an ideal way to spend an afternoon followed by dinner at any of the fine seafood restaurants just down the hill. The museum and related exhibits at Twin Lights provide the visitor with the story of not only one of America's most fascinating lighthouse structures, but also the best collection perhaps anywhere of photographs and equipment used by the U.S. Life Saving Service, forerunner of the U.S. Coast Guard. In addition, there's an excellent exhibit that deals with Guglielmo Marconi's famous demonstration of wireless telegraphy and superb examples of the unusual hunting and fishing boats built at the Jersey Shore many years ago.

Plan to visit Twin Lights on a clear day. Sitting on the bluffs overlooking the Shrewsbury River 200 feet above sea level, Twin Lights, like nearby Mt. Mitchill, offers a wonderful panoramic view of New York, Sandy Hook and surrounding waters. Those wishing to spend the better part of a day at Twin Lights might want to picnic on the grounds. Facilities for picnicking include tables and barbecue grills.

If you're coming from the Garden State Parkway and Route 36, you can reach Twin Lights by turning right just prior to the Highlands Bridge, which connects Highlands with Sandy Hook. This will lead you to Portland Avenue. Bear right onto Highlands Avenue and follow the signs to the entrance of Twin Lights.

The biggest attraction at Twin Lights is, of course, the double lighthouse. It is, as you'll quickly discover, not your typical lighthouse. Looking at it from the bottom of Highlands or from Sandy Hook, one might think the two tall towers to be those of an old fortress. The structure consists of the two lighthouse towers connected by a long, thin building, which once contained quarters for the keepers of Twin Lights and their families. Today, the building is the home of the Twin Lights museum and auditorium.

Look closely at the lighthouse towers, and you'll see that despite the term *twin lights*, they're not *really* twins. No one knows for certain why architect Joseph Lederle chose to give the North Tower an octagonal shape and the South Tower a square one, but he did. One should also know that the present Twin Lights were constructed in 1861-1862 and are not the original towers that stood atop Highlands. Those were built in 1828 and consisted of two unconnected towers.

Visitors to Twin Lights are permitted to climb the North Tower, which, although the lighthouse was officially decommissioned in 1949, still blinks from dusk to dawn. The steps are steep and narrow—there are 64 of them—but the climb is worth your effort. As one might expect, the view from the top is superb. Special permission is needed to enter the South Tower.

After climbing the North Tower and enjoying the vista, plan to spend some time in the Twin Lights Museum. It is one of the best museums on the Jersey Shore and contains a number of interesting artifacts, photographs, documents and exhibits that chronicle the history of Twin Lights. There's also a working replica of Guglielmo Marconi's original wireless telegraph equipment.

In 1899, due to the Twin Lights' high elevation and proximity to New York, Marconi built the first wireless telegraph antenna in the United States on the grounds. His wireless telegraphy equipment enabled the citizens of Highlands to receive the first information about the return of Commodore Dewey's fleet after its victory at Manila Bay during the Spanish-American War. The same equipment also enabled the *New York Herald* to be the first newspaper to report news of the 1899 America's Cup Race off the North Jersey Shore.

Other interesting exhibits in the museum include the one that deals with the history of the U.S. Life Saving Service. (See below for more information on the U.S. Life Saving Service.) Be certain to check out the Francis Life Car, an iron container that was used to bring people ashore from sinking, wrecked ships. There's also an interesting collection of locally built skiffs that were used for hunting and fishing in bays and rivers along the coast. On display are examples of the Sea Bright Skiff, the Shrewsbury Crab Skiff and the Barnegat Sneakbox.

But the most fascinating exhibit is the one that deals with the boat, *The Fox*. In 1896, *The Fox* was the first known boat to cross the Atlantic Ocean without the use of sail or steam. Two Highlands fishermen, Frank Samuelson and George Harbo, accepted the challenge of rowing across the Atlantic initiated by the New York magazine, the *Police Gazette*. They completed their journey in 62 days and earned ten thousand dollars in prize money put up by the New York magazine's publisher, Richard Fox (hence the name of the boat).

The men rowed from New York harbor to LeHavre, France. A replica of *The Fox* is in the museum, plus a series of paintings dealing with their voyage by maritime artist, Henry Luhrs, and copies of photographs and equipment used by the men.

Just outside the museum you'll see a boathouse. It was the first lifeboat station built on Sandy Hook opposite Spermaceti Cove. Constructed in 1849, one year after the U.S. Life Saving Service was founded and began rescuing shipwreck victims off the New Jersey Coast, it is the only one remaining of the original eight Life Saving Service boathouses.

Approximately 50 yards south of the boathouse and main entrance to the museum is the Twin Lights Generating Station, which now contains an original Fresnal lighthouse lens from the South Tower as well as an audio program that explains the intricate development of the lens.

Just across from the generating station is the Twin Lights Auditorium where visitors can view films and slide shows depicting the history of Twin Lights and neighboring Sandy Hook. The films and slide shows are usually shown on weekends and holidays when attendance at Twin Lights is heaviest or upon request. Park staff announce what film or slide show will be shown as well as the starting time over the park's public address system.

After visiting the generating station, walk around to the front of the Twin Lights building, the side facing the ocean, where there is another audio program at the brick overlook. It gives a brief but valuable historical sketch of the Highlands area and should not be missed. Those not wishing or unable to climb the North Tower will want to check the view here.

Just behind the overlook is a cannon. Dubbed the Twin Lights Mystery Cannon after its discovery during a renovation of the original Twin Lights in 1841, its purpose at Twin Lights is still not known.

Finally, on the north side of the Twin Lights structure you'll find one last audio program, this one explaining the story of Marconi and his work at Twin Lights, told by his daughter, Gioia Marconi Braga. This is located just above the picnic area, on the spot where Marconi's antenna stood.

Twin Lights is open 9 a.m. to 5 p.m. daily. Site grounds are open until sunset. The park is closed on Thanksgiving, Christmas, and New Year's Day. There is no admission charge. For more information, call (201) 872-1814 or (201) 872-1886.

The U.S. Life Saving Service

What would become known as the U.S. Life Saving Service began in 1848 after a New Jersey Congressman, Dr. William A. Newell, convinced the federal government to appropriate $10,000 to construct and equip lifesaving stations along the Jersey Shore.

New Jersey was the logical birthplace for the U.S. Life Saving Service. During the eighteenth and nineteenth centuries, before the advantages afforded ship captains with the use of modern navigational equipment, there was a large number of shipwrecks off the Jersey Coast. Many people lost their lives and millions of dollars worth of cargo went to the bottom.

Although shipwrecks occurred with unsettling regularity from Cape Cod to Cape Hatteras, New Jersey recorded some of the worst disasters and proportionately more of them. The reason was twofold. First, New York possessed one of the country's busiest harbors with a large amount of ship traffic even back then, and much of it passed along the Jersey coast. Second, the Jersey coast was notorious for its dangerous, shifting sandbars and shoals. When the wind blew out of the northeast, as it frequently does during storms, sailing ships were blown toward shore or forced to seek refuge close to it. Often they hit a sandbar and, because of gales and particularly rough seas, were wrecked.

The money Congress spent on creating the Life Saving Service went to purchase lifesaving equipment and the construction of lifesaving stations. Originally, the stations were simple and rather crude; they contained provisions and lifesaving equipment. When a wreck was spotted, surfmen would launch boats from the beach and rescue shipwreck victims.

If the ocean was too rough, the surfmen would fire a shot line to the ship, rig other lines, and pull people to safety using the Francis Life Car. Over the years hundreds of people escaped death by riding to safety in one of these containers. You can see two original Francis Life Cars at the Twin Lights Museum.

Originally, eight stations were built for the Life Saving Service on the Jersey Coast. They were located from Sandy Hook to the southern edge of Long Beach Island. As the Life Saving Service matured, stations were constructed approximately 3½ miles apart on the coast, with foot or horse patrols covering the beach area in between. New Jersey eventually had 41 lifesaving stations in all.

The U.S. Life Saving Service was gradually extended to cover not only New Jersey's coastline, but the remainder of the Atlantic Coast, the Gulf and Pacific Coasts, and even the shorelines of the Great Lakes. After a reorganization of the Life Saving Service was completed in 1872, better records of rescues and rescue attempts were kept. From 1872 to 1915, when the Life Saving Service merged with the U.S. Revenue Cutter Service to form the U.S. Coast Guard, over 175,000 people had been safely rescued from the angry sea.

Search for Captain Kidd's Treasure. If you spot a solitary figure scanning the sand with a metal detector at the edge of a Highlands street, there's a chance he's searching for a few old doubloons, though he may not admit it. Legend has it that the notorious pirate, Captain Kidd, buried treasure somewhere on the bay side of Sandy Hook. Few people actually searched for the buried treasure until 1948 when an old fisherman found some gold coins in the sand off Cedar Street. When news spread of his discovery, it was widely assumed the coins were part of the lost treasure of Captain Kidd. People flocked to the bay beaches of Highlands and sifted the sand there with hopes of striking it rich. Other coins were found, but the treasure wasn't.

Although the gold coins were never truly linked with Kidd's treasure, the legend lives on.

Go Fishing for Jersey Jumbos. Jersey Jumbos are bluefish. They're not only exciting fish to catch, but they're good eating fish, too. The Jersey Shore is noted for its excellent bluefishing. They are inshore fish and travel in schools. You can spot a school by looking for flocks of seagulls overhead; they eat what bluefish in a feeding frenzy don't. The bluefish is a fighter, so don't count on a particularly easy catch. But that's what makes bluefishing fun—and challenging. Be careful handling bluefish. They have sharp teeth and can do damage to an unsuspecting fisherman whose fingers are in the wrong place. Most of the Highlands' party boats advertise bluefishing. Two of the best bluefishing grounds on the north Jersey Shore are the Shrewsbury Rocks and Ambrose Light Tower. The best time to go for bluefish is July through September.

SANDY HOOK

Back before Giovanni de Verrazano and Henry Hudson explored the waters around Sandy Hook, the Lenni Lenape Indians regularly visited the thin, everchanging strip of barrier beach to exploit its natural resources. The Indians came to fish, to gather shells and beach plums, and to cut down dead cedar trees in order to make canoes.

Even though Richard Hartshorne acquired use rights for Sandy Hook in 1678, it wasn't until 1762 that merchants from New York City purchased the northern tip of Sandy Hook to erect a lighthouse in order to make navigation into and out of New York harbor easier for visiting ships. The Sandy Hook lighthouse began operating two years later. Today, it is the oldest operating lighthouse in America.

Sandy Hook's strategic location was realized as early as the late 1600s when plans were drawn to erect a fort there. A sandy peninsula

---

DID YOU KNOW THAT ... WHEN THE SANDY HOOK LIGHT-HOUSE WAS COMPLETED IN 1764, IT STOOD 500 FEET FROM THE TIP OF SANDY HOOK? TODAY THE LIGHTHOUSE STANDS 1¼ MILES FROM THE TIP. A GIANT SAND BUILD-UP AT THE NORTH END OF THE PENINSULA, DUE TO OCEAN CURRENTS AND WAVES, HAS ENABLED SANDY HOOK TO GROW SUBSTAN-TIALLY OVER THE YEARS.

---

jutted out into the lower reach of New York harbor. Gun emplacements could easily guard entrance to the harbor, because the channel leading to it passed right by the tip of Sandy Hook. But the fort was never built.

The British knew how valuable Sandy Hook was, and during the War for Independence, British regulars and Loyalists or Tories controlled it, despite attempts by the Americans to take the sandspit. It proved particularly valuable to British Gen. Henry Clinton, who, after the Battle of Monmouth in 1778, fled to Sandy Hook where he and his troops then escaped to New York.

Shortly before the Civil War, construction of a large fort was begun at Sandy Hook. It was to be used as the first line of defense of the New York and New Jersey harbor area, supplementing the other coastal forts closer to the New York City port. Never officially named, because it was never completed, the partially erected fort was simply known as "Fort at Sandy Hook."

The only permanent fort built at Sandy Hook was **Fort Hancock**. The U.S. Army Proving Ground command used land there as a base of operations as guns, ammunition and armor plates of all types were tested on Sandy Hook beach from 1874–1919. During World Wars I and II, Fort Hancock was an important coastal defense fort and heavily fortified with the most powerful guns of the era.

Early in World War II, it was especially feared that Germany might try to attack New York and bomb its harbor; therefore, the gun emplacements at Fort Hancock were extremely important in the defense of the city. Many of the gun batteries and bunkers can be viewed today, decaying amid beach grass and sand dunes. Some are extremely dangerous to walk on and explore. Obey the warning signs.

After World War II, Fort Hancock's big guns were dismantled, made obsolete in coastal defense due largely to the superiority of air defense. In the guns' place came first anti aircraft guns, then Nike Ajax missiles and, still later, larger Nike Hercules missiles. The Nike missiles at Sandy Hook were part of the last defense system seen there. In 1962 the southern two miles of Sandy Hook was leased by the State of New Jersey from the U.S. Army for use as Sandy Hook State Park. In 1972 Gateway National Recreation Area was created, which included Sandy Hook. And in 1975, Fort Hancock was officially turned over to the National Park Service and made a National Historic Site.

Despite the historical significance of Fort Hancock, most people who come to Sandy Hook for the day come to go swimming. If you plan to visit Sandy Hook in the summer, expect large crowds. Try to avoid visiting the park on summer weekends or holidays, since there is no guarantee you'll get in unless you arrive very early. For those not interested in swimming, the best time to visit Sandy Hook is in spring or fall. The weather is usually pleasant, and there are no crowds, except, perhaps, on weekends.

There is also no reason why one should not consider a visit to Sandy Hook in late fall or even winter. Fishermen use the facilities at Sandy Hook year round. What you'll find in the off-season are uncrowded hiking trails, excellent beachcombing and the opportunity to visit Fort Hancock and its sites at your own pace. Be advised, however, that in January and February Sandy Hook can be bitter cold. Icy winds often blow across the barrier beach, making hiking or exploring Fort Hancock enjoyable only if you're properly dressed.

If you arrive by car during the summer season (Memorial Day through Labor Day), there is a recreation user fee. Bicyclists are free; so are those who walk in. Actually, bicycling around Sandy Hook is an excellent way to see and enjoy the sites. The roads are flat and well paved, which makes for easy cycling. Those who cycle also have easy access to many of the sites without having to worry about parking, a major problem at Sandy Hook in the summer.

In order to familiarize yourself with Sandy Hook and learn about the wide range of programs and activities available to visitors (see below), your first stop should be the Spermaceti Cove Visitor's Center. It's located on the right side of the park's main thoroughfare, just beyond Parking Area D and directly across from Spermaceti Cove on the bay side. The building, once a U.S. Life Saving Service Station, was built in 1894. Plan to spend enough time here to catch the 15-minute slide show, which provides a good introduction to Sandy Hook, and to visit the displays that deal with the ecology and history of the area. Antique beach apparatus, once used by the Sandy Hook surfmen (as men of the U.S. Life Saving Service were called) are also on display.

On your way out, pick up the free brochures and pamphlets available to visitors. They range from self-guided walking tours to information pertaining to seashells found on Sandy Hook beaches. The ranger on duty there will also be able to answer any questions you might have.

Leave the Visitor's Center and continue into the park. A half mile or so up the road is what's known as Parking Area F, a fishing beach. Even if you're not an angler, proceed up the road. Just before the parking lot adjacent to the beach, notice the old ammo bunkers once used to store artillery shells for battery guns. Across from the ammo bunkers are what *look* like machine gun bunkers. Actually, they were sentry checkpoints.

Although there are no markers indicating such, this South Beach Area was where, some say, World War II was really won. It was here that a top secret radar testing site existed in the 1930s. Experiments carried out here helped scientists from nearby Fort Monmouth (see chapter 3) complete the all-important development of radar. This, of course, enabled Allied forces to pick up on screen bleeps indicating the approach of enemy aircraft. Radar might not have *really* won the war for America and her allies, but there can be no doubt it played a significant role.

Returning to the main road, continue heading north into the park. Eventually you'll come to a fork in the road. One route will take you directly to the Fort Hancock National Historic District; the other will take you there, too, but by way of Gunnison Beach, Battery Gunnison and North Beach. Take the latter route.

Battery Gunnison is the remains of two 6-inch gun emplacements built in 1904. One can climb atop the battery, walk through the maze of rooms and tunnels, and view the guns up close. Gunnison Beach separates the battery from the ocean. North Beach is the northernmost beach on Sandy Hook that is protected by lifeguards and open to swimmers. If you plan to swim or spend the day on the beach, take the time to ride up to North Beach. It is the nicest of all Sandy Hook beaches and has the best views of ships approaching New York harbor.

West of North Beach is Fort Hancock. Continue on the main road—you'll see Sandy Hook's famous lighthouse standing tall against a backdrop of blue sky—and follow it to the fort. (For a complete tour of Fort Hancock, see below.)

Once you've visited the sites at Fort Hancock and spent some time in the museum there, you'll be on the bay side of Sandy Hook. If it's a clear day, you'll be able to see across Sandy Hook Bay to Atlantic Highlands and Highlands, including Twin Lights. Heading south on the main road, you'll pass by Horseshoe Cove and the Halyburton Monument where the remains of British sailors dating back to the Revolutionary War were found years ago.

Further down the main road, to your right, is the **Sandy Hook Holly Forest**. This is a wildlife sanctuary. This means it's illegal to pick plants or harm the wildlife in any way. In the forest you might catch a glimpse of one of many types of birds that frequent Sandy Hook. Sandy Hook is on what's called the Atlantic Flyway, and a number of migrating birds seek shelter and food here. The oldest holly tree in the forest is estimated to be over 150 years old. Yet, because of the salt air, the trees are stunted and never reach the height of a normal holly tree.

After the Holly Forest are three bayside islands that lie close to shore. Skeleton Hill Island and South Island at Spermaceti Cove and Plum Island further south are all accessible if you don't mind wading out to them. You're apt to find some interesting marine life on them. A mile or two further down the road, and you'll come to the exit/entrance of the park.

Things to Do

Go on a Self-guided Tour of Fort Hancock. You can pick up the free pamphlet, *Fort Hancock History Tour*, at the Spermaceti Cove Visitor's Center or at the Sandy Hook Museum in Fort Hancock. Bicycling through the fort is better than driving, except, of course, during the winter. Walking is probably the best way to explore Fort Hancock, however. On the tour you'll pass a number of derelict buildings and undoubtedly wonder why they haven't been demolished or restored. The National Park Service, it seems, is in a frustrating bind. Presently, there's little money available to restore such buildings.

Some of Fort Hancock's buildings are in good shape; these have been renovated little by little since the Park Service gained control of the fort in the mid-1970s. There are a number of fine houses on Officer's Row, for example, the scenic boulevard that runs parallel with Sandy Hook Bay. The buildings that house the ranger headquarters and the

Sandy Hook Museum have also been restored. But much more money needs to be poured into Fort Hancock if its historical value is to be fully appreciated and preserved.

In addition to completing the Fort Hancock Tour, allow some time to view the following: Battery Potter—America's first and only "steam-powered, disappearing gun battery." From spring through fall rangers lead tours into the battery's tunnels. Rodman Gun—this huge Civil War-era gun was one of the largest muzzle-loading cannon ever made. The Fort Hancock gun is one of only two that still exist today. Sandy Hook Museum—located across from the parade field, this one-room museum contains small exhibits, photos, memorabilia, maps and illustrations depicting the history of Fort Hancock. Open daily 1–5 p.m. during the summer, and just weekends 1–5 p.m. in the winter. History House—currently the home of the Sandy Hook Veterans Historical Society, this building used to be the residence of a lieutenant and his family stationed at the fort around the turn of the century. Open only on weekends 1–5 p.m. Sandy Hook Lighthouse—located on the grounds of Fort Hancock, the lighthouse is still in operation under the jurisdiction of the U.S. Coast Guard. (The Sandy Hook Coast Guard Station and adjoining complex is on the bay side, northwest of Fort Hancock. It is off-limits to visitors.) Because it too is not open to visitors, the Sandy Hook Lighthouse hasn't captured the hearts of the public like "Old Barney," the Barnegat Lighthouse on Long Beach Island, has (see chapter 5). Yet the octagon-shaped Sandy Hook Lighthouse played an important role in the American Revolution; it enabled British ships to gain entrance to New York harbor with its strong beam, despite repeated attempts by patriots to destroy it.

Walk Old Dune Trail. Old Dune Trail begins at the Spermaceti Cove Visitor's Center. You can get a free copy of a pamphlet there that explains what plants you'll find along the one-mile loop. Stay on the path; over two-thirds of Sandy Hook is vegetated by poison ivy. Also, bring along insect repellent. Mosquitoes and nasty Green Head Flies abound in the summer. There are numerous other trails and walks on Sandy Hook. Ask a ranger for details.

Watch a Lifesaving Drill. During July and August, park rangers dress up as surfmen of the U.S. Life Saving Service and reenact a lifesaving drill on the beach near Spermaceti Cove Visitor Center. They fire an authentic reproduction Lyle Gun, an important piece of equipment in bringing to shore shipwrecked victims, and explain the various functions and lifestyle of a typical turn-of-the-century surfman. Call (201) 872-0092 for more information.

Go Bird-watching. Birds constitute the largest percentage of wildlife on Sandy Hook. Using a pair of binoculars, you might spot warblers, sandpipers, marsh hawks, a great blue heron, an osprey, a great horned owl, woodpeckers, black ducks and clapper rails. During the spring, there are ranger-led bird-watching expeditions on Sandy Hook.

Go Swimming. The most popular activity on Sandy Hook during the summer is swimming. Areas B, C, D, and E, Gunnison Beach and North Beach have lifeguards. There's even a nude beach south of Battery Gunnison. Although the sand isn't the best quality—grayish white in color and coarse—and the water isn't the cleanest found on the Jersey Shore, Sandy Hook's close proximity to New York still makes it a better choice than Jones Beach.

Go Surfing. Surfer's Cove, situated where the seawall ends near Parking Lot C, is the best spot on Sandy Hook to catch summer and autumn waves. On days when the waves are small, ride a longboard. When the swell picks up, thruster model surfboards perform best.

Go Sailboarding. Most of the sailboarding at Sandy Hook is done on the bay side of the peninsula, across from Area C. Beginners especially like the flat, glassy conditions that usually prevail and the shallow water. The privately run concession stand adjacent to the Parking Lot at Area C rents sailboards and gives lessons as well.

Go Jogging. Early morning or early evening joggers will find the roads and scenery on Sandy Hook to their liking. Don't run when traffic is heavy. You can get information on specified distances from rangers.

Hunt for Seashells. Before you do, pick up literature on shells found at Sandy Hook at the Visitor's Center. The pamphlets will help explain what you'll find walking on the beach. Common shells include Atlantic slipper shells, periwinkles, whelks, Eastern oyster shells, razor clams, Atlantic ribbed mussels and Atlantic bay scallop shells.

Enjoy a Puppet Show with the Kids. Twice a week during the summer, free puppet shows for children, starring Sissy Seagull, Clem Clam and others are presented on the beach in front of the Spermaceti Cove Visitor's Center. Call the center for details.

Learn the Art of Photography. Ranger-sponsored field photo sessions, followed by group discussions on ways to improve one's nature picture-taking, occur on selected weekends in the summer and fall. Call (201) 872-0115 for more information and reservations.

"Go Bunkers" on a Bunker Tour. Tours of gun batteries and bunkers within the Fort Hancock historical district are popular with history and military buffs. Tours are offered on selected Sundays during the spring and fall. Reservations are a must, as are flashlights. Call (201) 872-0092.

Star Gaze. Spend an evening peering through a telescope and view the heavens. A park ranger leads discussion on astronomy at the Spermaceti Cove Visitor's Center in the summer and fall. There's also a slide show that's presented to familiarize would-be astronomers with the basics of star gazing. It's recommended, but not necessary, that you bring your own telescope. For more information, call (201) 872-0092.

Go Fishing. There are special fishing areas for surf fishermen at Sandy Hook. Anglers can try their luck on the bay side, too. Night permits are available at the Ranger station. Rangers even provide surf casting instructions and workshops during the summer. Fish anytime, but autumn is best.

Go on a Canoe Cruise. On Sundays in July and August, one can spend several hours paddling around Spermaceti Cove. Bring something to eat, for the group stops on Skeleton Hill Island for lunch and explores the island afterwards. Reservations are required. Bring your own canoe or use one of the park's five canoes. This is an excellent activity for couples, families, and canoe clubs. For more information call (201) 872-0092.

Some Recommended Restaurants
in the Bayshore/Sandy Hook Area

Bahr's
2 Bay Avenue
Highlands
(201) 872-1245
Price Code: Moderate
Menu: Seafood

Bahr's is perhaps the Bayshore's most popular seafood restaurant. Dockside dining on the Shrewsbury River; nautical decor inside includes lots of Highlands memorabilia and old photos of ships.

Careless Navigator
1 South Bay Avenue
Highlands
(201) 872-1616
Price Code: Inexpensive
Menu: Mostly seafood

Careless Navigator has a very good lunch menu, including some most unusual and very popular seafood sandwiches. Located under Highlands Bridge, some tables have water view of Shrewsbury Bridge.

Chowder Pot
41 Route 36
Keyport
(201) 739-2002
Price Code: Inexpensive/Moderate
Menu: Seafood

Basic seafood menu, but large portions and all the shrimp you can eat. Chowder Pot is a good restaurant to take the kids.

Clam Hut
Foot of Atlantic Street
Highlands
(201) 872-0909
Price Code: Moderate
Menu: Seafood

The menu at the Clam Hut is similar to Bahr's; excellent lobster specials.

Service usually quite good, despite crowds.

Conners on the Shore
326 Shore Drive
Highlands
(201) 872-1500
Price Code: Moderate
Menu: Continental

Located at Conners Hotel, seafood and beef dishes are both quite good. You don't have to be staying at hotel to eat here.

Doris and Ed's
36 Shore Drive
Highlands
(201) 872-1565
Price Code: Expensive
Menu: Seafood

The best seafood on the Jersey Shore can be eaten at Doris and Ed's. Gourmet dishes, superb desserts, excellent wine list. Expensive, yes, but well worth it. Reservations highly recommended.

Hofbrauhaus
301 Ocean Boulevard
Atlantic Highlands
(201) 291-0224
Price Code: Moderate
Menu: German

Sauerbrauten, wiener schnitzel and other German specialties. For those tired of seafood. Excellent view of Sandy Hook Bay from across street.

Long John's Ltd.
18 Beach Boulevard
Highlands
(201) 872-1771
Price Code: Moderate
Menu: Seafood

Dockside dining, very good seafood buffet, free hors d'oeuvres. Competes with Clam Hut and Bahr's for the same seafood crowd.

Miramar at Pier 77
1 Willow Street
Highlands
(201) 291-8877
Price Code: Moderate
Menu: Northern Italian and seafood

One of the area's best kept secrets. Be certain to order dessert.

Moby's Restaurant
2 South Bay Avenue
Highlands
(201) 291-4430
Price Code: Inexpensive
Menu: Seafood

Paper plate dining, no waitress service, outdoor tables. Why bother, you say? The clam chowder is the best in town, so is the view.

Shore Casino
Atlantic Highlands Yacht Harbor, Simon Lake Drive
Atlantic Highlands
(201) 291-4300
Price Code: Moderate
Menu: Seafood and Italian

Nice harbor setting and good seafood without having to venture into Highlands. Veal dishes are recommended.

Ten Tips for Dining at the Jersey Shore

1. Read restaurant reviews. Magazines, such as *New Jersey Monthly* and *Atlantic City*, and Shore newspapers like the *Asbury Park Press* and *Atlantic City Press* regularly print restaurant reviews. Read and then file the ones that sound especially enticing.
2. Find out beforehand if the restaurant you choose to dine at has a liquor license. If you enjoy a drink with your meal, bring your own bottle of spirits.
3. Stay away from popular restaurants on weekends and especially on holidays.
4. Keep an eye out for days in which a particular restaurant offers "Lobster Specials" or "All the Shrimp You Can Eat"—and then select another evening to dine there if it's peace and quiet and good service you prefer.
5. Whenever possible, make advance reservations in order to avoid long lines. Wherever possible, ask for a table with a view of the water.
6. Choose a restaurant that's open year-round over one that's seasonal. You're more apt to get better service, bigger portions and higher food standards.
7. If it's seafood you enjoy, try and select a restaurant that has an adjoining fish market. This way you know what you order is fresh. Often you even get the chance to pick out your own fish or lobster.
8. If ordering seafood anywhere else on the Shore, don't be afraid to ask if the catch is fresh. Yes, there are Shore restaurants that use frozen fish.
9. Avoid eating dinner on the boardwalk. No matter how tempting the scents of sausage and peppers, foot-long heroes and fried clam sandwiches are, save the boardwalk eating experience for a snack or beach lunch.
10. Be wary of fish dinners that are smothered in sauce. It's not uncommon to get more sauce than fish.

2. THE NORTH JERSEY SHORE

Just south of Sandy Hook, and extending all the way down to the Manasquan Inlet, is what's usually referred to as the North Jersey Shore. It begins with Sea Bright, a town that's forever in danger of being swept away by the sea, and ends at Manasquan, a town that also acts as the southernmost coastal boundary of Monmouth County. In between is a string of towns—Belmar, Asbury Park, Deal, Spring Lake, Long Branch and others—that comprise the most densely populated section of the Jersey Shore, due to its large year-round residency.

As more and more workers opt for the commuting life, the seasonal stigma of the North Jersey Shore continues to disappear. Each day—in summer and in winter—the train that runs along the coast and ends up in New York City is filled with white-shirted commuters reading the *New York Times* and *Wall Street Journal*. Those whose place of work is northern New Jersey drive the Garden State Parkway. Finally, more and more commuters to Philadelphia and western New Jersey cities like Trenton and Princeton are living in the southern half of the North Jersey Shore and traveling across the state via Route 195.

The accessibility of the North Jersey Shore to Philadelphia and New York/North New Jersey has permanently altered the makeup of the area. Unlike beach towns farther south along the Jersey coast, there are no more "summer-only" beach towns on the North Jersey Shore. This, of course, does not mean that the North Jersey Shore doesn't attract hordes of tourists anymore or doesn't cater to tourism. On the contrary. In terms of sheer numbers, more visitors are vacationing in this part of the Jersey Shore than ever before. But a ride down to Spring Lake or Brielle in the middle of the winter will find thriving communities functioning just like anywhere else in the state.

The towns of the North Jersey Shore may be linked geographically and be similar in the transformation from seasonal to year-round living, but they comprise an area that is, nevertheless, one with many different personalities. This makes it all the more interesting for the visitor to explore. The North Jersey Shore is actually a study of contrasts. Asbury Park, despite being a mere four miles from Spring Lake, is a far cry from its neighbor in many ways. The same can be said about Deal and Long Branch, Bradley Beach and Sea Girt, Belmar and Brielle. And no town on the North Jersey Shore is like what one will find in Ocean Grove. One can spend days, even weeks, exploring the North Jersey Shore and never fully digest its grand diversity.

A hundred years ago when popular seashore resorts like Long Branch attracted wealthy New Yorkers and United States presidents, and huge mansions and luxurious summer cottages sat overlooking the Atlantic Ocean, the area was known as New Jersey's Gold Coast. It was the summer playground of the rich and famous. Millionaires like Solomon Guggenheim built outrageous summer palaces here; Diamond Jim Brady and the actress Lily Langtry were frequent visitors to Long Branch. Presidents Grant, Garfield, Arthur, Harrison, McKinley and Wilson summered on this part of the Jersey Shore. In 1881 Garfield came to Elberson, desperately hoping that the Jersey Coast salt air would help him recover from the gunshot wound he received from an assassin in Washington, D.C. Garfield, however, needed more than fresh air. He died 13 days after arriving.

DID YOU KNOW THAT ... WHEN IT WAS ANNOUNCED THAT PRESIDENT GARFIELD WOULD BE CONVALESCING FROM HIS GUNSHOT WOUND IN LONG BRANCH IN THE SUMMER OF 1881, TOWNSMEN CONSTRUCTED A LINE OF RAILROAD TRACK MORE THAN A HALF MILE LONG IN LESS THAN A DAY SO THE PRESIDENT'S CAR COULD BE PULLED RIGHT UP TO THE PORCH OF HIS SUMMER HOUSE?

Today little of that original splendor remains, yet in towns such as Deal, Spring Lake and Sea Girt there is no shortage of wealth or million-dollar homes. But it's a different class of people who reside in such homes and frequent the private beach and tennis clubs there. There is little real flaunting of wealth. Those who live in Deal and Spring Lake, for instance, prefer to keep their wealth behind the walls and shrubbery of their small estates.

Yet, despite the presence of such money on the North Jersey Shore, a place like Asbury Park gave rise to one of rock 'n' roll's greatest heroes, Bruce Springsteen. Singing about the woes of the working man, Springsteen and the characters in his songs symbolize the exact opposite of the grace and comfort of towns a few minutes north or south of Asbury Park.

But all this might very well change in the next few years. Towns like Asbury Park and Long Branch, both of which have suffered through decades of decline, appear ready to bounce back in a big way. Plans have already been drawn up to thoroughly renovate Asbury Park's Ocean Boulevard (aka "The Strip" made famous by Springsteen), replacing the rock clubs and seedy seaside bars with condominiums, health spas, restaurants and promenades. In Long Branch a 250-room Hilton Hotel is slated for completion in 1988. Can casino gambling be far behind? Insiders say Ocean Grove, with its tree-lined streets and Victorian homes, has the potential to become the Cape May of the North Jersey Shore.

Some of the contrasts found on the North Jersey Shore will never change, however. The residents of Sea Bright and Monmouth Beach, for instance, will always sweat out the frequent storms that hit the Jersey Coast. The two towns are protected by a large stone seawall. But over the years even this hasn't been enough to keep the Atlantic Ocean from flooding streets and destroying homes.

Farther south in a town like Brielle, the greenery is enough to make you wonder if the ocean is really just a half mile or so away. Unlike Sea Bright and Monmouth Beach, which are built on the same skinny strip of sand that includes Sandy Hook, Brielle is located on more stable ground and has no worries about shifting sands and failing seawalls.

Because of North Jersey Shore beach erosion, especially in towns such as Sea Bright, the beaches above Asbury Park are not as wide as they used to be, nor are they particularly suited to handle the hordes of sun worshippers and swimmers that swarm the area each summer. But what Long Branch, Asbury Park and Sea Bright lack in top-notch beaches, they more than make up for in nightlife. Few would argue the drawing power of the boardwalk and amusement areas in Long Branch and Asbury Park, specifically the water slides, miniature golf courses and arcades that dot Ocean Boulevard. If it's dancing and good music you're after, Asbury Park, Long Branch and Sea Bright together offer a wide selection of clubs, crowds and sounds.

South of Asbury Park the beaches do get somewhat wider, and, therefore, you'll probably find more room to lay your blanket on the sand. But not that much room. Belmar and Manasquan are often compared to Florida's Fort Lauderdale due to the inundation of college students during the summer months. If the beaches there get too crowded, you can always go fishing. Belmar has the largest party boat fleet in New Jersey; Manasquan has the Manasquan Inlet.

You won't find beaches in Spring Lake and Sea Girt quite as packed as Belmar and Manasquan's though. And back we go to the contrasts of the North Jersey Shore. Even if you don't choose to swim in Spring Lake or sun in Sea Girt because of the exorbitant fees to get on the beaches there, a Sunday bicycle ride through these two towns is highly recommended. The point is the North Jersey Shore is steeped in variety. And variety, they say, is the spice of life.

SEA BRIGHT

Sea Bright sits just south of Sandy Hook. Because of the large stone and concrete seawall on its ocean side, those driving along Ocean Avenue, the town's principal thoroughfare, have no view of the beach. There's little beach to see, however. Erosion has been particularly cruel to Sea Bright. It's not unusual during a storm for waves to actually break on the seawall, which means that passing cars get hit with salt-water spray as seawater floods Sea Bright's streets.

Sea Bright is one of the Jersey Shore's skinniest towns. In some parts of it, the distance from the seawall to the Navesink and Shrewsbury

DID YOU KNOW THAT ... SOME SCIENTISTS EXPECT THE
ATLANTIC OCEAN TO RISE EIGHT FEET BY THE YEAR 2100?
THAT WOULD MEAN SEA BRIGHT AND MONMOUTH BEACH'S
SEAWALL WOULD NEED TO BE RAISED TO A HEIGHT OF 41 FEET
BEFORE THEN IN ORDER TO KEEP THE OCEAN FROM WASHING
AWAY HOMES AND ROADS.

Rivers on the town's west side is no more than a couple hundred yards.
In between is Ocean Avenue and a small collection of side streets.
Despite this, Sea Bright is a popular North Jersey Shore beach town.
Virtually all available space has some sort of construction on it, be it
summer homes, year-round homes, condominiums, restaurants, bars or
beach clubs.

Downtown Sea Bright consists of a number of shops and is a bustling
area of activity in the summer. It's also a good place to eat. Check out
the **Sunflower Country Kitchen** (1125 E. Ocean Avenue) for a delicious
breakfast or lunch; the accent is on health food. The **Peninsula House**
(1049 Ocean Avenue), with its Edwardian decor, is also recommended
for supper or an evening drink. If it's a view of the river you prefer,
the **Rum Runner** (816 Ocean Avenue) and the **Riverhouse on the
Quay** (280 Ocean Avenue) are both good places to dine.

Sea Bright is known for its nightlife more than anything else, however.
Most of the town's nightclubs cater to the young, upwardly mobile set
and, on the whole, are a bit classier than what you'll find farther south
in Long Branch and Asbury Park. **Icabod's** (1 East Church Street) and
the **Good Side Cafe and Wine Bar** (10 East Ocean Avenue) are popular
haunts. Inside the former you'll find hanging plants against a backdrop
of brick walls and stained glass. The Good Side Cafe and Wine Bar
attracts a cocktail lounge crowd.

The Peninsula House is also a favorite nightspot in Sea Bright. One
of the town's most popular clubs is **The Trade Winds** (1331 Ocean
Avenue)a teen club which serves no liquor. Here you'll find a crowded,
lively dancefloor, an excellent sound system, and a disc jockey blaring
out Top 40 tunes. Outside, there's a swimming pool and hot tub, which
are part of the Trade Winds' Beach Club.

Speaking of beach clubs, there are a bunch of them in Sea Bright.
All of them, however, are private. In fact, there's only one public beach
in town. But Sea Bright isn't the place to go to swim. It's best to drive
up to Sandy Hook or down to Seven Presidents Park in Long Branch
where the beaches are public and wider. Come back to Sea Bright after
the sun sets for dinner and a few rounds at the bar.

MONMOUTH BEACH

Monmouth Beach is another beach club town. If you're a local, or a
regular summer visitor who stays the season, membership in one of
the clubs is the way to go. But for the day or weekend visitor to

Monmouth Beach, the "members only" signs that can be found in front of the entrance to the clubs can lead to frustration and even anger. You won't even be able to catch a glimpse of the ocean because the wooden platforms that are perched atop the seawall are private. There you'll find "No Trespassing" signs.

If you're driving through Monmouth Beach on your way to Sandy Hook to the north, or Long Branch and Asbury Park to the south, notice the juxtaposition of old and new as you pass by. Old whitewashed summer homes stand next to eye-catching contemporary structures with large windows and skylights. The building which is now the Marine Police headquarters of the New Jersey State Police on Ocean Avenue used to be the area's Life Saving Service Station a century ago.

LONG BRANCH

It's difficult to say which town—Long Branch or Cape May—was America's first seashore resort. Both claim the honor. The problem is that in the 1800s resorts didn't simply pop up one year and suddenly people began to flock to them. Instead, resort development of both Cape May and Long Branch took years—and occurred pretty much around the same time. Therefore, these two Jersey Shore towns must share the title of the "Nation's First Seashore Resort."

In the 1830s and 1840s, Long Branch was on its way toward becoming a summer resort. The draw, however, wasn't necessarily the ocean. Rather, it was the small gambling parlors and billiard halls that had begun to open in the town as well as the horse racing that went on, usually on the beach. For years thereafter, Long Branch attracted a particularly fast and lively crowd; society-types could be seen strolling the streets of Long Branch, and fashion and theater personalities were the object of the latest gossip.

But it wasn't until the arrival of President Ulysses S. Grant in 1869, who decided to make Long Branch the summer capital of the nation, that the town began its Golden Age. It was then that the resort's political importance rivaled its social prestige. Over the next couple of decades it was possible to see socialites such as Jim Fisk, Diamond Jim Brady and Lillian Russell on the same street as some of America's most important government officials and army generals such as Winfield Scott, George Meade and Phil Sheridan. American artist Winslow Homer sketched all this activity on his drawing pads for publication in *Harper's Weekly*.

After Grant left office, Rutherford B. Hayes, James A. Garfield, Chester A. Arthur, Benjamin Harrison and William McKinley all summered, at one time or another, at Long Branch during their terms in office. Woodrow Wilson summered in West Long Branch when he was president.

In the meantime, Long Branch's reputation as a gambling mecca continued to grow. The Monmouth Park Jockey Club was begun in

1870; almost at once betting on horses proved wonderfully popular. Smoke-filled gambling houses were places where fortunes were won and lost over the course of a summer at Long Branch. Some people went as far as calling the town the "Monte Carlo of America."

Long Branch's era of splendor lasted until the early part of the twentieth century. Eventually, laws forbidding gambling stopped the flow of money on card and dice tables, which, in turn, stopped the flow of the rich and famous into Long Branch during the summer. After President Wilson, no other president used Long Branch as the country's summer capital. From then on, the eyes and ears of the nation turned elsewhere during June, July and August for its dose of political hearsay and social scuttlebutt.

Long Branch's decline as a major seashore resort was gradual but steady. Storms eroded its once fine beaches. Other resorts on the Jersey Shore now were more promising to summer visitors. By the late 1960s organized crime had settled into Long Branch, and not always surreptitiously. A couple of gangland murders seriously tarnished Long Branch's image. Urban blight, in the form of run-down buildings and shabby streets, and the problems associated with too many people on welfare tarnished its image even further.

Despite these problems, Long Branch has survived as a resort town. Families from northern New Jersey and New York still spend summers in bungalows that have been handed down from generation to generation. A boardwalk and amusement center attract crowds to the beachfront at night. In the daytime, people still go to the beach to swim and sun.

The feeling in Long Branch is that if the town can hold out a little longer, it will experience a rebirth that could very well bring back memories of its glory days. Developers are seizing upon the opportunity to re-create a first-class resort that, hopefully, will encourage the return of the monied class in a big way. Presently, there are plans to construct a large oceanfront Hilton Hotel in Long Branch that could initiate the town's renaissance.

Things to Do

Spend the Day at Seven Presidents Oceanfront Park. Seven Presidents Oceanfront Park, named for the nation's chief executives who summered in the Long Branch area, possesses the best public beaches on the North Jersey Shore between Sandy Hook and Belmar. The 33-acre park is small, but it has three bathing beaches and three surfing/sailboarding beaches. There are sand dunes (but not for walking on, though) and two usually crowded kiddie playgrounds filled with wooden apparatus and sand pits. In addition, shower and changing facilities are available and concession stands sell fast food and drinks.

Maintained by the Monmouth County Parks System, the park is meticulously kept and quite clean because of it. During the week the beach area is populated mostly by locals. However, during the weekends and especially on holidays, beach blanket space can get scarce due to the arrival of those unable to get into Sandy Hook. Open year-round, there is an admission charge during the summer. The entrance to the park is at the intersection of Ocean and Joline avenues.

Stroll the Long Branch Boardwalk. Most of the concession stands and wheels of fortune are crowded around the Long Branch Amusement Pier on Ocean Avenue. You'll find a few kiddie rides, novelty shops, baseball batting cages and bars. **Stuff Yer Face** is the best place to eat lunch or dinner if you're hungry and don't wish to leave the immediate area and lose your parking space. Dig into a **Boli Express** (folded up pizza with vegetable filling) if your appetite is a large one. Try **Scoop's** on Ocean Avenue, just across the street from the boardwalk center, for creamy homemade ice cream and **Criterion Candies** for take-home sweets such as saltwater taffy and homemade chocolates.

Just north of the amusement pier and across the street on the west side of Ocean Avenue is a statue of President James A. Garfield. According to town officials, there are plans to restore the statue and renovate the grounds on which it stands.

Take the Kids to Kid's World. Located on the Long Branch Amusement Pier, this kiddie paradise of state-of-the-art play paraphernalia is both educational and entertaining. Kid's World is supposedly aimed at 2- to 13-year-olds, but most of the exhibits and things to do seem much more suitable to the younger half of the age group. At Kid's World, kids frolic in the soft play park, which includes a ball pit, punching bag forest, rope climb, sliding tube and canoe ride; get spooked in the Haunted Mansion (one of the few amusements *not* suited for the little ones); attend a circus; visit the petting zoo; participate in Romper Room; and slide down the water slide.

Entrance to Kid's World is not cheap; expect to pay in the neighborhood of $8 per person (kids *and* parents). But the fee is for the day and includes beach privileges. To take full advantage of Kid's World, arrive early and plan to spend the day there.

Fish Off the Long Branch Pier. There is only one pier off the Long Branch boardwalk. Fishermen call it the Long Branch Fishing Pier; all others refer to it as either the Long Branch Pier or Long Branch Amusement Pier. The southern corner of the pier is the area to fish, because a shoal about 150 feet away is where fish congregate. Depending on the season you're apt to catch fluke, weakfish, bluefish or mackerel. A bait and tackle shop and deli are on the premises. Open 24 hours a day year-round.

Sample the Shore's Best Hot Dogs. Funny that Long Branch, a predominantly Italian seaside community with more than its share of Italian restaurants and pizza parlors, should possess the two best places on the entire Jersey Shore for hot dogs. **Max's** is a veritable Long Branch institution. For years it was on the Long Branch pier. But due to a fire a few years ago, it moved a few blocks inland to Ocean Boulevard (not to be confused with Ocean Avenue) and opened for business where the Surf Lounge once stood—a notorious mobster hangout. The hot dogs at Max's are long and tasty; the hamburgers are thick and delicious.

But the *tastiest* tube steaks and burgers are found a few blocks south on Ocean Boulevard at the **Windmill**. Here, the dogs taste as close to perfect as you'll get anywhere, and the sauerkraut is absolute tops. Charcoal-broiled hamburgers, California-style, are big favorites, too.

Competition between the Windmill and Max's is understandably keen. But Max's has the edge because it offers sit-down counter space and waitress table service. At the Windmill, you'll have to stand at the counter or else eat in your car. That can get awfully messy if you bring the kids along. Windmill diehards don't seem to mind the inconvenience, though.

Visit the Church of the Presidents. The history of Long Branch's Golden Age is recalled via memorabilia, photographs, documents and furnishings at the **St. James Chapel** (1260 Ocean Avenue). It is also known as the Long Branch Historical Museum. Open only by appointment, call (201) 229-0600 for reservations. While at the museum, visit the Garfield monument on nearby Garfield Terrace which marks where the house stood in which the president was taken to recover from his gunshot wound. He died there on Sept. 19, 1881.

Visit the West End/West Long Branch Area. West End's shops carry a wide selection of contemporary fashions, popular with those students who attend Monmouth College in West Long Branch (see below). West End also has two of the more popular nightspots in the area: The **Inkwell** (665 Second Avenue), a former 1960s coffeehouse, still retains much of its original charm and is open until 4 a.m. Delicious omelets are the Inkwell's specialty.

The **Brighton Bar** (121 Brighton Avenue) is not for everyone; the

---

DID YOU KNOW THAT ... ALTHOUGH BRUCE SPRINGSTEEN IS WIDELY ASSOCIATED WITH ASBURY PARK, HE WAS BORN AND RAISED IN FREEHOLD, A TOWN TEN MILES WEST OF ASBURY?

---

main brand of music heard blaring from the claustrophobic stage on most nights is punk rock. If slamdancing is your thing, though, there is no other rock club on the Jersey Shore anything quite like the Brighton Bar. On occasion the Brighton does host other forms of rock, too. Some of the best new original bands on the Shore play the Brighton on these nights, before graduating to bigger clubs in the area.

See Where the Movie *Annie* Was Filmed. West Long Branch's Monmouth College sits on perhaps the prettiest campus in New Jersey outside of Princeton. Once the Shadow Lawn Estate, which contained the Guggenheim Mansion and where President Woodrow Wilson ran the affairs of the nation during the summer, the building is now a historic landmark. Today it contains classrooms and offices. But for a few months a few years ago, it was taken over by the cast and crew of *Annie* as the mansion was transformed into the home of Daddy Warbucks.

Spend a Day Winning (or Losing) at Monmouth Park. Located in the nearby town of Oceanport on Oceanport Avenue, Monmouth Park features thoroughbred flat, turf and hurdle racing Monday through Saturday during the summer. Those interested in observing the inner workings of Monmouth Park will want to take the free tram tour every Monday, Wednesday and Saturday morning during the summer. The tour begins at 7:15 a.m. and runs for approximately two hours. Complimentary breakfast is served and visitors receive a small souvenir. For more information, call (201) 222-5100.

DEAL

Driving south of Long Branch on Ocean Avenue, one might think he or she was suddenly transformed somehow to a millionaire's row in Newport, Rhode Island, or perhaps to the west coast in the heart of Bel-Air. Mansions are on both sides of the road. You'll find colonial, seashore, Victorian and southern-styled mansions—most on large, immaculately kept, perfectly manicured pieces of property. The town is Deal, and if its residents could figure a way to wall off the community and separate it from the rest of the world, they probably would.

Deal is one of the most private communities on the Jersey Shore as well as one of the richest. Because of this, there isn't much of a welcome for tourists, although do not forsake a drive along Ocean Avenue and through the town's equally impressive sidestreets for such lack of hospitality. Some people attribute this to a perpetual state of snobbery that encompasses Deal. There is a certain degree of snootiness, for sure. But then again, there is no need to lure tourists to Deal, say its residents. The town is well off without an influx of summer visitors each year, so they simply aren't encouraged to spend vacations there.

The **Deal Casino** takes up much of the prized beachfront not otherwise privately owned. It is a private beach club as one might have guessed, and extremely difficult to get membership. One has to be a resident, and, even then, the screening process is rigorous to say the least. Deal has no hotels and very few places to eat. Drive through Deal and admire its opulence. But if it's overnight or weekly accommodations on the North Jersey Shore you're looking for, you'll have to search elsewhere.

The same is fairly true for such neighboring communities as Elberon, Allenhurst, Interlaken, Loch Arbour and Rumson. One writer described these towns as "straight out of *The Great Gatsby*." He wasn't far off the mark.

ASBURY PARK

Fifty years ago Asbury Park was the pride of the North Jersey Shore. Its mile-long boardwalk was filled with strolling couples enjoying the clean, crisp air and perhaps some sticky saltwater taffy made in one of the nearby shops. **Convention Hall**, the boardwalk centerpiece, hosted such great names in big band music as Glenn Miller and Harry James, and on Saturday nights the dancing went on until late at night. Beyond the boardwalk, the city's lovely lakes and parks were where families went to enjoy Sunday picnics, while the downtown section was crowded with shoppers the other days of the week.

It was a well-planned city, too. The streets are wide and tree-lined, and the churches large and impressive. Asbury Park was founded in 1871 by New York brush manufacturer James A. Bradley, who, a year prior, visited neighboring Ocean Grove and liked the area so much that he purchased 500 acres of land just north of the Methodist camp meeting colony. Bradley called his then undeveloped parcel of land Asbury Park, named for the first Methodist bishop in America, Francis Asbury. He forbade liquor and gambling, two vices, according to Bradley, that corrupted Long Branch. He also encouraged people with high religious and moral standards to populate the city and buy the homes he built. Many of the fine examples of Victorian and Queen Anne architecture in Asbury Park can be traced back to these formative years. Later these homes would stand side by side with those featuring Georgian and Art Deco designs, along with the traditional-styled seaside cottages that dotted the Jersey Shore.

Asbury Park's importance to the North Jersey Shore was unchallenged until the 1960s when the city suffered a rapid decline. Neglect, mismanagement and keen competition for tourists from other communities on the Shore took a heavy toll. Finally, race riots in the late 1960s and the failure of businesses downtown due to the construction of shopping malls nearby stripped Asbury Park of much of its former glory.

During the 1970s, Asbury Park's character took on a strange new look. Its blue-collar beer joints and seaside bars nurtured a rock 'n' roll scene that was eventually to give rise to one of America's biggest rock performers, Bruce Springsteen (see below). In the 1960s Convention Hall was the North Jersey Shore's only auditorium that permitted rock concerts. Bands like the Dave Clark Five, the Rolling Stones, the Jefferson Airplane and the Doors performed there, inspiring local rock 'n' rollers to develop their own brand of rock. By the time Bruce Springsteen had become an international rock 'n' roll hero, Asbury Park was generally considered a rock mecca and mentioned in the same breath as Memphis, Detroit and Liverpool.

Asbury Park's new status may be short-lived, however. A bold new renaissance is in the making that would all but end the rock culture that currently thrives in the city. Developers and investors such as country singer Johnny Cash have made a tremendous commitment to bring back Asbury Park's original splendor and notoriety as a first-class resort city. This will mean the construction of seasonal and year-round condominium complexes, widespread public improvements, such as the renovations of streets, parks and Asbury Park's downtown section, plus a complete overhaul of the city's beachfront. The 550 million dollar redevelopment plan will give Asbury Park a chance to once again become a thriving community and make it practically unrecognizable in ten years to those who recall only neon lights and the all-night sounds of rock 'n' roll.

Plans call for the closing of Ocean Avenue and the tearing down of the bars, nightclubs, pizza parlors and amusements that currently occupy the thoroughfare. Other nearby streets will be closed and a large public plaza is planned. Public parks adjacent to Deal, Sunset and Wesley lakes will be expanded and improved. New hotels are to be built with ocean views; Convention Hall is slated to be restored. Commercial development, the kind usually associated with beach resorts (novelty shops, amusement areas, arcades) will be contained to the south end of the boardwalk, and even there, quite limited.

It's an ambitious project, to say the least, but town officials and developers are determined to see it a reality. All of this will take years to complete, but already there is progress. Asbury Park's largest hotel, the **Berkeley-Carteret** on Sunset and Ocean avenues, has been completely renovated and now offers truly first-class accommodations. There are 254 rooms, elaborate conference centers, a ballroom and restaurant, and a decor that emphasizes elegance. Says a promotional pamphlet found in the lobby of the hotel, "All eyes will focus on this Grand Old Lady for she is the flagship that heralds Asbury Park into its future." That certainly seems to be the case.

Asbury Park: An American Rock 'n' Roll Town

In 1975, Bruce Springsteen's face graced the covers of both *Time* and *Newsweek* — in the same week. Rather than help his career, the instant notoriety nearly destroyed it. The pressure to live up to all the advance hype, plus the suspicions aroused in rock circles that Springsteen and his music were nothing *but* hype, proved heavy and unfair. Fortunately, the album that was released at the time, the classic *Born To Run*, was everything it was made out to be — and more. And looking back, Springsteen overcame his obstacles and rallied to become rock's greatest live performer and its most important artist since Bob Dylan and the Beatles.

The media blitz was tough on Springsteen, but it was just what the doctor ordered for Asbury Park and its music scene. Immediately after the appearance of the Springsteen *Time* and *Newsweek* cover stories, record companies sent scouts to scour the bars and rock clubs of Asbury

Park in search of other Bruce Springsteens singing songs about lost, broken dreams and boardwalk love affairs. What they found was the house band at the Stone Pony, Southside Johnny and the Asbury Jukes, which went on to record a number of albums and garner critical praise for their earthy, rhythm and blues-influenced sound.

After the record company scouts came the fans. They had heard of places like the Stone Pony and hoped to catch a glimpse of Springsteen or members of his E Street Band sitting in with local groups on the club's stage. Others went in search of the places Springsteen wrote about like Madam Marie's. All this brought much attention to Asbury Park and helped it assume its place in the rock 'n' roll history books.

Since Springsteen and Southside Johnny's rise to stardom, there have been other Jersey Shore, Asbury Park-based rock artists who have followed their paths. David Sancious, a former piano player with Springsteen's E Street Band, made a number of acclaimed jazz-rock albums in the mid and late 1970s. Miami Steve Van Zandt aka Little Steven officially left the E Street Band in 1984 to pursue his own solo career. Thus far, it has resulted in one band, the Disciples of Soul, and three fine albums, *Men Without Women*, *Voice of America* and the antiapartheid gem, *Sun City*. John Bon Jovi, whose band, Bon Jovi, is an established act in mainstream rock and heavy metal, began his career at Asbury Park's The Fast Lane (now defunct). Although not Shore rock 'n' rollers per se (they're from Rhode Island), John Cafferty and the Beaver Brown Band were once regulars at the Fast Lane and Stone Pony before they got the opportunity to score the soundtrack for the rock movie, *Eddie and the Cruisers*. (*Eddie and the Cruisers* dealt with the rock life at the Jersey Shore.) Other artists, although not as known as those mentioned above but with Asbury Park in their rock 'n' roll veins, include Billy Chinnock, John Eddie, Glen Burtnick and Norman Nardini as well as LaBamba and the Hubcaps.

Things to Do

Visit the Boardwalk Before Renovation Begins. Anyone interested in the rock culture of Asbury Park will want to visit **Madam Marie's**, the gypsy fortune-teller made famous by Springsteen in the song, "Fourth of July, Asbury Park (Sandy)." The tiny structure with the beaming eye painted on the side of it is where she stares into her tarot cards and predicts the future. Purchase a T-shirt at any of the boardwalk shops with the inscription "Greetings From Asbury Park, N.J.," the name of Springsteen's very first album, and the title of the city's most popular postcard, which also graced the cover of the record. Munch on some fudge or taffy. Asbury Park has the best selection of such sweets north of Atlantic City. Criterion Candies is the best shop on the boardwalk for such treats. On the south end, behind the Casino Arena, is one of Asbury Park's two historic carousels. The other is located across the street in the Palace Amusements Center. Ride one or both of them and wax nostalgic as they're certainly a part of the Asbury Park boardwalk tradition.

Visit the Berkeley-Carteret and the Statue of James A. Bradley.
The Berkeley-Carteret is certainly worth a walk-through. Its main lobby
area has been smartly restored and promises to become the hub of
activity in the beachfront area of Asbury Park in years to come. Across
the street from the hotel's main entrance is a statue of Asbury Park
founder James A. Bradley. One can imagine the park behind it filled
with flower gardens and paths that lead to Sunset Lake once restoration
of the park has been completed.

Go Swimming. Asbury Park isn't exactly known for its Class A
beaches, but that doesn't mean one can't enjoy a day's worth of sun
and surf at them. The beach area has been spared the worst effects of
erosion due to the jetties that jut out into the ocean every hundred
yards or so. Swimmers and sunbathers do take advantage of Asbury
Park's relatively clean and rather safe beaches. But serious swimmers
and body surfers might want to consider Seven Presidents Oceanfront
Park in Long Branch as an alternative to Asbury's rather weak breakers.

Run in the Asbury Park 10K or Jersey Shore Marathon. These
are two of the largest and best-organized road races in the Mid-Atlantic
states. Sponsored by the highly regarded Shore Athletic Club, runners
from all over the world participate in the races, which also command
widespread media coverage. The 10K is usually held in August, while
the marathon is held sometime in late autumn. For specific dates of
the two races, check *New Jersey Runner* magazine, or write to the Shore
Athletic Club, P.O. Box 308, Oakhurst 07755.

Spend the Night Dancing at the Stone Pony. They call the Stone
Pony the House That Bruce Built. "The Boss" is known to hang out
and jam at the Pony when he's not on tour or in the recording studio.
Those who make the pilgrimage to this legendary rock club aren't
disappointed once inside where they'll find photos of Springsteen,
members of the E Street Band, Southside Johnny and the Jukes and
other Asbury notables. Located at 913 Ocean Avenue, the Stone Pony
is the most prestigious rock club not only on the Jersey Shore, but in
all of New Jersey. A visit to Asbury Park would not be complete without
visiting the Stone Pony. Few first-timers leave the Pony without purchasing one of the club's popular T-shirts.

OCEAN GROVE

Ocean Grove might very well be the most unique town on the North
Jersey Shore. Unspoiled by mass development, Ocean Grove is a walk-in
museum. When you enter the gate on Route 71, you step back in
time—back to an era of lovely Victorian cottages and guesthouses,
quiet summer evenings and peaceful strolls along the boardwalk.
Teeming with tradition, Ocean Grove represents a most interesting
slice of home-town America circa 1890, much the same way that Cape
May does some seventy-five miles to the south.

Nestled between Asbury Park to the north and Bradley Beach to the south and flanked by Wesley and Fletcher lakes, Ocean Grove is not for everyone, however. Begun as a camp meeting retreat by Methodists in 1869, a strong sense of religious commitment remains in Ocean Grove. It's also a summer resort that attracts an unusually large proportion of senior citizens. And it's a dry town, to boot. So, if you come to the Jersey Shore to unwind, relax and simply slow down the pace of your life, then Ocean Grove is most appropriate. If, on the other hand, it's nightclubs and bright lights you want, best to stay elsewhere on the Shore. Asbury Park, Manasquan or Belmar would be good bets. But do make a point of spending at least part of a day walking around Ocean Grove and admiring its historical treasures. You won't regret it.

Ocean Grove's history extends back to 1870, the year the first Methodist Camp Meeting took place. Those who attended stayed in tents, listened to religious orators preach the Good Word, and joined together in daily prayer meetings. Everything took place in tents or outdoors until the **Great Auditorium** was constructed in 1894. A huge, wooden Victorian structure, it was built to seat close to seven thousand people, and it is still used today.

Over the years Ocean Grove's reputation as a summer retreat grew significantly. Hotels, guesthouses and summer homes replaced the tents, although, to this day, there remains a summer tent colony around the Great Auditorium. Many of the nation's most noted religious leaders came to preach at the Great Auditorium. Billy Sunday, Billy Graham and Norman Vincent Peale have spoken from the auditorium's pulpit. President Ulysses S. Grant made frequent visits to Ocean Grove; his mother and sister had a cottage there. Future presidents James A. Garfield, Teddy Roosevelt and Woodrow Wilson also spent time in Ocean Grove. Stephen Crane, Enrico Caruso, William Jennings Bryan, Will Rogers and Dr. W. E. B. DuBois spoke at the Great Auditorium, sat in the audience there, or simply visited Ocean Grove during the summer. In 1970, President Richard Nixon gave a speech there in which he explained his plans to bring the Vietnam War to a halt.

Ocean Grove's heritage and history was directly influenced by the Camp Meeting Association until 1974. Since 1869 the association administered all governmental proceedings within the community. It was the association, for example, that directed the prohibition of liquor in the town. It also passed an ordinance that prohibited cars on the streets of Ocean Grove on weekends.

But in 1974, a court ruling ended the governing powers of the Camp Meeting Association. It was widely assumed that because of this, Ocean Grove would quickly move in line with the rest of the North Jersey Shore. Tradition, however, dies slowly in towns such as Ocean Grove where generations of families lived a life they thought righteous and most desirable. Today, despite the relaxation of some mores and the abolishment of some laws, Ocean Grove retains many of its original camp meeting customs. And for one week during the summer, the

Ocean Grove Camp Meeting still meets like it did for more than a century. Sermons, prayer meetings, guest speakers and Christian socializing fill Sunday to Sunday; for many in Ocean Grove it still is the highlight of the year.

Things to Do

Visit the Great Auditorium and Auditorium Park. You may or may not want to partake in any of the religious gatherings that occur in the Great Auditorium, but a visit to it is certainly a must, since it is a Jersey Shore landmark. Constructed mostly of wood, the auditorium is known for its fine acoustics. If you're interested in attending a concert there, pick up a copy of the Ocean Grove Summer Program, which lists the musical as well as nonmusical events that take place in the auditorium during the summer. Choir groups, string ensembles and symphonies perform at the Great Auditorium June through August. The New Jersey Mozart Festival is a very popular concert series.

In front of the auditorium is the Beersheba Well. It was the first well dug in Ocean Grove; today the gazebo and fountain there stand as a monument to the first Methodists to attend camp meetings in Ocean Grove. Check out the statue of Ellwood Stokes nearby. He was one of Ocean Grove's first and most recalled spiritual leaders.

Visit Centennial Cottage. An excellent example of a typical Ocean Grove Victorian summer home, the cottage is now the town's museum. Built in 1874, the cottage has been fully restored and contains artifacts, photographs, furniture, toys and household items from Ocean Grove's Victorian era. The Centennial Cottage is located on the corner of Central Avenue and McClintock Street. Open only during the summer, there is a small admission charge. For more information, call (201) 774-0042 or (201) 775-0035.

Take a Self-guided Walking Tour of Ocean Grove. Pick up the pamphlet *Walking Tours of Ocean Grove*, which maps out three tours of the town. All three take you through picturesque Victorian streets that contain some of the finest examples of Victorian architecture found north of Cape May. Pamphlets are available at the Tourist Center on Main Avenue.

Stroll the Boardwalk. Ocean Grove's boardwalk is ideal for a leisurely early morn or evening walk. There are no concession stands, no amusements. It's you, the boards, some benches and the beach.

Go Swimming. Ocean Grove has some of the best swimming beaches in the area. Very family-oriented, they are clean, not as crowded as beaches in neighboring towns and guarded. There's also a municipal pool at the north end of the beach. Beach badges are required. For information and current rates, call (201) 988-5533.

Relax in a Rocker. Have you been itching to get through Tolstoy's *War and Peace*? Rent a room in any one of Ocean Grove's many guesthouses and relax away an afternoon on a front porch rocking chair with book in hand. If possible, select a guesthouse on either Pilgrim Pathway or Ocean Pathway where the views are best.

Have Lunch or Dinner at the Sampler Inn. Cafeteria-style dining—this is the place to eat if you're on a budget. Meals are priced incredibly low and are quite good, too. Big senior citizen gathering place. Located at 28 Main Avenue.

Participate in a Sand Castle Contest or a Volleyball Tournament. Ocean Grove sponsors a number of community activities for both adults and children. In addition to the two mentioned above, there's an inner tube race, a biathalon, craft shows, kite-flying contest, scavenger hunt and puppet show. Write to the Ocean Grove Chamber of Commerce, P.O. Box 415, Ocean Grove 07756 for a calendar of events.

BRADLEY BEACH

Many visitors to the North Jersey Shore drive right through Bradley Beach. It isn't difficult to do. Situated south of Ocean Grove, the town hardly possesses the type of tourist attractions found in Asbury Park or Long Branch—namely, large amusement areas, nightclubs or historical sites. What Bradley Beach does possess, however, is a comfortable, family-oriented atmosphere and beach area.

Bradley Beach is a middle-class resort. Most people who summer in the town have been doing so for years. Families rent the same summer house each season, or else have summer homes of their own there. Most of them are far from fancy; but they're all within close proximity to the beach and main shopping area on Route 71.

Aside from the beach, Bradley Beach has a mile long boardwalk, good for jogging and walking, and a number of special events like weekly concerts at the **Boardwalk Band Shell**, located on Brinley and 5th Avenue on the boardwalk. The town also conducts local talent shows and a Little Miss Bradley Beach Contest. All of the events are small-scale, yet fun. For a list of summer activities and information pertaining to beach badges, contact the Borough Hall, 701 Main Street, Bradley Beach 07720.

BELMAR

For many, Belmar means deep-sea fishing. The **Belmar Marina** on the Shark River and off Route 35 is home to more than 50 party and charter craft, all of which make daily trips out onto the ocean in search of blues, weakfish, blackfish, even albacore and shark. Many operate year-round. You won't find more fishing boats in one area anywhere else on the Jersey Shore.

The Belmar Marina also has five docks worth of slips for private boats, a launch ramp, a fine bait and tackle shop called the **Fisherman's Den**, and a small luncheonette where anglers sip hot coffee and swap fish stories. Just across the highway is **Pat's Riverview Diner**, which some folks say has the best menu of any of the Shore's diners, and the **Windmill**, a sister of the original and more known Windmill in Long Branch, the place to taste the Shore's best hot dog. All of this makes the Belmar Marina and vicinity a pretty busy area during the summer months, especially on weekends and holidays.

Yet, others come to Belmar and never so much as bait a hook. This group of vacationers comes for Belmar's beaches and nightlife. The town has an interesting blend of families and college age kids on its beaches each season. The families come for the same reason families come to Bradley Beach each summer—affordable accommodations in the way of apartments, guesthouses and bungalows, and perhaps a bit of family tradition, too. The college age crowd comes because Belmar permits group rentals. That means the limit on the number of people who can sleep and shower in one bungalow or beach house is greater here than in towns which do not permit group rentals. The more that stay, the tighter the space, it's true. But the more that stay, the cheaper the rent, providing everyone kicks in. Wherever you find group rentals on the Jersey Shore, you're apt to find college age kids. Lots of them.

And where there are college age kids, there are nightclubs where the music is usually good and the scene quite lively. Belmar has a number of nightspots that cater strictly to the under-30 crowd. **Bar Anticipation** (703 16th Avenue) and **D'Jai's** (1805 Ocean Avenue) are particular favorites for those with music on their minds. Wear your dancing shoes. **Montego Bay** (4th and Ocean avenues) contains somewhat more sophistication and atmosphere than the other two, but don't expect the mood there overly romantic or quiet. Montego Bay, after all, bills itself "The Party Paradise of the Jersey Shore." For the Irish and those who pretend to be Irish, there's **Ryan's Pub** (701 Main Street) which attracts a slightly older crowd.

Belmar has a boardwalk, although the only amusements in town are found across the street from it at **Belmar Playland** (14th and Ocean avenues). There you'll find roof-top miniature golf and just enough video games and pinball machines to keep the addicted happy on nights they don't journey north to Asbury Park and Long Branch, or south to Point Pleasant Beach and Seaside Heights.

Shark Fishing

Ever since the movie *Jaws*, no other fish has so captured the interest or imagination of sport fishermen as well as the general public as that so-called monster of the deep, the shark. Visions of landing a 20-foot, two-ton Great White danced wildly in many an angler's head, although experienced fishermen knew the chances of that happening were quite remote and the risks involved in battling such a fish were great indeed.

The shark hysteria that inundated America in the midseventies gradually wore off. But those who go out and specifically fish for shark still find it an immensely rewarding experience. As a result, today the shark is one of the most popular big game fishes taken off the Jersey

Coast. Each summer boat basins in Brielle (Hoffman's Anchorage) and Point Pleasant Beach (Clark's Landing) sponsor shark fishing tournaments with thousands of dollars in cash prizes. The entry fees are rather steep (anywhere from $250 to $500 per boat), but the number of boats is usually limited, therefore increasing one's chances of hitting the jackpot. Win or lose, the excitement level knows no bounds.

A number of sharks are regularly found off the Jersey Coast. Blue, dusky and brown sharks are the most common. It's not unusual, however, to hook into a hammerhead, tiger or thresher shark. But the most prized shark is the mako. The mako is a classic fighting fish in every sense of the word, and a delicious eating fish, too; some people can't tell the difference between mako and swordfish.

The best time to fish for shark is June and July. Unlike other gamefish that often require all sorts of specialized gear, sharking can be done using 30- or 50-pound class tackle. The preferred way to attract sharks is with a chum slick. The best bait: whole or chunks of bluefish.

Of course you'll have to go offshore to have any real chance of landing a mako (good news for swimmers, since makos have been known to attack humans). Spots such as the 28 Mile Wreck, the Mud Hole, and the shelf of the Hudson Canyon are favorites with shark fishermen. One, however, need not confine himself to just these three locations. Sharks can be found virtually anywhere 10 or 15 miles offshore with a good chum slick that includes plenty of blood.

Those not inclined or able to venture out in a boat can still enjoy shark fishing. The dogfish is a small shark that can be caught in the surf and large bays. Regular tackle and squid for bait can get anyone started in shark fishing.

Unlike the dogfish shark, which is harmless because it does not have teeth, the mako or any other shark caught offshore can cause serious problems for the fisherman who does not take the proper precautions once a shark has been landed. Take care to tie up securely the shark's jaw and tail even if the fish appears dead. Taking unnecessary chances miles offshore is foolhardy.

Since the growth in popularity of shark fishing, thousands of sharks have been hooked and killed needlessly. Those not interested in eating the fish (not all sharks make desirable dinners) and not wishing to keep, say, the jaw as a trophy (as many do), should consider tagging and releasing the sharks they catch. This helps marine biologists study the behavior and feeding patterns of the shark, a most mysterious creature. For more information on shark tagging, contact the American Littoral Society, Sandy Hook, Highlands 07732, or NMFS Cooperative Shark Tagging Program, NOAANMFS, Narragansett Laboratory, South Ferry Road, Narragansett, Rhode Island 02882.

SPRING LAKE

They call Spring Lake the Irish Riviera. And with good reason. Whereas Deal is predominantly Jewish, many residents of Spring Lake—year round and seasonal—wouldn't be caught dead without green on each St. Patrick's Day. Neither would many in neighboring

Sea Girt. You hear Irish in the last names: Kelly, O'Halloran, McManus. You see Irish at the bars: green beer parties, boisterous sing-alongs. And you feel a bit of Ireland in the air: an old country warmth permeates Spring Lake, a town where visitors can be made to feel like old friends.

That's not to say, however, that the whole world is welcome in Spring Lake. It's not. If it were, beach badge fees wouldn't be outrageously high—$5 a day per person; $6 on weekends. There would also be more middle-class type motels and hotels to accommodate weekend or week-long visitors. But if you're willing to pay for the privilege of summering in Spring Lake, then you're accepted kindly. Some eagerly pay the cost; others would rather swim, sunbathe and socialize elsewhere.

There might be one or two better beaches on the North Jersey Shore than Spring Lake's beaches; they tend to grow a bit smaller each year due to erosion, this despite the presence of groins or jetties built to prevent the swiping of sand by fast currents and storms. But no North Jersey Shore community can boast a nicer boardwalk to walk or jog or bicycle on, especially in the early morning when most of the town is still asleep.

People come to Spring Lake for its boardwalk and sand duned beaches, which are really a rarity in these parts of the Shore. But they also come for what lies behind all this, too. Walk a block or two away from the beach and the beautiful homes, the fancy, well-kept gardens and shrubbery, and the irresistibly quiet streets all give Spring Lake an extra special charm. Many of Spring Lake's stately old homes and seashore cottages have been restored; most are privately owned. But some have been made into delightful guesthouses and bed and breakfasts. Actually, no Jersey Shore town outside of Cape May offers a wider or finer selection of bed and breakfasts than Spring Lake.

The **Normandy Inn** (21 Tuttle Avenue) might be considered the cream of the Spring Lake bed and breakfast crop, especially if you're an admirer of beautiful nineteenth-century antiques which can be found in each and every room to go with the distinctive Victorian ambiance that drifts through the 100-year-old mansion. Also on Tuttle Avenue, one of Spring Lake's prettiest streets, is the **Sea Crest** (19 Tuttle Avenue) and the **Johnson House** (25 Tuttle Avenue). Neither possesses the extravagance or Victorian passion found in the Normandy Inn, but both the Sea Crest and Johnson House offer Spring Lake visitors comfort and hospitality plus in traditional-styled seashore colonial cottages.

The **Ashling Cottage** (106 Sussex Avenue) was built by George Hulett, the man responsible for many of Spring Lake's stunning late nineteenth-century homes. He built Ashling Cottage with lumber from the dismantled Agricultural Exhibit of the Philadelphia Exposition of 1876. Eight other Hulett-constructed homes, similar in architectural design, are scattered about Spring Lake.

The **Kenilworth** (1505 Ocean Avenue) offers spectacular "English

Weekends" on occasion. For three days guests revel in such English delights as high tea, Devonshire breakfast, live chamber music, sing-alongs and "pub night." The **Victoria House** (214 Monmouth Avenue) has an enticing wraparound porch with gingerbread accents, gothic shingles, floor-to-ceiling windows and stained glass. The **Alexander Lodge** (15 Mercer Avenue) has large, spacious rooms and private balconies with views of the ocean. Other Spring Lake bed and breakfasts include **La Maison** (404 Jersey Avenue), the **Villa Park House** (417 Ocean Road) and the **Sandpiper** (7 Atlantic Avenue).

Lodging in Spring Lake can be a memorable experience. And if the town's bed and breakfasts don't meet your fancy, perhaps a few nights in one of Spring Lake's classic hotels might. The **Essex-Sussex**, one of Spring Lake's grandest hotels, was recently made into a condominium/hotel in an attempt to generate revenue so it can be restored to its former elegance. Such elegance used to mean evening gowns for women and white coats and black ties for men, and uniformed doormen and graciousness beyond compare.

> DID YOU KNOW THAT ... THE MILOS FORMAN FILM, *RAGTIME*, WHICH STARRED JAMES CAGNEY, WAS SET IN THE ESSEX-SUSSEX HOTEL? OTHER MOVIES THAT HAVE USED SPRING LAKE AS A SETTING INCLUDE WOODY ALLEN'S *STARDUST MEMORIES* AND *ONCE UPON A TIME IN AMERICA*, WHICH STARRED ROBERT DeNIRO.

The Essex-Sussex Hotel might not have the 300 rooms it once had for public use, and it might have forever lost its grand tradition in the condominium conversion, but the Spring Lake seashore hotel charm can still be found in the other hotels in town. The **Shoreham** (115 Monmouth Avenue), for instance, is a large hotel that attracts a regular clientele; it has a terrific collection of rocking chairs spread the length of its long porch. The **Allaire Hotel** (Ocean and Union avenues) does its best to keep the Spring Lake tradition alive. It, too, has a large porch, old-fashioned rockers and a large dining area.

The **Warren Hotel** (Mercer Avenue) has a lobby filled with wicker and antiques, while many of its 200 rooms have ocean views. Other landmark hotels in Spring Lake include the **Hewitt-Wellington** (200 Monmouth Avenue) and the **Colonial Ocean House** (First and Sussex avenues).

There are other things to do in Spring Lake besides go to the beach, walk the boardwalk or let an afternoon drift by sitting in a wicker rocking chair—although, for many of Spring Lake's visitors, this is all they need to be satisfied and all they really came for.

Still, one can visit the **Spring Lake Historical Society Museum**, located on the second floor of the municipal building (5th Avenue and Warren Street). There you can view a collection of old photographs, furniture and memorabilia pertaining to Spring Lake's past. In the summer the museum is open Tuesdays 9:30 a.m.–12:30 p.m. and the first Sunday of the month from 2 to 4 p.m. In the winter, it's the first Tuesday and Sunday of the month, 9:30 a.m.–12:30 p.m. and 2–4, respectively.

The society also sponsors one of the most popular events in town, the Annual Spring Lake House Tour, which includes visits at a number of vintage homes, churches and public buildings. Often the tour culminates with lunch at the private and quite prestigious Spring Lake Bath and Tennis Club on Jersey Avenue. For more information on the tour, contact the Historical Society at the Municipal Building or the Greater Spring Lake Chamber of Commerce (P.O. Box 694, Spring Lake 07762).

Since Spring Lake is saturated with Irish culture, stop at the **Irish Centre** (1120 Third Avenue) and pick up a fine, imported woolen sweater or perhaps an Irish folksong record or two. A stroll around the willow tree–dominated paths and the gardens that hug the shore of Spring Lake, the body of water after which the town is named, is ideal for romantically inclined couples tired of the boardwalk. You can also board the Spring Lake Trolley and tour the town as it winds its way through some of Spring Lake's finest streets, down through the town center, and out along Ocean Avenue. The trolley runs from 8:30 a.m. to 9:30 p.m. each day in the summer.

Finally, there's the highly popular annual five-mile run called the Spring Lake Five. Sanctioned by the Athletic Congress, the race attracts the best runners in the New York–New Jersey metropolitan area and even beyond. For this year's race date, write to The Spring Lake Five Mile Run, P.O. Box 534, Spring Lake 07762.

SEA GIRT

Some of Spring Lake's charm and Irish heritage can be found in Sea Girt. Unlike Spring Lake, however, Sea Girt is almost exclusively a residential community. Sea Girt entertains no notions of becoming a tourist beach town, either. There are no public facilities near or at the beach. Parking is restricted. Beach badge prices are as high as they are in Spring Lake. And with the possible exception of the Parker House, Sea Girt has none of the beautiful inns and bed and breakfasts that attract summer visitors to Spring Lake.

About the only attraction in Sea Girt, aside from viewing its immaculately kept streets and expensive homes, is the Sea Girt Lighthouse on the corner of Ocean and Beacon avenues. Perched atop a traditional beach house, the light began beaming in 1896 and continued until decommissioned in 1955. It's recently been restored and is now owned by the borough of Sea Girt. It is not, unfortunately, open to the public on a regular basis. Lighthouse buffs, though, can usually arrange a tour of it by contacting the Sea Girt Lighthouse Foundation (P.O. Box 84, Sea Girt 08750).

The National Guard Training Center and the New Jersey State Police Academy are located in Sea Girt. It was here in a beautiful white mansion, dubbed the Little White House, that New Jersey governors summered, including the only one to eventually move to the *real* White House, Woodrow Wilson. The Training Center/Academy, however, is off-limits to tourists.

Those finding themselves in Sea Girt might want to have brunch or dinner at the **Yankee Clipper** (1 Chicago Boulevard), where the view of the ocean is excellent. The **Parker House** is a popular spot for drinks, especially with the yuppie crowd. But Sea Girt's most famous nightspot and drinking establishment is **Jimmy Byrne's Sea Girt Inn** on Route 71. Here you can partake in traditional Irish sing-alongs, listen to Top 40 rock or dance to big band music.

MANASQUAN

Each summer Manasquan swells with a crowd that's predominantly single, young and active. The rickety bungalows along Brielle Road and First Avenue, especially the north side of First Avenue, are sardine-packed with mostly the under-30 generation. Manasquan, like Belmar, is one of the few towns on the Shore that still permit group rentals. And in Manasquan, where it's possible to pass a beer through the window of one bungalow and into the hands of someone next door, the close proximity often makes Manasquan seem like one giant group rental.

On any given summer night, you'll hear hard rock, punk rock, heavy metal or pop blaring out of stereo systems as you walk down First Avenue. You might also catch the scent of a midnight barbecue in progress and see more than one Budweiser can pyramid precariously erected on the edge of a bungalow porch. If the party is a private one, then walk over to the **Osprey** on the corner of Main Street and First Avenue, or to **Leggett's**, just a couple of doors south, and there'll be enough suds flowing and enough rock 'n' rolling to keep anyone well-stocked with fun.

Manasquan isn't necessarily overrun by the younger generation, however; there are family-style rentals in town, and you can find

---

DID YOU KNOW THAT ... THE MANASQUAN INLET MARKS THE BEGINNING OF THE INTRACOASTAL WATERWAY, A WATERWAY THAT STRETCHES CLEAR DOWN TO FLORIDA? A BOATER CAN SAIL OR MOTOR ALONG THE ENTIRE PASSAGE WITHOUT EVER HAVING TO VENTURE OUT ONTO THE ATLANTIC OCEAN.

children digging in the sand on the beach. In fact, Manasquan does much to keep the family resort image balanced with the perpetual party atmosphere on First Avenue and Brielle Road.

The best way to get around Manasquan in the summer is by bicycle, especially if you plan to go anywhere near the beach. Manasquan has a severe parking problem and no place is it more evident than on First Avenue and adjoining streets on the weekend. If you arrive at the beach early enough, you'll probably find space in a pay lot, but expect to pay dearly for the privilege. If you park illegally on the street, you're certain to get a ticket and perhaps even a towing bill.

First Avenue runs parallel with Manasquan's one-mile beachfront. If you take it to its southern end, you'll wind up on Riverside Drive and the Manasquan Inlet. Here, you can fish and watch the boats pass by in the popular waterway. Those wishing to get out of the sun and still take in the sights should walk up to Manasquan's "boardwalk," a macadam walkway, which everyone calls a boardwalk because it has virtually everything a boardwalk is supposed to have except boards. Here, you'll find a small pavilion where one can sit and enjoy the view all day long.

You'll see all kinds of boat traffic in the inlet: pleasure boats, commercial fishing boats, racing boats, sail boats, Coast Guard boats (the white building across the inlet on the Point Pleasant Beach side is the Manasquan Inlet Coast Guard Station). Directly in front of the pavilion is Manasquan's fishing and surfing beach. The quality of fishing varies, but when the surf's up, nowhere on the North Jersey Shore possesses the power and hollow shape of Manasquan's waves. The famed "Manasquan Bowl" will test any surfer's abilities when the breakers are big. Due to the protection offered by the inlet jetties, the waves here are often glassy smooth when there's a southerly wind, which is most of the time, while in Point Pleasant Beach and beaches south, the surf is choppy and difficult to ride.

If Manasquan's inlet beach is used mostly by surfers and surf fishermen, the Main Street beach is where the bulk of the beach action is. If you desire a little more peace and a bit more space, try Manasquan's north beach section. It is usually less crowded there, but parking, once again, is a big problem. Wherever you lay your blanket, you'll need a beach badge to do so. Badges can be purchased at the Manasquan Beach Police Headquarters on Main Street and the boardwalk. Day, week and season badges are available.

When one tires of the ocean, there's always the **Wild Mountain Water Slide** at the intersection of Brielle Road and First Avenue. It's one of the best in the area as far as speed and radical turns go. A good time to ride a mat down the slide is on a warm, sticky summer night when there's little wind. During the day, Wild Mountain is usually crowded with kids.

Rainy days in Manasquan can be spent sipping tropical drinks at

Casablanca, a very popular, classy watering hole, due to its Moroccan design and yuppie atmosphere. Long lines, however, are not uncommon outside the Casablanca (Brielle Road, west of the **Draw Bridge Restaurant**). A good alternative is the **Main Street Saloon** on East Main Street. The decor isn't as sophisticated as what you'll find at Casablanca, but the beer is just as cold, and the Saloon is noted for its clambakes.

If you want to purchase your own spirits to bring back to your cottage or bungalow, the **Gross Winery Outlet** on Route 35 is where you can pick up some of New Jersey's finest wines without having to travel all the way down to Gross's main outlet in Absecon (see chapter 8).

Finally, shoppers shouldn't miss **Peddler's Village**—rain or shine. Also located on Route 35 (on the Manasquan Circle), Peddler's Village consists of a slew of small shops and markets where one can find virtually anything—usually for good price, too. Open Friday through Sunday year-round.

BRIELLE

Set back behind Manasquan, Brielle is a small town of shady streets and green lawns with no real connection to the summer bustle that dominates her neighbor from Memorial Day to Labor Day each year. Brielle is a pleasant residential area, filled with fine homes sitting on the edge of the Manasquan River. It also has a beautiful country club and golf course and just enough restaurants to keep locals from having to deal with the summer crush at other area restaurants.

Boaters and fishermen, however, know Brielle for its fleet of party and charter boats and its excellent marinas. With the exception of **Bogan's Boat Basin**, which is located directly under the Manasquan River Bridge and is the most popular dock in the area for party boat fishing, all the other marinas are located east of the bridge on Green Avenue. There you'll find the **Brielle Yacht Club**, the **Brielle Marine Basin** and **Hoffman's Anchorage**. The latter two run charter boats out onto the Atlantic. The Brielle Marine Basin also contains a complete marine shop and boat repair facilities. The Yacht Club's restaurant and bar are open to the public; it's a good place to have a drink, take in the sights on the river, and chat with local sailors. Hoffman's Anchorage is noted for its quality charter boats, experienced captains and annual fishing tournament.

If you continue along Green Avenue, you'll come to Brielle Road and a picturesque old draw bridge that's still in operation. The setting in the harbor, which is known as the Glimmer Glass, is postcard perfect, especially in spring and fall when cars don't crowd the bridge. Right next to the bridge is an excellent restaurant called, fittingly enough, **The Draw Bridge**. If you cross the bridge, pass the restaurant, and continue down Brielle Road, you'll come to the Manasquan beachfront.

One of Brielle's biggest events—Brielle Day—is held every September, usually a weekend or two after Labor Day. It's a popular event that attracts not only Brielle residents, but tourists, too. There is a fun run to enter, a crafts show to browse through, and plenty of good things to eat.

Some Recommended Restaurants on the North Jersey Shore

Casa Comida
336 Branchport Avenue
Long Branch
(201) 229-7774
Price Code: Inexpensive/Moderate
Menu: Mexican

Without a doubt the most popular Mexican restaurant on the North Jersey Shore. Menu includes shrimp veracruzana, chile colorado, BBQ ribs and much more. For dessert, try a piece of kahlua pie, no matter how full you might be.

The Draw Bridge
361 Brielle Road
Manasquan
(201) 223-8434
Price Code: Moderate/Expensive
Menu: Steaks and seafood

Seafood and steaks made to order. Excellent salad bar. Make your own desserts.

Evelyn's
507 Main Street
Belmar
(201) 681-0236
Price Code: Moderate
Menu: Seafood

Evelyn's is an institution on the North Jersey Shore. Not exactly gourmet cooking, but you can't go wrong with any of the fried fish dinners. Because it's so popular, Evelyn's does get quite crowded; be prepared to wait.

Garruzzo's Inn
420 Higgins Avenue
Brielle
(201) 528-5464
Price Code: Moderate/Expensive
Menu: Italian

A favorite with locals, Garruzzo's best dishes are those listed on the blackboard as specials.

Harry's Lobster House
1124 Ocean Avenue

Sea Bright
(201) 842-0205
Price Code: Moderate/Expensive
Menu: Seafood

Harry's has been around since 1933. That says something about the food and service. Noted for its delicious lobster bisque with fat chunks of lobster on the bottom.

Jody's Seafood
121 Parker Avenue
Manasquan
(201) 223-3927
Price Code: Inexpensive
Menu: Seafood

Located next to Jody's Fish Market, so you know what you order is fresh. Small, even cramped dining room, but everything on the menu is good and the price is right. Another local favorite.

Maria's
165 Main Street
Manasquan
(201) 223-2033
Price Code: Moderate
Menu: Italian

Standard Italian dishes and pizza, but prepared with care. Excellent tomato sauce—zingy and tasty. Family-run operation.

Peninsula House
1049 Ocean Avenue
Sea Bright
(201) 842-2100
Price Code: Moderate/Expensive
Menu: Seafood and beef

There are five different rooms, each with its own charm; mostly standard menu, but dinners well-prepared. Entertainment on the premises.

Ristorante Bellavista
228 New Ocean Avenue
Long Branch
(201) 229-4720
Price Code: Moderate
Menu: Italian

Both northern and southern Italian dishes are served. Everything homemade; pasta imported from Italy.

Riverhouse on the Quay
280 Ocean Avenue
Sea Bright
(201) 842-1994
Price Code: Expensive
Menu: Imaginatively international

The Riverhouse possesses one of the most interesting menus on the North Jersey Shore. You'll find Greek dishes alongside those from Jamaica and France. Beautiful setting on the Navesink River.

Sampler Inn
28 Main Avenue
Ocean Grove
(201) 775-1905
Price Code: Inexpensive
Menu: Cafeteria

Okay, so the food served at the Sampler isn't exquisite. But for cafeteria food, it's quite good. The place to go when the word economical really means economical.

Tuzzio's
224 Westwood Avenue
Long Branch
(201) 222-9614
Price: Inexpensive/Moderate
Menu: Italian

Long a favorite with Long Branchers, Tuzzio's dining room is set back behind the bar in a terribly bland setting. But appetizers like mussels and clams and the veal scaloppine and marsala make up for the drabby surroundings.

Union Landing
622 Green Avenue
Brielle
(201) 528-6665
Price Code: Moderate
Menu: Seafood

Most people who order mako shark (in season) rave about it. Solid seafood dishes, very good appetizers. Situated on the Manasquan River.

Yankee Clipper
1 Chicago Boulevard
Sea Girt
(201) 449-7200
Price Code: Moderate/Expensive
Menu: Steaks and seafood

Gorgeous view of the ocean gives whatever you order an extra special touch. Prime ribs are very good, seafood is fresh.

3. THE INLAND SHORE

While the North Jersey Shore, which is actually the Monmouth County coastline, provides visitors with beaches, boardwalks and resort towns that range from extravagant (Spring Lake) to economical (Bradley Beach), the inland part of the county provides the visitor with something entirely different.

The Inland Shore, or western Monmouth County, is an area of green rolling hills, winding country roads, lazy rivers, babbling brooks, vegetable and fruit farms, sleepy towns with general stores and corner malt shops, and an ambiance that is a far cry from what one finds closer to the ocean.

The Inland Shore is also steeped in colonial and Revolutionary War history. Towns such as Freehold and Englishtown still retain a colonial charm, which often reminds visitors of areas in Vermont and Massachusetts. Many old farmhouses date back to the eighteenth century, some of which are open to the public and well worth visiting. A crucial Revolutionary War engagement, the Battle of Monmouth, was fought just outside Freehold. Today, Monmouth Battlefield State Park tells the story of the battle—the only one in which the leader of the American forces, Gen. George Washington, met the leader of the British forces, Gen. Henry Clinton, in combat.

Speaking of parks, Allaire State Park is one of New Jersey's best. Few state parks anywhere have more things to do and see. The Monmouth County Parks system is also superb, quite possibly the best county parks system in New Jersey. Turkey Swamp offers some of the finest camping in the area and many of its most interesting hiking trails. Deepcut Park is a horticultural center; it consists of over 40 acres of gardens and greenhouses. Longstreet Farm is a turn-of-the-century working farm. It's especially popular with young children because they can partake in farm chores. In all, there are 16 county parks in Moumouth with a total of more than 4,000 acres.

The Inland Shore is also famous for its flea markets, antique shops, horse farms, stables and racing facilities. Freehold Raceway features harness and thoroughbred horse racing. Raceway Park and Wall Stadium offers drag and stock car racing, respectively. Englishtown, Collingwood and Howell are first in everyone's mind when it comes to flea market bargains. When one includes the activities and area of the North Jersey Shore (chapter 2) with those of the Inland Shore, it's easy to see why Monmouth County is the most alluring of all Shore counties, perhaps the prettiest, and certainly the most varied.

The Inland Shore is actually a fine alternative to the typical beach attractions. When people vacation at the Shore, very often they think of the area as nothing *but* sand and sun. An overly familiar commitment to go to the beach today and the boardwalk tonight, then back to the beach tomorrow is all too common. Rainy days or dull, cloudy ones do provide respite. But more times than not, the day not spent on the beach is dedicated to poker games on the front porch of the bungalow or late mornings in bed.

Now, nothing is wrong with these pleasant passings of time—provided that is indeed what one wants to do. Unfortunately, that's not always the case. Many Shore visitors simply don't realize that a 15- or 20-minute drive due west—whether it be Monmouth County's Inland Shore or Ocean County's Pine Barrens (see chapter 6)—unveils a whole set of exciting things to do and see. That's why this chapter and the Pine Barrens chapter are part of this book.

Few people who vacation at the Shore actually rent accommodations inland. For one thing, there aren't nearly the number or variation of lodgings, in say, Englishtown, that you'll find in any of the beach towns. For another, during the months of July and August, when more visitors come to the Jersey Shore than at any other time, it can get uncomfortably hot inland. That's why the truly best time to visit the Inland Shore is on those cloudy, nonbeach days, or during the fall when not only is it cooler, but the area's farms are busy harvesting and the scenery is spectacular.

Finally, one of the real secrets of this "other" part of the North Jersey Shore is its restaurants. There are many excellent ones. In fact, according to readers of *New Jersey Monthly*, the second best restaurant in the entire state can be found in Rumson. It's called **The Fromagerie.** (Taken from the *New Jersey Monthly*'s Second Annual Reader Poll, August, 1985, "The Best Restaurants in New Jersey Are ... " The number one restaurant was judged to be **The Manor** in West Orange; the number three was the **Ram's Head** in Absecon, just outside Atlantic City. See chapter 6.) Rumson's **Pear Tree**, Red Bank's **Little Kraut**, and **Koh's Shanghai Wok** in Ocean Township also received especially high marks.

The names of such restaurants should tell you something about their cuisine. Those who don't enjoy much the taste of fried shrimp, broiled scallops or clam chowder will find Inland Shore restaurants wonderfully attractive. Bon appétit!

MATAWAN

Cheesequake State Park. Located in Middlesex County just off the Garden State Parkway (Exit 120), Cheesequake State Park is often overlooked by Shore visitors on their way to points further south. Although the park doesn't possess the number of things to do and see that, say, Allaire State Park (see below) or Island Beach State Park (see chapter 4) offers visitors, a morning or afternoon visit is, nevertheless, worthwhile.

Cheesequake has three main hiking/nature trails, each of which is interesting and quite easy to walk. The park is known for its valuable salt- and freshwater marsh areas, and trail guides available at the park office help explain the flora and marsh activity you'll see on your walk. The Green Trail is the longest trail in the park (3½ miles) and has the widest range of plantlife. You'll pass through a white cedar swamp, and an extreme northern reach of the Pine Barrens forest, and view a most interesting variety of vegetation. This is possible because Cheesequake is located where the state's northern vegetation zone ends and the southern one begins.

As for the marsh area, hikers might come upon numerous kinds of birds (Pick up a copy of the handout, "Birds of Cheesequake" at the park office before you set out) as well as small animals found in the park. Marshland is an extremely valuable part of nature since it is the earth's second most productive ecosystem. Only the underwater coral reef contains more life and produces more nutrients that plants and animals feed on. The Cheesequake marshland is particularly valuable to central New Jersey ecology because it acts as a water purifier in an area where rapid commercial and residential development has often endangered water supplies.

Despite its interesting hiking trails and marshland, Cheesequake is far more popular in the summer for its swimming and picnicking facilities. Hooks Creek Lake is a rather small swimming hole and it does get crowded. But it's an ideal place for families with young children. There's no threat of swift currents or punishing breakers that frighten toddlers at ocean beaches. A bathhouse for changing and showering and a concession stand are on the premises. Nearby is a play and ballfield area.

Cheesequake's picnic facilities are well used in the summer, too. Most sites have tables and grills or stone fireplaces. A number of sites, though, are quite close to the Parkway. If you desire a site set away from the sights and sounds of passing cars, ask the ranger at the entrance gate to suggest a more peaceful spot.

Few people realize it, but Cheesequake also has a camping area. There are 53 campsites in the park and two large group camping areas. Once again, ask a ranger to recommend a site so that you're away from civilization, if that's what you wish. Some campsites are a stone's throw away from an apartment complex that hugs the eastern boundary of the park.

Despite this, campers should seriously consider Cheesequake. With the exception of Allaire State Park further south, there are no other camping areas on the North Jersey Shore that are as close to the beaches and resort areas as Cheesequake is. The few private campgrounds in the area are found further west in Freehold as are such county parks as Turkey Swamp, which also has camping.

Cheesequake is a fine place to bicycle, too, especially during the autumn when the leaves are changing colors. Its roads are well paved and usually void of traffic in the off-season. It's impossible to lose your way on the park's road system, as it is well marked and simple in design.

For information on special park activities and camping reservations, call (201) 566-2161 or write Cheesequake State Park, Matawan 07747. Admission is charged during the summer months.

HOLMDEL

Garden State Arts Center. The Garden State Arts Center, the large amphitheater located in Telegraph Hill Park just off the Parkway at Exit 116, is one of New Jersey's most impressive and respected performing arts venues. Each season, from June through September, the Arts Center plays host to an incredible array of performers, and special events. Singers such as Liza Minnelli, Connie Francis, Tom Jones and Peter Allen; rock bands like Crosby, Stills and Nash, Air Supply, Santana, and Southside Johnny and the Jukes; symphonies such as the London Symphony Orchestra and the New Jersey Symphony Orchestra; and special events such as an evening with Mikhail Baryshnikov, Itzhak Perlman, the Boston Pops or even Bill Cosby make the Garden State Arts Center one of the premier cultural centers, not only in New Jersey, but in the entire mid-Atlantic region.

In addition to all this, the center also sponsors annual heritage festivals, which celebrate the ethnic roots of Italians, Poles, Ukranians, Jews, the Irish, Germans, Scots and Slovaks among others. The festivities include a number of exhibits and displays, plus various forms of live entertainment and music. Most of the festivals occur in either June or September, before or after the summer lineup of main events.

Finally, there are many free daytime programs sponsored by the Garden State Arts Center Foundation and Cultural Fund aimed specifically at children, senior citizens and the handicapped. For information about what free events are scheduled for this year, call (201) 442-8600, extension 222.

The Garden State Arts Center seats 5200 while another 4000 are permitted to purchase "lawn tickets" and, with a blanket, sit on the grassy knoll that surrounds the amphitheater. Tickets for Garden State Arts Center events go very fast. Thus, it's to your advantage to check the season calendar as early as possible. The *Asbury Park Press*, the Shore's largest newspaper, usually publishes the calendar Memorial Day weekend. You can request specific information pertaining to concerts and such listed on the calendar by calling the main number listed above, or by stopping at the Arts Center ticket office.

Veteran concertgoers to the Garden State Arts Center usually purchase all their tickets at once before the season opens, thereby guaranteeing them seats for the shows of their choice. The Arts Center has a habit of adding more shows as the season progresses, so it's a good idea to check periodically with the ticket office to see if anything that's been added appeals to you. The price of tickets varies with the performer and seat location. Lawn seats usually cost between $10 and $12.

Holmdel Park. Aside from being a delightful county park with all the standards—hiking trails, fitness trails, picnic areas, a fishing and skating pond and open playfields—Holmdel Park has the Longstreet Farm, a 300-year-old "living history" farm that has been restored to its 1890–1900 period. Owned by the Longstreet family, one of the very first Dutch families to settle in the area, the farm was a prosperous one from the mid-1700s to the 1920s.

Today, visitors can wander through the old barns and sheds and watch park personnel dressed in 1890s farmer's garb perform farm duties the way Monmouth County farmers would have done them nearly a century ago. Chickens, pigs, goats, sheep, cows and geese inhabit the pens and pastures, although it should be noted that Longstreet Farm is not a petting zoo.

Open to the public is the Longstreet Farmhouse, restored to its late Victorian period and furnished appropriately. Guided tours of the house are available. In addition, Longstreet Farm provides a number of educational programs that deal with the history of the farm and the task of running it. "Down on the Farm," for instance, is a popular special event that caters to visitors wishing to experience first-hand such farm chores as milking cows, feeding hogs and planting a garden.

As you tour the farm and farm buildings, pay special attention to the collection of turn-of-the-century machines and carriages; much of these were actually used by those who worked the fields and barnyard at Longstreet. The Longstreets, being "gentlemen farmers" and quite wealthy, rarely dirtied their hands doing chores. Hired help and tenant farmers performed the duties of running the farm.

Holmdel Park and Longstreet Farm are open year-round and are free. They are located on Longstreet Road, a few miles west of the Parkway, Exit 114. For information pertaining to Longstreet Farm's special programs, call (201) 842-4000.

Holmes-Hendrickson House. A few hundred yards up Longstreet Road is the Holmes-Hendrickson House. Built about 1754, the house contains a compromised architectural style, taking from both Dutch and English eighteenth-century designs. This is proof, say historians, that by the mid-1700s, Dutch and English settlers were accepting and even integrating elements of each others' customs. Prior to this, much tension existed between the two groups of settlers. The English controlled the government of the New Jersey colony and hoped the Dutch settlers would assume English traditions. For years the Dutch stubbornly resisted, preferring instead to isolate themselves totally from the English whenever possible.

The Holmes-Hendrickson House has been restored and contains furnishings from the mideighteenth century, the kind that might have been in a farmhouse of this type. The kitchen area contains displays dealing with the way Dutch settlers prepared food. Information on the uses and types of furniture in the bedroom and sitting area is presented by the house guide. One can also view antique farm tools on the second floor.

The Holmes-Hendrickson House is run by the Monmouth County Historical Association. It is open June to October, Tuesdays and Thursdays, 1–4 p.m., Saturday 10 a.m.–4 p.m., and Sunday 1–4 p.m. Small admission charge. For more information, call (201) 462-1466.

MIDDLETOWN

Deep Cut Park. Gardeners, horticulturalists and ordinary people who appreciate fine flowers will be interested in Deep Cut Park and its Horticultural Center. Nestled in one of Middletown's nicest areas, this 40-acre Monmouth County park of gardens and greenhouses, walks and water lily ponds, is especially nice in spring when many plants and flowers are beginning to bloom. Deep Cut, however, is open year-round and usually has something of interest in the greenhouses or perhaps a seminar or class going on to warrant a visit during the other three seasons.

Before you stroll through the gardens, stop at the Visitor Center where a guide can arrange an orientation slide program for you to view. Guided tours of the gardens and greenhouses are available for groups, provided reservations are made in advance. There's a horticultural reference library on the premises as well as volunteers who conduct the day-to-day activities at the center.

Be sure to visit the All America Rose Selections Trial Garden, where new strains of roses are grown and tested. This garden is one of only 24 of its kind that exist in the United States. Also at Deep Cut: perennial gardens, a shade garden, a winter garden, a vineyard and vegetable garden, and a special greenhouse where endangered orchids are cared for; the flowers are sent to Deep Cut by the U.S. Customs Service.

Deep Cut conducts a number of seminars and classes designed to improve horticultural appreciation and awareness, and home gardening. It also has a Horticultural Hotline ((201) 671-6906) manned by trained horticulturalists who will answer any home gardening questions you might have. Deep Cut is located 1½ miles east of the Garden State Parkway on Red Hill Road, just across from Tatum County Park. No admission charge.

Marlpit Hall. Marlpit Hall was, at different times in its history, the home of two influential politicians in colonial Middletown. The house was originally a tiny Dutch dwelling built in the late seventeenth century by James Grover, Jr., a justice of the peace and grist-mill owner. Later when John Taylor, a merchant and also justice of the peace, purchased the house, he enlarged it considerably, using plans drawn from the Georgian architectural style, so popular with English settlers.

Thus, like the Holmes-Hendrickson House in Holmdel, Marlpit Hall possesses both Dutch and English architectural features.

Marlpit Hall has been restored so that it resembles the 1700–1820 period of the house's history. Inside, you'll find numerous examples of eighteenth-century furniture, including drop-leaf and tilt-top tables, chests and a dressing table, Windsor chairs and the Taylor family clock, which was made in Monmouth County and listed in the 1818 inventory of the house.

Located at 137 Kings Highway, Marlpit Hall is open April through December on Tuesdays and Thursdays 1–4 p.m., Saturday 10 a.m.–4 p.m., Sunday 1–4 p.m. Admission charge. For more information, call (201) 462-1466. Marlpit Hall is under the supervision of the Monmouth County Historical Association.

ENGLISHTOWN

Englishtown Auction. You'll find everything from antiques to zories (rubber beach sandals), from hubcaps to bargains on houseware items, from fresh produce to homemade apple pies, and from plants to peanuts at the Englishtown Auction. Even if you're not looking to buy anything, an early Saturday morning sojourn to Englishtown is an experience you're not apt to forget quickly. This 50-acre, nationally known flea market and auction is packed solid with well over 700 vendors each Saturday and Sunday morning, year-round. Those with things to sell arrive as early at 4 a.m. to get a strategic selling spot and set up before the first buyers arrive at 7 a.m.

Don't be fooled by the flea market environment; not everything sold is used merchandise or junk that's often discarded if its owner can't unload it. Many of the vendors, especially those with inside stalls, sell brand new merchandise, usually at prices below what you can expect to pay at retail stores. Of course, there are hustlers at Englishtown, and you'll have to check thoroughly whatever you buy for damages, stains or scratches. Sometimes damaged goods are sold at Englishtown. But more times than not, you'll go home with a bargain you couldn't possibly find anywhere else.

Those wishing to sell instead of buy or browse should contact the Englishtown reservation office, which is open every Friday, 9 a.m.–12 p.m. and Saturday and Sunday, 9 a.m.–4 p.m. Call (201) 446-9644. Once you have a reservation, plan to arrive early enough to secure the best space available.

If it's antiques you're looking for, be prepared to get to Englishtown when the sun comes up. You'll want the first crack at anything of value that might have come out of granny's attic and be considered junk by an unknowing seller. Be advised that other antique hunters will surely arrive when you do, thus any "steals" go quickly.

Saturdays are often better than Sundays for both buyers and sellers. Parking can be a problem and so can crowds, especially during the holiday season. Englishtown Auction is located at 90 Wilson Avenue, off Route 9 and 527.

OLD BRIDGE

Raceway Park. Some of the finest drag racing on the Eastern Seaboard occurs at Raceway Park, which straddles the Englishtown–Old Bridge boundary on Route 527. During July, the four-day National Hot Rod Association Summer Nationals are held here and attract thousands; it's the biggest racing event from Maine to Florida. Race categories include funny cars, dragsters and pro stock.

Regular racing at Raceway Park takes place on Wednesday nights from April to October, and on Sundays from March to November. Mostly time trials are held on Wednesday nights and Sunday mornings. Sunday afternoons are the eliminations and finals on the quarter-mile drag strip. Motorcross and truck races are also popular at Raceway Park. These events take place throughout the racing season.

The Raceway Park season schedule is published in February. To get a copy, send a self-addressed, stamped envelope to Raceway Park, Pension Road, Englishtown 07726. Raceway Park's Information Hotline is (201) 446-6370.

SHREWSBURY

Allen House. The Allen House stands on what once was a Lenni Lenape Indian trail and later a highway used by Dutch and English settlers to get from the settlement of Shrewsbury, one of the very first on the Jersey Shore, to Middletown. The Allen House was built by Judah Allen in the late seventeenth century. A subsequent owner turned it into a highway tavern. Called the "Sign of the Blue Ball," the tavern catered to travelers and provided the area with an important meeting place.

During the Revolutionary War, a skirmish between surprised Continental soldiers and attacking Tories (those loyal to the British crown) led to the death of two soldiers and the capture of nine others. The incident was referred to as the "Allen House Massacre."

The Allen House has been restored to the period in the mid- and late eighteenth century when it operated as a tavern. Because the building was in such bad disrepair, little of the original house remains. The two-floor structure has since been furnished with period furniture, and tours of the house are conducted by Monmouth County Historical Association guides.

The Allen House is located on one corner of what is known as the Historic Four Corners of Shrewsbury. On the other three corners stand the **Quaker Meeting House** built in 1816; **Christ Church**, built in 1769; and the **Presbyterian Church**, built in 1821. The Four Corners is at the intersection of Route 35 and Sycamore Avenue.

You can visit the Allen House from April through December on Tuesdays and Thursdays 1–4 p.m., Saturdays 10 a.m.–4 p.m. and Sundays 1–4 p.m. For more information, call the Monmouth County Historical Association at (201) 462-1466.

FORT MONMOUTH

Army Communications-Electronics Museum. Fort Monmouth is the home of the U.S. Army's Communications Electronics Command, the main research center for further development in the field of military-related communications. It was here, back in the 1930s, where army scientists and technicians developed radar (many experiments were conducted at Sandy Hook, see chapter 1), and where the U.S. Army Signal Corps had its communications school until it relocated to Georgia in 1976.

The Army Communications-Electronics Museum depicts the history of Fort Monmouth from its origins in 1917 to the present, and traces the development of communications and electronic military equipment. The museum also contains communications relics that date as far back as the Civil War when the U.S. Army Signal Corps was created; foreign military communications equipment from the armies of France, Germany, Japan and North Vietnam, among others; and special exhibits like President John F. Kennedy's White House telephone, which he used on the first satellite telephone call between the United States and Africa, and a scale model of the type of radar used in Hawaii at the outbreak of World War II.

This is a specialized museum; communications buffs will find its displays most informative and interesting and will probably wish to spend more time there than the average visitor. However, those only mildly interested in communications will also find the museum somewhat rewarding.

To get to the museum, enter Fort Monmouth's Main Gate on Route 35 in Eatontown. Proceed down Avenue of Memories until Building 275, aka Kaplan Hall. The museum is located on the first floor. Hours are Monday through Thursday year-round, from noon until 4. Admission is free. For more information, call (201) 532-2445.

For those interested in visiting another museum while on the base, the **U.S. Army Chaplain Museum** is also open to the public. Call (201) 532-3487 for details and hours.

COLTS NECK

Delicious Orchards. No trip to Monmouth County would be complete without a stop at Delicious Orchards. And at no time is a stop more worthwhile than in the fall when the apples are ripe, the cider fresh and the pies oh so tasty. Located on Route 34 (Box 4, Route 34, Colts Neck 07722), this large, popular country market is full of fresh Jersey produce, baked goods, cheese and homemade breads and contains more than enough proof why New Jersey is known as the Garden State.

Delicious Orchards is extremely popular on weekends in the fall when people seem to make a day out of shopping at the market. You can buy your Halloween pumpkins here and bushels of apples. Many people order pies for the holidays. In addition to the delicious apple pies, be sure to try some apple donuts and apple cake. And don't leave without a gallon of New Jersey apple cider in your arms.

Delicious Orchards is open Tuesday through Sunday, from 10 a.m. to 6 p.m. For more information, call (201) 542-0204.

Seven Pick-Your-Own Fruit and/or Vegetable Farms

Battleview Orchards
R.D. #1, Wemrock Road
Freehold, 07728
(201) 462-0756
(apples, peaches, pumpkins, gourds, blueberries, strawberries, sour cherries)

Casola Farms
Route 34
Colts Neck, 07722
(201) 946-8885
(pumpkins)

Crest Fruit Farm
R.D. #5, Thompson Grove Rd.
Freehold, 07728
(201) 462-5669
(apples, peaches, plums)

Eastmont Orchards
Route 537
Colts Neck, 07722
(201) 542-5404
(apples and peaches)

Holmdel Nurseries
110 Main Street
Newman Springs Rd.
Holmdel, 07733
(201) 946-4271
(pumpkins and gourds)

Menzel Brothers
Route 34
Holmdel, 07733
(201) 946-4135 or (201) 946-3060
(broccoli, cauliflower, lettuce, peas, pumpkin, spinach, strawberries, tomatoes)

Shwahla Farm
R.D. #4, Fort Plains Rd.
Howell, 07731
(201) 462-7587
(blueberries)

LINCROFT

Monmouth Museum. Located on the Brookdale Community College Campus (Newman Springs Road, Exit 109 Garden State Parkway), the Monmouth Museum likes to call itself a Museum of Ideas. Unlike the Monmouth County Historical Association Museum in Freehold (see below), which deals with Monmouth County history, the Monmouth Museum has no permanent collections and no historical exhibits. Instead the museum is concerned with ideas and concepts stemming from the world of art, science, nature and human culture. Revolving exhibits might include watercolor paintings done by local artists, a display centered around the theme of migration, or an overview of customs, mores, dress and folk art of a particular people. Recently a special exhibit entitled "Ukranian Folk Art" was borrowed from the Ukranian Museum in New York City.

In the Junior Gallery, children are encouraged to look as well as touch. One of the gallery's most popular exhibits is one that deals with land planning. The exhibit encourages youngsters to build their own communities—and then confronts them with problems like pollution and waste disposal.

Open year-round, six days a week, Tuesday–Saturday from 10 a.m. to 4:30 p.m. and on Sundays from 1 p.m. to 5 p.m. (closed Mondays), the Monmouth Museum provides a vastly interesting alternative to the historical museums in the area. For more information on current exhibitions and guided tours, call (201) 747-2266. There is an admission charge.

FREEHOLD

Monmouth County Historical Association Museum. The Monmouth County Historical Association oversees upkeep, tours and special exhibits in four county historical houses—the Holmes-Hendrickson House (Holmdel), Marlpit Hall (Middletown), the Allen House (Shrewsbury) and the Covenhoven House (Freehold, see below). In addition, it also runs the main museum and library at 70 Court Street in Freehold.

The museum contains paintings, ceramics and furniture from the colonial era, many of which, as one might expect, have a direct relationship to Monmouth County history. Its collection of 23 pastels of Monmouth County Dutch colonial farmers by the noted artist Micah Williams is the toast of the museum along with Emmanuel G.

Leutze's famous painting, *Washington at Monmouth.* Leutze (1816–1868) also painted *Washington Crossing the Delaware,* which hangs in the New York Metropolitan Museum. Another exquisite piece is a locally built Wainscot chair, which is the oldest major piece in the museum's collection. It was built in the late seventeenth century. Upstairs in the museum's attic is a potpourri of relics, curiosities and toys donated to the museum, but not on formal display.

During museum hours, Tuesday through Saturday 10 a.m.–4 p.m., Sunday 1–4 p.m. year-round, a guide will walk you around the museum, sketching out a capsuled history of Monmouth and pointing out the significance of the displayed items and paintings. There is an admission charge.

The association also sponsors a number of excellent annual events, including the American Decorative Arts Lecture Series, various folk art workshops and a popular Christmas exhibit at the museum. For more information, call (201) 462-1466.

Covenhoven House. William Covenhoven was a well-off Dutch farmer, whose house was built in 1753, although it is believed the kitchen area dates back as early as 1710. Significant not only because of its age and its blend of Dutch and English architecture, but because British Gen. Henry Clinton occupied the house and his troops plundered it just prior to the Battle of Monmouth. Because of this, the house is often referred to as Clinton's Headquarters.

Considered a mansion by eighteenth-century Monmouth County standards due to its unusually large size, the house is in excellent condition and is furnished according to a 1790 inventory of Covenhoven's property taken after his death. The inventory also included furnishing plans, so the Monmouth County Historical Association was able to furnish the house upon restoration with pieces the Covenhoven family might have used (the originals were destroyed or stolen by the British) and placed precisely where they would have stood in the house in the late eighteenth century.

As you tour the house, notice that it contains closets, even a large, walk-in one. In the colonial era, closets were taxed as if they were rooms and rarely constructed because of this. Clothes and such were kept in drawers and chests. It's suspected that Covenhoven chose to have closets in his house despite the additional tax to show off his wealth.

There are two floors to tour, which a guide will take you through, plus an attic where there's a display of the material and tools used to build the house and a photographic story of the restoration of it by the Monmouth County Historical Association.

The Covenhoven House is located at 150 West Main Street and is open from June through October, Tuesday, Thursday and Sunday from 1 to 4 p.m. and on Saturday 10 a.m.–4 p.m. There is a small admission charge. For more information, call the Monmouth County Historical Association at (201) 462-1466.

National Broadcasters Hall of Fame. It seems odd to find the National Broadcasters Hall of Fame here amid so much colonial and Revolutionary War history, but here it stands. The Hall of Fame and museum were initiated in 1977 with the induction of 21 members, including Red Barber, Lowell Thomas, Arthur Godfrey, Kay Kyser, Edward R. Murrow, Walter Winchell, Jack Benny, and George Burns and Gracie Allen. Since then, more than 45 other radio personalities and pioneers have been so honored. Selections are made by an executive board, and then members of the Hall of Fame organization vote to choose finalists.

The Hall of Fame boasts the largest collection of antique radios in the world, along with hundreds of hours of taped radio shows like "The Lone Ranger," "Amos 'n' Andy," "The Eddie Cantor Show," and "Burns and Allen." You can also hear the voices of all the Hall of Famers and many more sportscasters, newscasters and famous voices in radio history. A display of broadcasting microphones, photographs of radio personalities and a video program give visitors a quick overview of the Golden Age of Radio.

The National Broadcasters Hall of Fame is located at 19 West Main Street. Due to a lack of funds, however, the museum is only open on Sundays from noon to 3 p.m. (The National Broadcasters Hall of Fame is supported solely by admission revenue and donations.)

Freehold Raceway. Harness Racing at Freehold Raceway began in 1853 and has been a major source of gambling entertainment in New Jersey ever since. In 1984 a fire destroyed the grandstand, but it has recently been rebuilt with better views of the 11 races that are held Monday through Saturday from August to the end of May. Post time is 1 p.m. except after daylight saving time when it is moved back to noon.

Freehold Raceway's biggest race is the James B. Dancer Memorial Pace with a $350,000 purse. Held each Labor Day, the race commands widespread attention in the racing world. Guided tours of Freehold Raceway are available to groups provided reservations are made in advance. The tour includes an overview of pre-race stable activities,

---

DID YOU KNOW THAT ... THE ONLY DAYTIME HARNESS RAC-
ING IN THE UNITED STATES IS AT FREEHOLD RACEWAY?

---

preliminary nonbetting races and a film on harness racing. Children find the tour especially interesting. Call (201) 462-3800 for more information on the races as well as reservations for the guided tour. The Raceway is located at the Freehold Circle, where Route 9 and Route 33 intersect.

Turkey Swamp Park. Set back in western Monmouth County, yet only 35 minutes from the beach resorts of the North Jersey Shore, Turkey Swamp Park is the only county park at the Inland Shore to offer camping. It has 64 campsites, 32 of which can be reserved, while the remaining 32 are taken on a first come, first serve basis. In addition, there's also a wilderness camping area, but it's mainly used for youth group camp outings.

As might be expected, the park has some five very good hiking trails of various degrees of length and difficulty. They all wind through the pine forest at Turkey Swamp and pass by swamps and bogs, wild blueberry patches and other plantlife associated with the Pine Barrens. Guided nature walks are led by park naturalists providing reservations are made in advance. There is also a 13-acre lake that's stocked with catfish, sunfish and bass, and fishing, of course, is permitted. Canoes, rowboats and paddleboats can be rented, too.

Turkey Swamp Park is noted for two popular annual events: Turkey Swamp Park Day, held in early October, consists of a special set of activities related to the park's ecology, plus a small fair and a crafts show; and the Jersey Devil Hunt, also held in the fall, is just that, a fun-filled search for that legendary creature of the Pine Barrens. (For the story of the Jersey Devil, see chapter 6.)

Turkey Swamp Park is located on Georgia Road, off Route 524, and is open year-round, although camping is only permitted March through November. There is no fee to enter the park, although there is a camping charge. For further information, call (201) 462-7286.

MONMOUTH BATTLEFIELD STATE PARK

On June 28, 1778, a pivotal Revolutionary War battle raged just outside Freehold between the Continental forces of George Washington and British regulars under Gen. Henry Clinton. The confrontation gave Washington's troops the desperately needed confidence to continue fighting for America's independence from England after the brutal, demoralizing winter spent at Valley Forge.

Washington's battle plan was formulated after receiving word that General Clinton's forces were enroute from Philadelphia to New York City through New Jersey. Clinton feared the arrival of a French fleet off America's shores and wanted his troops in New York City where they would be better able to withstand an attack or siege.

Washington and his army left Valley Forge on June 19. He ordered Gen. Charles Lee to head an advance unit and attack Clinton's supply wagon train and rear guard. For some still unexplained reason, Lee did not follow out the orders Washington gave him until the very last moment, thus losing valuable time. He finally did attack on June 28, but retreated when told of approaching British reinforcements from Clinton's main force. Clinton regrouped his army and immediately went on the offensive.

By this time Washington and his troops had arrived at the scene of battle. Angered at Lee for not following his orders, Washington assumed command and regrouped the American forces. The British attacked;

each time they assaulted the American positions they were, however, repelled.

The shooting subsided when darkness overcame the battlefield, and during the night cover, Clinton and his troops escaped from the American grasp. They made it to Sandy Hook where they boarded ships, crossed Sandy Hook Bay, and made it to New York City without further incident.

Both sides suffered heavy losses at the Battle of Monmouth, yet both claimed victory. Washington had much to rejoice over; his men, once he rallied them, performed admirably in the field, taking the British head on and standing their ground. Clinton, on the other hand, fulfilled his objective of getting to New York City and managed to outfox Washington when it seemed he and his men were doomed.

A visit to Monmouth Battlefield State Park is a return to that day in June when Washington's Continental Army battled the British to what really amounted to a draw. The park sits on land where much of the fighting occurred. The Visitor's Center contains the full, detailed story of the battle, using displays and an electronic map of the battlefield that depicts troop movements while a narrator reveals the day's heroics. A gift shop in the building sells books and pamphlets relating to the battle for those wanting even more information on what some historians consider one of the turning points of the war.

Monmouth Battlefield State Park is located on Route 33 and is open year-round. Admission is free. For further information, call (201) 462-9616.

Battleview Orchard's Apple Cake

5 apples, sliced thin
5 tbsp. sugar
2 tsp. cinnamon
(combine and set aside)

Combine, then beat 3 minutes:
3 cups flour
2½ cups sugar
½ tsp. salt
4 eggs   Add:
1 cup oil   1½ tsp. baking soda
2 tsp. vanilla   1½ tsp. baking powder
⅓ cup orange juice   Beat 1 more minute.

Layer in greased angel cake pan ⅓ batter, ½ apples, ⅓ batter, ½ apples, ⅓ batter. Bake 1½ hours at 350°. Cool in pan. Remove to plate and sprinkle with powdered sugar. May be made ahead and kept in refrigerator.
(Courtesy of Battleview Orchards)

Things to Do

Take a Walk Around the Battlefield. Paths around the park give a good overview of the battlefield. Before you wander around the grounds, however, listen to the account of the battle in the Visitor's Center. Then gaze out at the fields and imagine Washington's troops holding back waves of British soldiers as they attempt to rout the Americans. Let your imagination go even farther and hear the boom of cannon and the pops of muskets.

Have a Picnic. The battlefield grounds have two picnic areas with a total of 60 tables. Spring and fall or early and late summer are the best times to picnic at the park. The midsummer sun often makes it too hot to enjoy fully the scenery and sense of history all around you.

Take the Kids Fishing. If your children are under 14 years of age, they're permitted to fish in the Liberty Grove Pond, which is conveniently located between the two picnic areas.

Attend the Annual Battle of Monmouth Reenactment. Each year on the weekend closest to the battle date, volunteers don the red coats of the British and the blue of the Continental Army and act out the battle. It's a grand affair, certainly the highlight of the park's summer season. This is a popular event, so do expect crowds. Bring a hat along and wear cool, comfortable clothing as you'll be standing in the sun most of the day.

Attend the Annual Flintlock Competition. In April, the same reenactment groups wear their colors, set up camp and stage a series of competitive shoots. Using replicas of the weaponry of the late eighteenth century, the groups determine which among them have the deadest eyes. Just as much fun as the battle reenactment.

Visit the Craig House. John Craig was the Paymaster for the Freehold area militia and fought with Washington at the Battle of Monmouth. During the strife British troops took control of his farm after his family fled and used the farmhouse as a temporary hospital. The Craig House has been restored and is open to the public Thursday to Sunday 10 a.m.–5 p.m. in the spring, summer and fall and Saturday and Sunday (Thursday and Friday by appointment) during the winter. To get to the Craig House, one has to leave the main area of the park, make a left on Route 33 and head to the Freehold Circle where Route 33 and Route 9 meet. Head north on Route 9 until Schibanoff Road. The Craig House is located on that road, west of Route 9.

Visit Molly Pitcher Spring. Molly Pitcher, well placed in Revolutionary War history and legend, is said to have drawn water from the spring on Wemrock Road to quench the thirst of her husband, a gunner with the Continental forces, during the heat of battle. When he went down with a wound and could no longer man his cannon, Molly Pitcher took his place. For her bravery and duty to her country, General Washington made her an honorary officer in the American army. View the marker near where Wemrock Road intersects Route 522.

Visit the Owl Haven Nature Center. Although not under the jurisdiction of Monmouth Battlefield State Park, the center is on park property. Owl Haven is run by the New Jersey Audubon Society and is situated on Route 522, just up from Molly Pitcher Spring. Open Tuesday through Sunday from 1:30 to 4:30 p.m., the center has ecological exhibits that pertain to local wildlife, especially owls. The center even has live owls on the premises; these have been injured somehow in the wild and are nursed back to health by Audubon members. Owl Haven sponsors a series of special birding outings throughout the year. For more information, call (201) 780-7007.

Visit Old Tennent Presbyterian Church. The church is not on park property but is related to the battle and is just a couple miles away from the Molly Pitcher Spring and Owl Haven Nature Center. Located on Tennent Road off Route 522, the church was built in 1751 with the generous financial support of William Covenhoven, owner of Covenhoven House (see above). On June 28, 1778, the church was used as a hospital for Americans wounded during the battle.

Although the church isn't open to the public except on Sundays when religious services are still held there, a walk through the oldest sections of the cemetery will reveal a number of barely readable markers. In the graves are the remains of American and British soldiers killed during and immediately after the battle, including one Lt. Col. Henry Moncton, a British officer whose sword hangs on display at the Monmouth County Historical Association Museum in Freehold (see above).

Visit Battleview Orchards. Not many out-of-staters are truly convinced that New Jersey is indeed the Garden State, but regulars to such pick-your-own farms and orchards as Battleview Orchards know better. Each year, from May through October, Battleview, which borders Monmouth Battlefield State Park on Wemrock Road off Route 33 (hence the name), offers pickers a chance to select some of the area's best fruit. More than 40,000 bushels of apples, its specialty, in addition to 10,000 bushels of peaches, 100,000 quarts of strawberries and blueberries, pumpkins, sour cherries and gourds are harvested annually. All fruit picked is sold by the pound and weighed in the orchards. Battleview supplies containers. Purchase a Battleview Pick-Your-Own Club Membership Card for one dollar and you'll receive a newsletter containing regular announcements concerning harvests and best picking times as well as special discounts and canning and freezing information.

Battleview Orchards consists of 100 acres of apples (McIntosh, Red Delicious, Golden Delicious, Stayman Winesap and Rome Beauty), which are harvested from September through October; 70 acres of peaches (freestone and semifreestone), which are harvested from mid-July to mid-September; 12 acres of strawberries from late May through late June; 12 acres of pumpkins and gourds, from mid-September through October; 10 acres of blueberries; and 3 acres of sour cherries, both of which are harvested in July.

Battleview Orchards Country Store sells its special blend of delicious apple cider (comparable to Delicious Orchards cider, see above), which is pressed on the premises and contains no preservatives. Also sold are cider donuts, homemade pies, jams and jellies, local honey, produce, and, of course, all fruit harvested but not picked by pickers. You can even buy canning, freezing and jelly-making supplies, too.

For more information, call (201) 462-0756. For weather and picking conditions, call (800) 662-3075. Picking hours are from 10 a.m. to 5 p.m. every day.

WALL

Wall Stadium. Each Saturday night from April through October, stock car racing fans gather at Wall Stadium to watch finely tuned, revved-up cars, driven by professional and amateur racers alike, race around the oval track. There are heats, consolation races, finals and featured races, and you can rest assured that the action is heavy and the excitement hot when the checkered flag is lowered.

The four divisions of stock car racing at Wall Stadium are Modified (the fastest, most expensive cars), Modified Affordable Division or M.A.D. (restricted modified cars in terms of cost and equipment), Modern (six cylinders) and Street (street cars). First heats begin at 7 p.m. The night's racing ends when the last of the featured races is over.

Many of the race slots in the various divisions are filled by professional circuit racers from the Mid-Atlantic region (New Jersey, New York, Pennsylvania). But anyone with a properly equipped car can enter. One needs a Wall Stadium Pit License, which costs $25 but is good the entire racing season; one must also pay a small fee to use the pit on the night one races.

Wall Stadium also hosts a number of special racing events, including popular demolition derbies that are held four or five times a year. There's plenty of fun, and the crack-ups are incredible. Just as incredible are the relatively few serious injuries suffered by drivers in these "you smash me, I'll smash you" contests.

Wall Stadium is located on Route 34. Take Exit 98 off the Garden State Parkway. For more information on races and demolition derbies, call (201) 681-6400.

FARMINGDALE

Collingwood Auction and Flea Market. Many of the same things you're apt to find on a vendor's table at Englishtown can also be bought at the Collingwood Auction & Flea Market. There are indoor and outdoor vendors at Collingwood, just like at Englishtown, but usually not as many at the former. Regular flea marketeers say, however, that good to excellent bargains on used items can be found at Collingwood. Books, dishes, glassware, automotive parts and household items are best bets.

Collingwood is open on weekends and Fridays throughout the year. It's located at the intersection of Routes 33 and 34, south of the U.S. Naval Weapons Station at Earle. For information on selling space at the flea market, call (201) 938-7941.

ALLAIRE STATE PARK

From 1674, when the first New Jersey blast furnaces began smelting ore, until little more than a century and a half ago, the Shore iron industry was an important one. The Central and South Jersey coastal plains possessed large, rich iron ore deposits, the result of decaying vegetation in the many low-lying swamp areas. Many Shore settlers worked in the industry—either smelting the iron ore by running large furnaces, or crafting iron products.

On what is now Allaire State Park stands the remains of Allaire Village, once a profitable iron ore community that was self-sustaining to the point of issuing its own currency to be used in the village. It began in 1822 when James P. Allaire of New York purchased the Howell Works, the original iron works on the land, from Benjamin Howell of Philadelphia. Under Allaire, the big furnaces turned out quality iron castings for such household items as caldrons, pots, kettles, stoves and piping. It was a prosperous operation indeed; more than 450 workers and family members inhabited Allaire Village during its heyday in the early to midnineteenth century. In addition to iron workers, the village provided employment for carpenters, millers, harness makers, coach drivers, a baker, even a schoolteacher to educate the village children and a minister to preach at the Allaire Chapel on Sunday mornings.

Allaire's bog iron business and the community that grew up around it thrived until 1846 when things turned bad for the New Jersey bog iron industry. By then coal had been discovered in Pennsylvania's Allegheny Mountains. Allaire, Batsto (see chapter 6) and other New Jersey bog iron foundries burned charcoal from pitch pine to fire their furnaces. Coal, however, was cheaper to use than charcoal. Allaire suffered severe financial difficulties and in 1848 was forced to quiet its furnace forever. When it did, Allaire Village became known as the Deserted Village.

Many buildings remain from the village's heyday, and one can visit them here at Allaire State Park. Buildings such as the carpenter's shop (1835), where wooden utensils were repaired and wagon wheels made; the blacksmith's shop (1836), where tools were made and horses shod; the bakery (1835), which later served as the village school; the General Store (1835), where villagers did their shopping and gossiping; and the foreman's cottage (1827), where the foreman of the iron furnace and his family lived, have all been restored, along with other village buildings. Together, they provide a most interesting glimpse back to the days when bog iron was king in these parts.

During the summer, Allaire Village and its surroundings are a beehive of activity. Blacksmiths, weavers and quilters work on the premises, depicting methods used 150 years ago. On weekends, craftspeople set up displays, usually in front of the bakery, and sell their work. You'll find all sorts of lace and hand-sewn items, carved wood pieces such as duck decoys, handmade brooms, and watercolor paintings of local scenes.

In the fields adjacent to Allaire Village are held antique fairs, flea markets and still more specialized craft shows. Concerts, a Theatre on the Green production, square dance festivals and farmer's markets round out the events hosted by the park in late spring, summer and early fall.

November brings Christmas Stocking Stuffer Sales and December, "Saint Nicholas Day," when Old Saint Nick greets the children. The Allaire General Store remains open daily until December 22 each year (call (201) 938-3311 for confirmation) and sells a wide variety of old-fashioned Christmas gifts and ornaments to hang on the Christmas tree.

Of all the parks at the Inland Shore, none is as popular as Allaire. The park is approximately 20 minutes away from the beach towns of Belmar, Spring Lake, Sea Girt and Manasquan and is the closest state park to the ocean that offers camping. There are 55 sites, which are open all year, and it's no secret that many more are needed to meet the demand. If you plan to camp at Allaire during the summer, expect to find few, if any, sites left by late afternoon. From June 14 to Labor Day, one-third of the sites may be reserved for 7 or 14 night periods. The remaining two thirds of the sites are available on a first come, first serve basis. Campers usually queue up early in the morning to secure a site. For more information on camping and camping reservations, call (201) 938-2371.

Allaire State Park is open year-round. During the peak summer months there is an admission charge. The park is located in Farmingdale on Route 524, just three miles from the Parkway South Exit 98.

Things to Do

Visit Alaire Village. A self-guided map of Allaire Village is available at the Visitor Center. Be sure to visit the blacksmith shop, general store and the chapel. Church sessions are held there on Sunday mornings from July to Labor Day. Notice that the steeple is located in the back, rather than the front of the church. To make your visit even more rewarding, select a day when one of the many seasonal special events is held. Each year Allaire Village publishes a Calendar of Events, which lists the times and dates of all shows and special activities. To request a calendar, write to Allaire Village, Allaire (Farmingdale) 07727, or call (201) 938-2253.

Ride the Pine Creek Railroad. The Pine Creek Railroad is located adjacent to the Allaire Village. Children and train buffs will enjoy a ride on either the coal-burning or diesel-powered locomotive that winds its way through a scenic area of Allaire. Passengers sit in antique rail cars and board at Allaire Station where there's a small museum.

The volunteers who operate the Pine Creek Railroad also stage three events each year that are worth investigating. In June there's the Great Locomotive Chase, a Civil War reenactment; in September the Railroad sponsors Railroader's Day, a celebration of America's railroad heritage; and in December, The Christmas Express brings Santa Claus to Allaire. For more information on these, call (201) 938-5524.

Take a Wagon Ride Through Allaire. A horse-drawn wagon takes visitors on a lazy ride over one of the park's horse trails. Fun for the kids. Wagons depart from the Visitor's Center throughout the day in the summer and on weekends in late spring and early fall.

Go Fishing at Lower Mill Pond or on the Banks of the Manasquan River. Lower Mill Pond is stocked with fish each April so youngsters under the age of 14 can enjoy participating in a Junior Fishing Contest. (Call park for details.) Adults are permitted to fish the Manasquan River, which is also stocked weekly—with trout. The Manasquan runs throughout the park's interior and offers better than average fishing during trout season. There are no bait and tackle shops in the area; bring all the gear you need with you.

Canoe the Manasquan River. Contrary to popular belief, Allaire does not rent canoes or any other small boats. But there are areas on the river bank to launch canoes, providing you bring your own. The scenery is quite nice and the water calm. A good way to spend a summer afternoon.

Go Hunting. Allaire is the only park at the Inland Shore that allows hunting. A specified hunting area is in the south section of the park. Permits and licenses are required; only deer hunting is permitted.

Hike Allaire's Nature Trails. A number of fair hiking trails wind throughout much of the park's 3000 acres. Much of Allaire's wilderness area is thick forest that contains a fine representation of northern Pine Barrens plantlife. If you take the Green Trail, which begins at Lower Mill Pond at the entrance to the Deserted Village, you'll come to the Allaire Nature Center a quarter mile into your walk. There you'll find exhibits dealing with Allaire's natural history. Naturalist-led nature walks are held during the summer season. Guides are informative and interesting.

Go Horseback Riding. Monmouth County has more than its share of riding stables and academies. Many of them permit horses to be brought to Allaire via trailer, or the stables themselves actually sponsor rides in the park on the well-marked, easy-grade horse paths. Allaire does not rent horses. The horse trails are turned into cross-country paths in the winter.

Have a Picnic. Like all county and state parks on the Jersey Shore, Allaire has a picnic area, complete with tables and stoves. To keep the kids occupied, there is a playground just beyond the picnic area and pony rides (which tend to be expensive and short, however). Picnicking is a popular activity at Allaire, so expect the tables around you to be occupied as well. If it's privacy you prefer, take your lunch into the woods and eat on the trail. No fires of any kind are permitted in the wooded area (strictly enforced), and do bring out what you brought in, meaning any and all trash.

Play golf. Allaire has the only state-owned golf course. The 18-hole, par 69 Spring Meadow Golf Course has its own entrance on Route 524, a few hundred yards west of the park's main entrance. Included on the premises—a clubhouse, which offers meals, and a Pro Shop.

HOWELL

Howell Antique Village and Flea Market. Yet one more worthwhile flea market to visit is the Howell Antique Village and Flea Market, which features much of the same merchandise found at Collingwood and Englishtown, altnough you'll probably find more produce and eggs, and better bargains here than at the other two markets. As for antiques, you'll find them at Howell, but don't expect too many deals or steals. These days the demand for antiques has increased dramatically. This has driven up prices and forced even amateur collectors to search even harder for good buys. Howell is open weekends. Located at 2215 Route 9. For further information, call (201) 367-1105.

Some Recommended Restaurants at the Inland Shore

American Hotel
20 East Main Street
Freehold
(201) 462-0819
Price Code: Moderate
Menu: Beef, seafood

For those who enjoy a Currier and Ives atmosphere. The American Hotel is a Freehold landmark; those who eat there regularly swear by its buffets.

Battleground Country Club
Route 527 (Millhurst Road)
Tennent
(201) 462-7575
Price Code: Moderate/Expensive
Menu: Continental

Restaurant overlooks golf course. Recent change of ownership has meant tastier food and better service.

Colts Neck Inn
Routes 34 and 537 (Freehold Road)
Colts Neck
(201) 462-0383

Price Code: Moderate/Expensive

Menu: Steaks, chops, seafood

Colts Neck Inn has a solid reputation among the equestrian set. Ample servings, country colonial setting.

The Farm House
438 Branch Avenue

Little Silver

(201) 842-5017

Price Code: Expensive

Menu: Steaks, chops, seafood

The Farm House is a 150-year-old authentic farm house. Delicious Yankee-styled homemade cooking.

The Fox & Hounds
29 Route 34 South

Colts Neck

(201) 431-4900

Price Code: Expensive

Menu: American/French

For those who prefer elegant country dining. Men are required to wear jackets. The service is excellent, the food prepared with utmost care.

The Fromagerie
26 Ridge Road

Rumson

(201) 842-8088

Price Code: Expensive

Menu: French

Delightfully rich sauces, exquisite veal dishes, French decor. Voted one of the three best restaurants in New Jersey. What more needs to be said?

Koh's Shanghai Wok
Route 35 and Deal Road

(Middlebrook Shopping Center)

Ocean Township

(201) 493-8118

Price Code: Moderate

Menu: Chinese

The best Chinese restaurant in the area—Szechuan, Cantonese and Hunan cuisine. Routinely voted one of the top Chinese restaurants in state by *New Jersey Monthly* readers.

Lincroft Inn
700 Newman Springs Road

Lincroft

(201) 741-8170

Price Code: Moderate

Menu: Continental

Very good prime ribs of beef; every Wednesday night, there's a prime ribs special, which includes complimentary glass of wine.

Little Kraut
115 Oakland Street
Red Bank
(201) 842-4830
Price Code: Moderate
Menu: German/Continental

Small, storefront restaurant has excellent German dishes such as Wiener Roastbraten and Wiener Schnitzel. Also some Continental dishes. Large portions. Love those German Potato Pancakes with apple sauce or sour cream.

Molly Pitcher Inn
88 Riverside Avenue
Red Bank
(201) 747-2500
Price Code: Moderate/Expensive
Menu: American/Continental

The Inn overlooks the Navesink River and has a delectable colonial charm. Order the prime ribs or scrod.

Olde Union House
11 Wharf Avenue
Red Bank
(201) 842-7575
Price Code: Moderate/Expensive
Menu: Continental

Another one of Monmouth County's century-plus old restaurants. Most noted for its seafood dishes and steak.

The Pear Tree
42 Avenue of Two Rivers
Rumson
(201) 842-8747
Price Code: Expensive
Menu: Northern Italian and French

The Pear Tree has quickly become one of the Inland Shore's most popular restaurants since new owners have upgraded the quality of food. This is the place to order breast of quail and lobster cardinal. Superb desserts.

The Shadowbrook
Route 35
Shrewsbury
(201) 747-0200
Price Code: Expensive
Menu: Continental

Yet another of Monmouth County's elegant country restaurants. Set on a 20-acre estate in a Georgian mansion. Veal and duck dishes are recommended.

Whiskers Restaurant
30 Monmouth Street
Red Bank
(201) 747-3300
Price Code: Moderate/Expensive
Menu: Beef, seafood

Victorian ambiance and unusually friendly service only serve to accent a fine menu with portions that don't disappoint.

4. THE BARNEGAT PENINSULA

A funny thing about the Barnegat Peninsula—technically speaking, it's an island. It *used* to be a peninsula, before the Point Pleasant Canal was dug, linking the Manasquan River with Barnegat Bay. Since then, the long, thin barrier beach has been cut off from the New Jersey mainland. Manasquan Inlet, which is part of the Inland Waterway, and the Manasquan River are to the north. Barnegat Inlet is to the south. The Point Pleasant Canal and Barnegat Bay are to the west. To the east, of course, is the Atlantic Ocean.

There are, however, five bridges that connect the 22-mile island with the rest of the Jersey Shore. The Manasquan Bridge spans the Manasquan River and connects Brielle and Manasquan and the rest of Monmouth County with Point Pleasant Beach and Ocean County via Route 35. The Point Pleasant Canal has two bridges across it: one crosses on Route 88 and connects Point Pleasant with Point Pleasant Beach, and the other crosses a half mile south and links Point Pleasant with Bay Head.

The final two bridges are further south. The Mantoloking Bridge goes across Barnegat Bay as does the Thomas B. Mathias Bridge. The former bonds Bricktown with Mantoloking and is the most centrally located of the bridges. The latter brings cars from Toms River to Seaside Heights and Island Beach State Park via Route 37.

During the summer months, the Barnegat Peninsula (we'll use "peninsula" to be consistent) becomes one of the most popular sections of the Jersey Shore for vacations from the New York-New Jersey metropolitan area. The island is quite long as already noted, but only in Point Pleasant Beach and parts of Island Beach State Park is the land mass any wider than a mile. Then, take away 12 miles for Island Beach State Park at the southernmost part of the peninsula. That means the many thousands who vacation here from June to September crowd themselves onto a 10-mile strip with only one very congested artery, Route 35, running from top to bottom of the peninsula.

Why then would people want to buck the traffic that inevitably backs up all the bridges each summer? And why would people want to come to a part of the Jersey Shore whose resources are taken to the limit beginning Memorial Day Weekend? Because of its beaches, its boardwalks, the bay and the ocean.

The Barnegat Peninsula's beaches, from Jenkinson's in Point Pleasant Beach to the sand dune dominated stretch in Island Beach State Park, are, in a word, outstanding. Unlike those beaches to the north that are

narrower and constantly falling prey to erosion, the beaches of the
Barnegat Peninsula are wide and spacious.

Jenkinson's Beach compares favorably with the beaches of Wildwood,
generally considered to be the state's biggest, best beach area (see chapter
8). There is one major difference, though. Jenkinson's is a privately
owned public beach, which means a private corporation owns the beach
but opens it to the public—for a fee, of course. Wildwood, on the other
hand, is municipally owned and free.

Bay Head and Mantoloking's beaches are privately owned, too. But
unlike Point Pleasant Beach, Bay Head has not permitted access to the
public, until recently when a court order forced the town to sell a
certain number of beach badges to those living outside the town. The
whole idea of who has the right to beach access—and who doesn't—has
been a very sticky affair, especially in Bay Head. More about this later
on.

Heading all the way south to Seaside Heights, the beaches are private,
but the restrictions to beach access vary. Membership in beach clubs,
ownership of a summer cottage, or rental of one usually entitles you
to use of the beach, providing you purchase a beach badge. But the
day visitor who wishes to lay his or her blanket on the sand, say, in
Normandy Beach, will find that's not possible.

If it all sounds quite restricting, it is. But somehow everyone is
accommodated in the end. Seaside Heights and Point Pleasant Beach's
public beaches would probably remain the most popular beaches with
day visitors even if the restrictions were loosened. These two towns
have boardwalks and nightlife and naturally attract the largest amount
of vacationers. And then there's always Island Beach State Park, which,
of course, has public beaches—beaches that are undoubtedly the
prettiest on the peninsula and perhaps the entire Jersey Shore.

As for boardwalks, the Point Pleasant Beach boardwalk is entirely
family-oriented; it has a little of everything, which pleases both kids
and adults. The Seaside Heights boardwalk is a smaller version of the
one in Wildwood (see chapter 8). Wildwood has piers full of amusement
rides, some of which are the wildest and fastest on any boardwalk
anywhere. Seaside Heights isn't quite as spectacular, but it comes close.
No boardwalk north of Wildwood can match Seaside's arcades, amusements and action.

Seaside Park, Lavallette and Bay Head also have boardwalks, but
they're strictly for strolling. No rides or games of chance, just wooden
planks to walk on and wonderful views of the beach and ocean.

Finally, there's the bay. The Barnegat is a water playground for the
central Jersey Shore. On any given summer weekend, it is dotted with
colorful sails latched to the masts of sailboats and sailboards. Yacht
clubs in Bay Head and Mantoloking regularly sponsor regattas that
attract sailors from around the country. In addition, there are water-
skiers pulled by wake-creating motor boats, jet skiers, fishermen and

crabbers in rowboats, and those out in all sizes of pleasure boats soaking up the sun and scenery.

You don't even need your own boat, sailboard or jet ski to enjoy Barnegat Bay. Seaside Heights and Ortley Beach, for example, have rental facilities for all of the above. You can also fish on the edge of the bay without even getting your feet wet, or throw a crab trap over the side of one of the many finger-like lagoons in Ocean Beach. About the only thing people don't do in the bay in large numbers is swim. It's a bit dangerous with all the boat traffic, and besides, the ocean is only a few blocks to the east.

The towns on the Barnegat Peninsula cover the full range of resorts. Point Pleasant Beach is the largest town on the north end of the peninsula and possesses a small town center, excellent restaurants and a large fishing fleet to go with its fine beaches and boardwalk. It's a family resort, to be sure, with summer cottages and midpriced motels the main means of lodging.

Bay Head and Mantoloking are wealthy communities in comparison. They have glorious beaches, an Ivy League ambiance, and some of the most stately beachfront mansions that you'll find on the Shore. Except for Bay Head's couple of hotels and its bed and breakfasts, there is little in the way of other accommodations available. Mantoloking offers less than that.

Normandy Beach, Ocean Beach (Units 1, 2 and 3), Lavallette and Ortley Beach consist of row after row of brightly painted, tightly packed summer bungalows. These are rented by the week, month or season, or owned outright by families who have been coming to this neck of the Jersey Shore for years. People here enjoy the close proximity to Seaside Heights and to the restaurants in Point Pleasant Beach.

Seaside Heights has the nightclubs and the night action. Bars there stay open until early in the morning and almost always feature live music and dancing. Wheels of chance on the boardwalk spin until the last bettor goes home. Seaside Park is more residential, a striking contrast to its neighbor. It acts as a nice buffer between the Heights and Island Beach State Park where nature rules and early morning walks along the beach provide serenity and solitude.

POINT PLEASANT BEACH

Like the town of Highlands, Point Pleasant Beach likes to call itself the Seafood Capital of New Jersey. Proclamations such as these are difficult to prove, especially on the Jersey coast where virtually every town has its share of seafood restaurants, clam bars and fish markets. Point Pleasant Beach can flex its seafood muscles a bit more than most, though, because it is home to one of the three commercial fishing fleets in the state. (The other two are located in Belford on the Bayshore and Cape May.) What this means is that the fishing and restaurant industries in Point Pleasant Beach work hand in hand, which results in lots of delicious, fresh seafood on your dinner plate.

If you ride along Channel Drive and then around Inlet Drive, you'll see the commercial fishing trawlers, co-op fish markets and warehouses, repair shops and party and charter boats. Places like **Garden State Seafood** and **Fishermen's Co-op** sell fish that were probably pulled from the sea only hours before they're filleted and set on ice. Virtually any piece of equipment an angler or boater will ever need can be found in one of Channel Drive's supply stores.

It's also on Channel Drive and Inlet Drive that you'll come across Point Pleasant Beach's—and the Barnegat Peninsula's—best seafood restaurants. (See end of chapter for address and telephone number of restaurants.) The **Lobster Shanty** is well known and remains the area's most popular restaurant. But Jack Baker's **Wharfside**, located right across the street from the Lobster Shanty, **Barmore's Shrimp Box** on Inlet Drive and **Frazee's Seafood Restaurant** on Route 35 also offer delicious seafood dishes. These restaurants often have waits up to an hour or more in the summer, especially on weekends, so plan your dinner date accordingly. For those wishing simply to share a pot of steamers or a tempting shrimp cocktail in the evening, try Jack Baker's **Patio Bar**, behind the Wharfside Restaurant. It has a splendid view of the Manasquan River and possesses an informal, relaxed atmosphere.

So Point Pleasant does indeed have a valid claim to the Seafood Capital of New Jersey title. But, strangely enough, the town also has a superb selection of Italian restaurants—better, perhaps than any other Shore resort town north of Atlantic City. Add the two together and the odds are that if you're on the Barnegat Peninsula and wish to dine in a fine restaurant, you'll wind up in Point Pleasant Beach.

Filomio's and **Alfonso's** are the best choices. The former is located next to the Manasquan Inlet Coast Guard Station. All the portions served are large and savory, and the menu is far from just a list of the standards. Alfonso's is really in Point Pleasant, not Point Pleasant Beach. But it's so close to Point Pleasant Beach—and so good—that it deserves mention. A big favorite with locals, the sauces are zesty and the pasta is cooked just right. You'll find yourself returning to either of these two restaurants whenever you're in the area.

Speaking of food, there are two other establishments in Point Pleasant Beach that should not be missed. If you enjoy submarine sandwiches, consider it a must to sample one at **Mike's Sub Shop** on Arnold Avenue in Point Pleasant. With the notable exception of the White House Sub Shop in Atlantic City, you won't find a tastier hero on the Shore.

Jump from subs to ice cream. **Bob Hoffman's** on Route 35 is a Point Pleasant Beach landmark. All the ice cream is homemade; no matter what flavor you choose, it's bound to be rich and creamy. Bob Hoffman's is the only place on the Barnegat Peninsula worth waiting fifteen minutes or more on a summer night for that ice cream sundae or float.

On to less fattening things. If you're an antique collector or mere browser, Point Pleasant Beach is rapidly becoming one of the best places on the Shore to find that turn-of-the-century vase, lamp stand, chest or coat stand. The **Point Pleasant Antique Emporium** on the corner of Bay and Trenton avenues is, by far, the largest antique center in the area. Open seven days a week, the Emporium has over 100 dealers under its roof. Everything from exquisite Victorian furniture to pocket watches and rare books can be found here.

Across the street is **A Victorian Garden**, a small shop dwarfed by the Emporium, but worth a peek, nevertheless. The **Antique Den** on the corner of Bay and Arnold avenues probably ranks second to the Emporium in terms of merchandise and quality. A few stores down on Arnold Avenue, **The Antique Trading Center** (619 Arnold Avenue) and **Other Things** (613 Arnold Avenue), buy and sell antiques and have interesting collectibles. **Turn of the Century** (71 Broadway) sells antiques as well as jewelry. Finally, the **Yankee Stripper** on the corner of Channel Drive and St. Louis Avenue does dabble in antiques on occasion, though it's primarily a furniture stripping business.

Even though Point Pleasant Beach has fine restaurants and antique shops, it is still best known for its beaches and boardwalk. Of them all, Jenkinson's is the most popular. It's large enough to accommodate even the biggest Fourth of July crowds and still have room for volleyball, Frisbee or touch football games. It's also the only place where you can ride a classic beach train from one end of the beach to the other.

Seasonal beach badges or daily beach tags are required to gain entry on all Point Pleasant Beach beaches. Any of the booths situated on the boardwalk at the entrances to the beach have daily tags for sale. Fees are reasonable, considering what Spring Lake and Sea Girt charge day visitors.

> DID YOU KNOW THAT . . . AUTHOR ROBERT LOUIS STEVENSON IS SAID TO HAVE VISITED THE POINT PLEASANT BEACH AREA IN THE LATE 1800s AND WAS INSPIRED TO WRITE *TREASURE ISLAND* WHEN HE SAT ON THE MAINLAND VIEWING OSBORNE ISLAND IN THE MANASQUAN RIVER? THE ISLAND IS WEST OF THE MANASQUAN BRIDGE, JUST OPPOSITE POINT PLEASANT HOSPITAL. FOR YEARS LOCALS HAVE REFERRED TO THE ISLAND AS TREASURE ISLAND IN STEVENSON'S HONOR.

As already mentioned, the boardwalk, like most everything else in Point Pleasant Beach, is family fun. Ten years ago, boardwalk bars like the Hoffman House and the Riptide featured live music and drew a large, young, rather lively crowd to the boardwalk. But today there are condominiums where the Hoffman House stood, and the Riptide is now called **Park Place** and features only the softest rock. The college age crowd heads to Manasquan, Belmar or Seaside Heights for much of its nightly entertainment. That leaves the boardwalk pretty much a place to take the young ones on the amusement rides—two small parks, **Fun Fair** and **Jenkinson's South**, contain almost nothing but kiddie rides.

You can also feast on a spicy piece of pizza at **Cici's** (one of the best boardwalk pizza stands at the Shore), stop in for an ice cream at **Martell's**, chew on some saltwater taffy, spend a few quarters in **Frank's Arcade**, or play the **Heart of Gold**, one of the few wheels of chance still only ten cents to play. On Thursday evenings during the summer, the town sponsors fireworks on the beach. The best place to view the aerial display of colors is the boardwalk or on a boat just offshore. You'll see many party boats and private craft, their lights twinkling a hundred yards from the beach, and their horns honking in appreciation of a truly fine fireworks show.

Most of Point Pleasant Beach's motels, guesthouses and other accommodations can be found on three main thoroughfares: Broadway (motels), Ocean Avenue (bungalows, some motels), and Arnold Avenue (motels, guesthouses). Although the town has no information or welcome center, visitors can stop at the Chamber of Commerce (517 Arnold Avenue, (201) 899-2424) and pick up a Guide Book which lists and describes the various accommodations in town.

Those who come to Point Pleasant Beach to fish usually wind up staying at any of the motels on Broadway, because just about all of them are a stone's throw from the party boat docks. Anglers have a wide selection of party boats to choose from. Some boats specialize, for instance, in weakfish or fluke fishing; others concentrate on bluefish. Competition for business is keen among boats. You'll see mates standing on Broadway and Channel and Inlet drives waving you into their boat's parking lot. A good place to find out about different boats and the places they fish offshore is the **Cottage**, a luncheonette and breakfast nook at Ken's Landing (corner of Broadway and Inlet Drive). Here, you'll find local fishermen grabbing a bite to eat and talking fish year-round. Any of the other luncheonettes along Broadway are also good spots to pick up fishing tips.

Some fishermen prefer inlet fishing to party boat outings on the ocean. The Manasquan Inlet can be a good spot to fish. Due to strong tidal currents, however, be sure to use heavy sinkers and metal lures, and try to fish on the outgoing tide. It's then that fish look to feed on whatever comes their way from the Manasquan River backwaters.

Two events in Point Pleasant Beach should go on the vacationer's calendar. In July, the **Walsh Offshore Grand Prix** is held off the waters of Point Pleasant Beach and other Shore towns. The large powerboats are usually on display the week prior to the race as are the Budweiser Clydesdale horses, a throwback to the days when giant parades high-lighted the week of race festivities.

The Walsh Offshore Grand Prix is the largest powerboat race in the world; it brings top racers from around the country to Point Pleasant

Beach. The best place to view the start of the race is at Manasquan Inlet, as the boats pass through it on their way to the ocean course.

The other event is known as **Big Sea Weekend** and occurs in September after the summer season is over. The town sponsors a seafood festival, a five-mile run, an arts and crafts show, and the hilarious Tube Race and parade. Contestants compete in a mile long inner tube race off Jenkinson's Beach for the charity of their choice. It's a fun affair for spectators and participants alike and is a great way to end the summer.

BAY HEAD

New Jersey Monthly once claimed that Bay Head possessed the "snootiest" beach on the Jersey Shore. On the outside looking in, *all* of Bay Head might appear uppity. Most who summer in Bay Head are well off and regard the town as a special place indeed. And it *is* special. Think of Nantucket. Think of Martha's Vineyard. If Bay Head could somehow be moved to either of these famous Massachusetts summer retreats, few there would take notice. Bay Head contains virtually the same qualities that make these two islands off Cape Cod the pride of New England.

Consider the following. On Sunday mornings, the tiny town center of Bay Head is cluttered with Mercedes and Jaguars vying for parking spaces. Yachtsmen from the nearby **Bay Head Yacht Club** dressed in bright green or pink pants and Izod polo shirts can be found at **Mueller's Bakery** or **Fran's Deli** picking up buns and the *New York Times*. Nannies push carriages down the tree-lined streets, past cedar-shingled summer cottages nearly a century old.

Out on Barnegat Bay, a Bay Head Yacht Club–sponsored regatta might be getting under way. The club's tennis and squash courts are surely full. Doctors and lawyers team up against stockbrokers and company executives. On Twilight Lake, novice sailboarders are taking their first lessons. Meanwhile, teens head to the beach dressed in the latest swimwear. Such is life in Bay Head on a summer Sunday morning.

Bay Head's beaches aren't necessarily any better than the other beaches on the Barnegat Peninsula—except that they're less crowded, and when you turn your back on the ocean, you see million dollar mansions instead of a boardwalk overrun with amusement rides and arcades. The Bay Head beach is owned by the Bay Head Improvement Association, which, for years, offered membership and beach badges only to those who lived in Bay Head. Beachgoers in communities such as Point Pleasant and Bricktown cried discrimination and went to court to fight for the right to buy Bay Head beach badges. After a long, drawn-out battle, they won. Now Bay Head must sell badges to out-of-towners, too. But the fight wasn't over. Bay Head restricted parking regulations and has effectively discouraged all but the most stubborn outsiders from buying beach badges.

If you wish to stay in Bay Head in the summer, you'll have to rent a cottage (very expensive), rent a room in one of its classic, wooden hotels (there are only two), or stay in one of its bed and breakfasts (not exactly cheap).

Conover's Bay Head Inn (646 Main Avenue) is widely regarded as one of the best bed and breakfasts in the area; the warm hospitality and coziness found in the rooms goes unequaled. The **Bay Head Sands** (2 Twilight Road) is quite cheery and will take young children. The **Bentley Inn** (649 Main Avenue) is very popular with young couples. The **Bay Head Gables** (200 Main Avenue) is noted for its art deco and rooms with views of the ocean.

Nightlife in Bay Head is quite limited. Only **Pete's Bar and Grill** (Route 35), which becomes a disco after the dinner crowd has left, and the **Bluff's**, a hidden bar under the **Bluff's Hotel** on East Avenue, offer spirits and social play. A visit to the Bluff's is most recommended. The bar used to be a speakeasy during the days of Prohibition and has lost little of the atmosphere that made it a popular watering hole on the Peninsula 60 years ago.

Bridge Avenue, which intersects Route 35 midway through town, is Bay Head's village center. **Dorcas of Bay Head**, the corner cafe (Bridge and Lake avenues), is where you can get an outside table, eat lunch, and people watch. The old Bay Head theater is now the **Shopper's Wharf**; it houses a collection of shops that cater to the Bay Head visitor. **Bay Head Books**, farther up Bridge Avenue, will take care of your summer reading needs, while the **Bay Head Cheese Shop** serves customers with a wide variety of imported and domestic cheeses.

Even if you don't spend the weekend or even just a night in Bay Head, a stop or drive around this most picturesque of Shore towns is well worth it. Bay Head has a rare charm, one, perhaps of another era, that should be experienced by all Barnegat Peninsula visitors.

MANTOLOKING

Driving south on Route 35 through Mantoloking, you can't help but be awed by the magnificent homes that sit majestically overlooking the ocean and bay. Mantoloking is as private and low-key as Deal is farther up the coast. There are no hotels, no restaurants, nothing for the visitor to do except drive on through and admire such stately summer homes. The beaches are beautiful in Mantoloking, but the parking regulations are even more restrictive than in Bay Head. If you don't have a driveway in which to park, you're pretty much out of luck.

NORMANDY, OCEAN AND CHADWICK BEACHES

These tiny communities with matchbox-size bungalows on miniature lots, sardine-packed on row after row of narrow lanes and one-way streets, are a far cry from what is found a mile or two north in Mantoloking, where many homes sit on very large lots. These summer-only communities are bustling with activity June through September, but afterwards become ghost towns. Along the northbound section of Route 35 are fast food eateries, laundromats, surf shops, shell shops, pizzerias and lots of real estate offices. In the late afternoon, when everyone is returning from a day at the beach, traffic is backed up while crossing guards halt cars to let pedestrians get across the highway. The southbound section of Route 35 is less congested because it's less commercialized. Barnegat Bay activities such as fishing, crabbing, sailboarding and boating originate here.

The Ten Most Commonly Asked Questions About Windsurfing

Although windsurfing or boardsailing or sailboarding—they're one and the same—is a relatively new sport, created in 1967, there are more than a half million boardsailors in the United States and close to three times that many worldwide. Within the past few years, the sport has outgrown its cult status, become an Olympic event, and has evolved into a legitimate recreational water activity that people of all ages can enjoy.

One of the best places to windsurf on the Jersey Shore is Barnegat Bay. A fair breeze usually blows there in the afternoon, and because it is not wide open like the ocean to the east, yet still wide enough to have fun, the bay is actually ideal for windsurfing. In addition, the water is usually glassy so the novice can learn the basics quickly. Of course, those who want to take the art of windsurfing a step or two further can windsurf in the ocean where the advanced practice of wavejumping can be enjoyed.

Question: What exactly is windsurfing?
Answer: Windsurfing is a hybrid water sport that emphasizes the thrills of surfing and the finesse and grace of sailing. A board, much like a traditional surfboard, skims along the water as wind fills the sail, which is attached to a mast. The mast is attached to the board by way of a ball joint that enables it to move in all directions.

Question: Can anyone learn to windsurf?
Answer: Almost anyone. You need to be in fairly good physical condition. You need to know how to swim. There are no other limitations, not even age.

Question: Is it a good idea to take lessons?
Answer: Yes. Learn the proper way and avoid acquiring bad habits. An instructor from a reputable windsurfing shop like Windsurfing Bay Head (76 Bridge Avenue, (201) 899-9394) will often begin with a lesson or two on land. He'll explain to you the basics and help you get the "feel" of the board underneath your feet before you venture out into the water.

Question: How long will it take before I'm a capable windsurfer?
Answer: That depends. Like anything else, some people pick up windsurfing quicker than others. How much you practice is another

factor. Generally speaking, some initial lessons, perhaps 5 hours worth, followed by 30 hours of practice on your own is enough for the novice to feel fairly confident on a sailboard. Within three months of regular practice, one should be able to handle all but the most challenging bay conditions.

Question: Must I purchase a sailboard right away?
Answer: No. You can rent one to get started and make sure you enjoy the sport. But eventually you'll want your own equipment. Ask for advice before sinking money into a sailboard and related equipment. They come in many different lengths, weights and styles. A newcomer to the sport should consider a board that's approximately 12 feet long and 40–45 pounds in weight. As for sails, you'll want a large sail, which is best for light winds. The average sail size for a beginner is 59 or 60 square feet. Later on, you'll want to own other sails to meet specific wind conditions.

Question: How much must I spend?
Answer: Once again, that depends. You can expect to spend anywhere from $700 to $1200 for a board, sail, mast and boom. Buy only from a reputable boardsailing shop. Don't rule out used equipment, but know what you're buying.

Question: Is windsurfing dangerous?
Answer: Any water sport can be dangerous if proper precautions aren't taken. Generally, the worst that will happen to you is falling into the water. Good water safety is imperative as is a basic knowledge and respect of wind, wave and water conditions and, as already noted, an ability to swim. One important safety rule for novices: never sail alone.

Question: Do I need to purchase a wetsuit?
Answer: Only if you intend to sail in cold water or if exposure to the wind causes you to get cold prematurely. Wetsuits are bulky; you'll probably want to avoid them if you can.

Question: When is the best time to windsurf at the Jersey Shore?
Answer: The best seasons are spring and fall when the wind is most consistent. Windsurfing, however, is most popular during the summer when the air and water temperatures are warmest. You'll see, however, more and more boardsailors out on Barnegat Bay year-round.

Question: How do I find out about contests and regattas?
Answer: By checking with local shops in your area and subscribing to magazines like *Wind Surf* and *Wind Rider*. Also, each summer New Jersey sponsors the Garden State Games, an Olympic-type competition that includes boardsailing. There are different classes and levels of competition. Watch for announcements in the local newspaper and at YMCAs for specific dates.

Lavallette and Ortley Beach

Lavallette possesses some of the cottage culture that comprises small beach towns like Chadwick and Normandy to her north. But she has a bit of a year-round population and a pleasant shopping district on Grand Central Avenue (Route 35 South) that makes the town something more than a summer-only community. Lavallette takes advantage of both the bay and ocean sides of town, perhaps more so than any other on the peninsula. Unlike communities such as Bay Head and Mantoloking, Lavallette has not permitted residential development of most of her bayshore. Instead, there's a wonderful waterfront park that provides all the activity space one would need for fishing and crabbing (two piers), boating (two launch ramps) and even swimming (there is a guarded beach).

As for Lavallette's beaches, they are very good for bodysurfing, since the offshore sandbars are out far enough to prevent waves from curling on the shoreline like they do, say, in Point Pleasant Beach. Lavallette's waves break just right for catching a wave with just a few flaps of finned feet, or a few swift paddles while riding a raft, boogie board or surfboard. At the same time, children can frolic in the white water that gently washes ashore—the end product of the outside breakers—with little fear of being hit by one and knocked down.

Beach badges are available throughout the summer at Borough Hall (Grand Central and Washington avenues). One can purchase a badge for the season, half season, week or weekend. Badge fees are quite reasonable.

Ortley Beach is the next town south and is merely an extension of what is found in Lavallette. Its most noted landmark is **Joey Harrison's Surf Club** (1900 Ocean Avenue). With its extra large dancefloor and its nightly live entertainment in the summer, it is one of the most popular nightspots in the area.

Surf's Up!

Although surfers populate the entire coastline of New Jersey and surf waves from Sandy Hook to the tip of Cape May, it's here on the Barnegat Peninsula where they ride the biggest and most challenging waves. Dozens of surf spots along the peninsula handle all types of swells. Many of the "spots" are "beach breaks," meaning a location where the waves are formed on sandbars and break fairly close to the beach. The waves of Island Beach State Park and those in Lavallette and the Seasides hit sandbars and form especially neat, cresting curls, ideal for all levels of surfing.

Perhaps the only place on the entire peninsula not suited for surfing is Point Pleasant Beach. Years ago, Point Pleasant Beach *used* to have top-notch surfing. Today, most of what is there now is known as "shore break," waves that curl right *on* the beach, thus leaving no room in which to ride them. Due to the loss of its offshore sand bars, its relatively deep water, and the restructuring of the nearby Manasquan Inlet jetty, the only swell that produces rideable waves in Point Pleasant Beach is one from the northeast.

Bay Head usually has one or two beaches with waves that are quite good. But, once again, due to shifting sandbar patterns, it's difficult to say which beach will be the best for surfing this year. Check with local surfers for the latest surf report. From Mantoloking down to Lavallette, the sandbar situation improves dramatically. One theory why the sandbars are so pronounced at this section of the peninsula is because there is no inlet or manmade jetties to disturb the currents and natural flow of sand. Therefore, waves in Lavallette are apt to be much more consistent than farther up the peninsula.

In the Seasides, the best waves are found by the amusement pier, as already noted. During and immediately after storms or low pressure fronts, powerful waves often roll in on both sides of the pier creating challenging conditions for surfers. You'll see the area's best surfers gliding down the faces of waves here, cranking radical turns and cutting off the lip of the curl.

The biggest problem surfers encounter on the Barnegat Peninsula is not lack of waves, but the permission to get to them. Due to private ownership of the beach and restrictions on those public beaches, surfers are often denied access during the day in the summer months. Some towns do designate certain beaches as "surfing beaches" (Bay Head and Lavallette, for instance), but such beaches don't necessarily produce the best waves.

Fortunately for surfers, surfing conditions along the Jersey Shore are best in the early morning hours and in late afternoon, so surfers and swimmers usually keep out of each other's way, and badge checkers are either not yet on duty, or have gone home for the day. It's also during the early morning and late afternoon that the wind is most likely to be offshore, which makes for the best shaped waves.

The best place to find out about up-to-the-minute surfing conditions (wind, tide, swell direction, wave size) is at the local surf shop. The Barnegat Peninsula has four major shops that can give the visiting surfer advice as to where the best waves are and what the beach restrictions might be. Many of the shops also sponsor surf contests as does the Eastern Surfing Association. Check surf shop bulletin boards for details and entry blanks.

SEASIDE HEIGHTS

Seaside Heights's boardwalk is nearly as famous as its south Jersey Shore counterpart in Wildwood. Although the Wildwood boardwalk is longer (2½ miles as opposed to one mile in Seaside), and contains more amusement rides (five piers worth as opposed to one in Seaside), the summer Saturday night thermometer (if such things existed) would certainly register as high in Seaside as it would in Wildwood.

The biggest reason for the parity is Seaside's intense concentration of activity. Seaside is a small town, so the moment one enters it, one has a strong sense of being surrounded, even overwhelmed, with flashing neon lights, blaring music, traffic, hustle, shrieks echoing from the Casino Pier as the roller coaster races downward, and the alternating smells of salt air, pizza, caramel popcorn and amusement ride grease.

Seaside is a fast, lively, action-packed town from June through August. It's a place where summer loves are won and lost and where families from North Jersey come, as they always have, for their annual two-week vacation at the Shore. At Seaside they spend the day on the beach, but the night belongs to the boardwalk. Like a religious ritual, families will live out a tiny part of the American Dream by spending and splurging and injecting themselves with one thrill after another.

The boardwalk is like a large magnet that attracts visitors the moment they find a parking space—something that can be quite rare in the summer. Once you're on the boardwalk, though, it's just a matter of what appeals to you most—the rides, the wheels of chance, the arcades or the fast food stands.

If it's the amusement rides, head straight to the Casino Pier where the best ones are found. Here are some of the newest, fastest, most spine-tingling and stomach-shaking amusement rides north of Wildwood. Yet, despite all this, Seaside is most proud of the **Casino Pier Carousel**. Located in the **Casino Arcade**, between Grant and Sherman avenues on the boardwalk, the 80-year-old Carousel is truly a piece of Americana. A night spent on the boards wouldn't be complete without at least one ride on it. It is an antique amusement ride and certainly a classic; of the more than 10,000 carousels made during the golden age of carousels at the turn of the century, only 200 still exist. The wooden, brightly painted figures were handcarved, and the military band music you hear as you approach the carousel comes from an authentic Wurlitzer Band Organ built in 1923.

Carousel buffs from all over come to ride and photograph the Casino Pier Carousel. There's even a tiny gift shop where you can purchase figurines, books and even albums of military music. One can only speculate how long the carousel will remain in Seaside Heights. Each year there's talk of breaking it down and selling the wooden horses, which can command up to $15,000 per horse at auctions.

If it's the wheels of chance you prefer, you can lay bets down on a name or number for as little as a dime or as much as a dollar. The old saying, "You get what you pay for" certainly applies here. A dime placed on a winner will get you a towel, a box of candy or, worse, a small, plastic, naked doll. But if it's a buck you're willing to bet, it's possible to win videos, bicycles or cassette players. The competition for your bet will be keen, whether it be a dime or a dollar, so expect to be hawked and hollered at as you pass by the many stands.

You can find skeeball and pinball, and the latest selection of video games in any of the many arcades on the boardwalk. **Lucky Leo's** and **Sonny's and Rickey's** are popular haunts. The **Central Arcade**, the **Royal Arcade, Funtown Arcade** and **Big Top** are also worth exploring.

Finally, everyone succumbs to a boardwalk dinner at least once during their Seaside vacation. That might mean something as simple as a plain pizza or as complex as a sausage and meatball sandwich smothered in tomato sauce and topped with melted cheese, peppers and onions. For dessert, there's candy apples, cotton candy, caramel popcorn or all of the above.

Seaside's beaches are wide (as wide as Jenkinson's in Point Pleasant Beach), usually clean, and open to the public on a day or season basis. Tags or badges can be purchased on the boardwalk at the entrance to the beach. You'll find excellent surfing on either side of the Casino Pier (but especially on the north side), and one of the best surf shops in all New Jersey in neighboring Seaside Park. Called **Grog's Surf Palace** (910 Central Avenue), the shop boasts a broad selection of the latest state-of-the-art surf equipment and the latest fashionable surfwear.

Seaside is also the unofficial waterslide capital of the Jersey Shore. No less than three very good slides are in Seaside, all of which are loads of fun and provide a terrific way to cool off on a hot summer afternoon or evening. The best of the batch is **Rainbow Rapids**, an incredible maze of water tunnels and turns that will leave the unsuspecting mat-rider gasping for air. Sitting on your mat, you'll hit speeds upwards of 30 miles an hour or more as you twist and turn down the water-fed tubes and come splashing out the bottom in the wading pool. For an unusual thrill, the Rainbow Rapids experience is a must.

Aside from the boardwalk, there are four other main thoroughfares in town; each one runs north and south and gets very congested on weekends and holidays. Ocean Avenue and Ocean Terrace run parallel to each other and are closest to the boardwalk. Here can be found most of the bathhouses and pools, for those not inclined to sandy their feet or test the ocean's waters. The Boulevard contains the bulk of Seaside's nightclubs with **Baby'O** (406 Boulevard) and **Panache** (308 Boulevard) standing out among the others. A drink and a dance or two at Seaside's most famous nightspot, however, is also recommended. The **Chatterbox** (Lincoln and Boardwalk) was one of the first clubs on the Jersey Shore to bring in national acts to perform. Recently, the club has been booking classic 1960s groups.

Central Avenue is where you'll find Rainbow Rapids and many of the hotels in Seaside Heights. You'll notice rather quickly that your choice of lodgings is limited. Motels, apartments or bungalows are essentially it. Seaside, in other words, has no bed and breakfasts or higher-priced luxury hotels. For a free list of accommodations and rates, write to Accommodations Directory, Seaside Heights, Box 38R, Seaside Heights 08751.

Recommended Barnegat Peninsula Surf Shops

Brave New World
1208 Richmond Avenue
Point Pleasant Beach 08742
(201) 892-9833

Grog's Surf Palace
910 Central Avenue
Seaside Park 08752
(201) 793-0097

New Image Surf 'N' Wear
Route 35 & West Osprey Avenue
Lavallette 08735
(201) 793-4822

Ocean Hut Surf Shop
3111 Route 35 North
Lavallette 08735
(201) 793-3400

SEASIDE PARK

Although a neighbor of Seaside Heights, Seaside Park is much quieter and less hectic. It draws mostly summer residents who own bungalows or rent them for the season. Those who spend their summers there are in the enviable position of being within a short distance of Seaside Heights's boardwalk excitement and nightlife and of Island Beach State Park (see below).

Seaside Park's beaches are less crowded and take less abuse than those in Seaside Heights. The town's boardwalk has no amusements or concession stands, but it doesn't really need any of this, being so close to Seaside Heights. On the bay side of Seaside Park, windsurfing and sailing are quite popular.

ISLAND BEACH STATE PARK

The most frequently asked question of park rangers by first time visitors to Island Beach State Park is a good one: where is the island? The fact is Island Beach State Park is not an island; it's situated at the south end of the Barnegat Peninsula. But remember too, Barnegat Peninsula is not really a peninsula. It's an island. So, technically speaking, Island Beach State Park is *located* on an island, but is not an island in itself.

To make matters even more confusing, Island Beach was *once* an island. Back in 1720 during a particularly powerful storm, the ocean and bay met in what is now Ortley Beach; the two colliding bodies of water cut off Island Beach from the rest of the Barnegat Peninsula. The same storm closed New Inlet further south. The new waterway was called Cranberry Inlet and quickly became a primary route for ships

---

DID YOU KNOW THAT ... THE SUMMER MANSION OF THE GOVERNOR IS LOCATED IN ISLAND BEACH STATE PARK?

coming into or leaving Barnegat Bay. Historians tell us that pirates also valued the inlet and frequented Barnegat Bay by passing through it.

In 1812, however, another heavy storm hit the Jersey Coast and this time closed off Cranberry Inlet. Thus, Island Beach lost its island status, despite repeated attempts by man to reopen the waterway. Only one other time did Island Beach actually become an island again. That was in 1935 when the bay met the ocean in what is today Island Beach State Park. This time locals wanted it closed and filled in the new inlet. Area rumrunners and bootleggers didn't like the idea much because they, like privateers and pirates years earlier, recognized the strategic value of such a link with the ocean. In 1962 the famous March Storm temporarily cut Island Beach into 11 separate islands, and every now and then during winter storms, a new inlet will be formed somewhere in Island Beach State Park. But as soon as the storm subsides, so does the water.

Island Beach might never have become a state park had Henry Phipps, a steel-making magnate and contemporary of Andrew Carnegie, realized his 1926 dream of making the area a grand beach resort for the wealthy. Phipps envisioned seashore mansions and bayside marinas filled with yachts. Fortunately for future visitors to Island Beach, Phipps' dream was shattered after the stock market crash in 1929.

In the years following the crash, little thought was given to other schemes that would have exploited Island Beach's vast natural beauty. People did reside on Island Beach in small beach shanties until World War II when the Army came in and used the area to conduct experiments in antiaircraft rocketry. Immediately after the war, however, the Army gave up its interest in Island Beach. In 1953 the state purchased Island Beach from the Phipps Estate and six years later, made it into a state park.

Today Island Beach State Park is a vivid reminder of what the rest of the Barnegat Peninsula looked like prior to development. The park's precious sand dunes and such vegetation as red cedar, beach plum, American holly and wild black cherry, once common on the peninsula, are now just little more than a memory everywhere else.

Island Beach is not a large state park; it's approximately 12 miles long, but it's very narrow. The width varies, depending on where you are in the park. In some areas, it's barely more than a thousand feet from bay to beach; in the southern part of the park, it's more than a mile wide. The park's main artery is the two-lane road that extends from the entrance gate on Central Avenue down almost, but not quite all the way, to Barnegat Inlet. Virtually all of the bay side of Island Beach State Park is off limits to visitors. That's because Island Beach is as much a wildlife sanctuary and natural preserve as it is a day-use area for people.

Despite this restriction, Island Beach has plenty to offer. You'll find no place in New Jersey with more beautiful beaches. Long stretches of white, driftwood-dotted beaches with great sand dunes perched atop them make for a truly splendid setting. Behind these dunes is a secondary dune system overrun with dense thicket and berry bushes, which attract many different types of birds and small rodents.

During the summer Island Beach is an exceedingly popular day-use area. It's quite common for the park to fill up its 2400 parking spaces as early as 10 a.m. and therefore close Island Beach to vehicles. If you plan to visit the park, simply plan to get there as early as possible. Earlier than that on holidays. The park opens its gates at 7 a.m. on weekends and holidays, and 8 a.m. on weekdays. There is an admission charge year-round, although the fee is reduced in the off-season. Bicyclists and hikers are always admitted free.

One way to guarantee getting into Island Beach during the summer on weekends from July 4th to Labor Day is to take the Island Beach State Park Shuttle. If you're coming from the Garden State Parkway, get off at Exit 81, park your car in the parking lot there, and take the shuttle bus to Island Beach. Buses run 9 a.m.–6 p.m. and leave the parking lot every half hour. For more information on the summer shuttle, call (201) 793-0506.

DID YOU KNOW THAT ... EEL GRASS, WHICH ONCE GREW IN ABUNDANCE IN BARNEGAT BAY, WAS DRIED OUT AND USED FOR HOUSE INSULATION TO PROTECT AGAINST COLD WINTER WINDS THE SAME WAY FIBERGLASS INSULATION DOES TODAY? EEL GRASS HAS THE ADDED ADVANTAGE OF BEING ODORLESS AND NONFLAMMABLE. THE GOVERNOR'S MANSION IN ISLAND BEACH STATE PARK IS INSULATED WITH EEL GRASS. UNFORTUNATELY FOR THE EEL GRASS INDUSTRY, A BLIGHT WIPED OUT THE BAY'S EEL GRASS AND ENDED HARVESTING OF THE PLANT. TODAY, HOWEVER, EEL GRASS, SAY MARINE BIOLOGISTS, IS MAKING A GRADUAL COMEBACK.

Things to Do

Spend the Day on the Beach. Island Beach has both guarded *and* unguarded beaches. If you wish to escape the crowds and venture off on your own, you can. But be advised, the currents offshore are tricky and often swift. No one should swim alone in unguarded waters. The guarded beaches—Ocean Bathing Units #1 and #2—have changing rooms, lockers and showers as well as concession stands. Skip the fast food and enjoy a beach picnic. Island Beach is one of the precious few state beaches where you are allowed to bring food onto the beach and barbecue as long as the fire is at least 50 feet east of the dunes. This is one of Island Beach's biggest selling points in the summer, and many people take advantage of the liberal park policy.

Visit the Aeolium. Approximately a mile south of the park's entrance is the Aeolium, a welcome center of sorts that includes displays pertaining to the history of Island Beach and the fragile ecological balance of the park. You'll also see exhibits that point out the various forms of wildlife that live in the park, and you can pick up self-guided trail maps and information on such topics as bird-watching and beachcombing.

Walk a Self-guided Nature Trail. The trail that begins near the Aeolium is a good one to hike. Stay *on* the trail. If you walk through the brush and wander about on your own, you're certain to come into contact with poison ivy, damage plant life, and injure sand dunes. The dunes are any barrier island's most treasured resource. They protect the land from ocean storms and waves and beach erosion. The grass that grows on the dunes prevents the sand from being blown or washed away. To trample on it is to kill it. This seriously threatens the life of the sand dunes. If the sand dunes are threatened, then so is the very existence of the barrier island. (For more information on sand dunes, see chapter 8.)

For those who prefer guided tours, park naturalists conduct two a day during the summer. Each tour lasts approximately an hour, is limited to some 25 people and usually originates at the Aeolium.

Go Bird-watching. Like so many other natural areas on the Jersey Shore, Island Beach is located on the Atlantic Flyway. Thus, in April and May, and then again in September and October, the park is filled with resting migratory birds. Either spring or fall is a good time to bird-watch at Island Beach. The number of people visiting the park is low, the birds are usually plentiful, and the dreaded mosquito has not yet readied itself for his summer onslaught, or else has hopefully finished up his bloody business.

Island Beach also hosts bird-watchers in summer and winter. A number of nesting birds are in the thicket during the months of July and August, although much of this area is not open to visitors for obvious reasons. In the winter you can travel down to the southern tip of the park and search out sea birds like the kittiwake and gannet. You can also find snowy owls there as Island Beach seems to be one of their favorite haunts.

Go Scuba Diving. Scuba diving is permitted off Island Beach providing divers have proof of underwater diving training in the form of a valid certification card. Also, divers must adhere to certain rules in the park and waters offshore. Upon arriving, ask a park ranger for Island Beach's Diving Policy and Procedures Sheet.

Go Surfing. Island Beach offers experienced surfers the opportunity to enjoy their sport under challenging conditions and with beautiful backdrops of sand dunes and beach thicket. Only seasoned surfers should surf Island Beach due to its strong currents. The waves are of the beach break type and are usually best during a south swell.

Ride a Horse on the Beach. Island Beach is open to horses and horseback riders before and after the peak summer season, namely, from October 15 to April 15. Reservations must be made in advance by calling (201) 793-0506 as there are only a limited number of horses allowed on the beach at any one time. There is no extra charge for horses. Of course, horses are *not* to be ridden on the sand dunes. There is a beach access path for riders to use. Ask a ranger for directions.

Go Beachcombing. Island Beach is an excellent place to walk the beach and search for natural treasures. One can usually find an interesting assortment of shells and driftwood. Island Beach is also a particularly good place to find seahorses during late summer and early fall. Once dried, the seahorse, like the starfish, is considered a prized find. During the winter one might find what's known as *frost fish*. Frost fish are usually whiting that have either jumped out of the water onto the beach or have been beached by a wave. In any case, when the temperature is very low, these fish freeze almost instantly. Those who collect frost fish do so for eating purposes. Frost fish supposedly taste better than fish hooked and then frozen because the chemical interaction within the fish which changes the taste of the fish does not occur when the fish freezes to death.

Go Surf Fishing. Island Beach offers the angler some of the finest surf fishing on the Jersey Shore. Anglers are even permitted to take four wheel drive vehicles on the beach. Taking advantage of this will only enhance the fishing outing because you'll be able to follow bluefish and striped bass runs down the beach. These occur in autumn when mullet are found in large numbers just offshore. Mullet is what bring the blues into the surf. Some fishermen use metal lures, but the best bait, say experienced anglers, is exactly what the blues are looking to eat—mullet. Fishermen can get four wheel drive permits at the front gate, provided they show proof the vehicle will be used for fishing purposes only. In other words, you must have fishing equipment on hand. Three-day permits, good for three *consecutive* days, and annual permits are available for a fee. Island Beach is open to fishermen 24 hours a day. Those who prefer to fish off a jetty rather than off the beach can do so at the very end of the park where the north jetty of Barnegat Inlet is located.

If You Have a Boat. The bay side of Island Beach offers excellent crabbing. Beware, though, of very shallow water and the change of tides. One of the best places to snorkel on the Jersey Shore, believe it or not, is on the bay side of Island Beach. The water at Tice's Shoal is amazingly clear and full of marine life. Boaters also come to Tice's Shoal for a day of "boat parties." Often referred to as "Cocktail Cove," a number of boaters drop anchor here and spend the day sunning and sipping cocktails. Note: There is no boat launch at Island Beach State Park.

Some Recommended Restaurants on the Barnegat Peninsula

Alfonso's
1001 Arnold Avenue
Point Pleasant

(201) 892-4121
Price Code: Moderate
Menu: Italian

Alfonso's has a legion of locals who swear it's here you get the area's best pasta and Italian meat dishes.

Barmore's Shrimp Box
75 Inlet Drive
Point Pleasant Beach
(201) 899-1637
Price Code: Moderate
Menu: Seafood

Seafood of the traditional sort: stuffed flounder, lobster, fried clams. Waterfront dining. Almost always a wait in the summer.

Crab's Claw
601 Grand Central Avenue
Lavallette
(201) 793-4447
Price Code: Moderate
Menu: Seafood

A good place for seafood, especially for those in the Lavallette-Seaside area who don't wish to drive to Point Pleasant Beach for dinner.

Europa South
Route 35 and Arnold Avenue
Point Pleasant Beach
(201) 295-1500
Price Code: Moderate
Menu: Spanish and Portuguese

For a real change of pace, Europa South offers a most interesting cuisine. Rated best Spanish/Portuguese restaurant in South Jersey by readers of *New Jersey Monthly* in 1985.

Filomio's
17 Inlet Drive
Point Pleasant Beach
(201) 892-2723
Price Code: Moderate
Menu: Italian

Filomio's lasagne is legendary. Too many people, though, opt for the pasta at Filomio's; the real gems on the menu are the seafood dishes.

Frazee's
Route 35
Point Pleasant Beach
(201) 892-1021
Price Code: Moderate
Menu: Seafood

What you'd expect from a family-run restaurant with adjoining fish market: fresh seafood prepared with care.

Lobster Shanty
83 Channel Drive
Point Pleasant Beach
(201) 899-6700
Price Code: Moderate
Menu: Seafood

One of New Jersey's most popular seafood restaurants. Nautical decor, set on Manasquan River. Buffet is the best bet.

Offshore Inn
225 Ocean Avenue
Point Pleasant Beach
(201) 892-2848
Price Code: Moderate
Menu: Italian and seafood

In the mood for hot mussels? This is the place. Popular haunt for locals.

Pete's Bar and Grill
Route 35
Bay Head
(201) 892-3382
Price Code: Moderate
Menu: International

Don't let the name fool you; Pete's has far more class than a typical bar and grill. Delicious salads.

Sea Drift
128½ Ocean Avenue
Point Pleasant Beach
(201) 892-7820
Price Code: Moderate/Expensive
Menu: Italian

Linen tablecloths, flowers on table. One of Point Pleasant Beach's well-kept secrets. The house specialty? Veal.

Tesauro's
210 Ocean Avenue
Point Pleasant Beach
(201) 892-2090
Price Code: Moderate
Menu: Italian

Standard Italian menu, long a favorite with tourists.

Top of the Mast
23rd Avenue
Seaside Park
(201) 793-2444
Price Code: Moderate/Expensive
Menu: Seafood

Located just prior to the entrance to Island Beach State Park. Mussels in cream sauce, tile-fish, both excellent.

Wharfside
101 Channel Drive
Point Pleasant Beach
(201) 892-9100
Price Code: Moderate
Menu: Seafood

Wharfside has its loyalists, so does the Lobster Shanty. Both are on Channel Drive; both are Jack Baker creations. Take your pick.

5. LONG BEACH ISLAND

Long Beach Island is appropriately named. It is an island, a barrier island, which sits some four miles off southern Ocean County, connected to the mainland by only a causeway, which stretches across lower Barnegat Bay and Little Egg Harbor. Long Beach Island is indeed long—some 18 miles long from the northern tip of Barnegat Light State Park to the southern edge of the Holgate National Wildlife Refuge—not to mention skinny. Nowhere is it more than a mile wide. In fact, in many sections of the island, it's barely a half mile from beach to bay. And finally, Long Beach Island is mostly beach—some of the finest beach found on the Jersey Shore.

But what the name of the island doesn't do is reflect the intangibles, like Long Beach Island's unique character. Long Beach Island has little in common with its neighbors. There's virtually no resemblance to the bright lights and fast pace of Seaside Heights to the north, for example, or to the glamor and occasional gaudiness of Atlantic City to the south. There's even little to suggest any sort of relationship to southern Ocean County towns like Tuckerton and Manahawkin, which lie just across the bay, other than one of necessity.

Perhaps because it is an island somewhat removed from the mainland and is somewhat isolated from the rest of the Jersey Shore (there is only one way on and off the island—the Manahawkin Bridge), Long Beach Island has an identity all its own. Some claim it's similar to that found on Cape Cod. Like on the Cape, those who vacation on Long Beach Island usually return year after year. Most stay for weeks, rather than weekends or just the day. Many stay the summer.

On Long Beach Island people know their summer neighbors and frequently socialize with them. It's a family-oriented island; except on weekends and holidays, it's strangely quiet and even a touch tranquil, especially in northern island towns like Barnegat Light and Loveladies. Long Beach Island has no boardwalks, just sand dunes peppered with beach grass and cottages that snuggle up behind them. There are very few bars and nightclubs, although the island does have some very fine restaurants. It has only one amusement area, and it's a small one at that.

To spend a week or so on Long Beach Island is to sample a wonderful sense of community that's rare in beach resort towns during the summer months. To spend a month or longer on the island is to actually become a part of that community. What's amazing is that it's as strong as it is, despite the influx of people onto Long Beach Island each summer. The island possesses a winter population of approximately ten thousand.

DID YOU KNOW THAT ... BECAUSE LONG BEACH ISLAND IS APPROXIMATELY FOUR MILES FROM THE MAINLAND, IT IS RELATIVELY FREE OF POLLEN? THOSE WHO SUFFER FROM HAY FEVER WILL FIND LONG BEACH ISLAND MUCH TO THEIR LIKING.

In the summer, that figures swells to 10 or 12 times that size.

The island's main artery is Long Beach Boulevard, an asphalt ribbon that extends the length of the island. It loosely connects the string of beach towns, some of which have the most unusual of names (Ship Bottom, Harvey Cedars). On the boulevard is where you'll find many of the island's eateries, its specialty and gift shops, and the stores that provide just about all of the essentials for one to remain on the island the *entire* summer. That means never *once* having to go over the Manahawkin Bridge and onto the mainland. It's no secret that islanders value their self-sufficiency, even if it doesn't run as deep as some would believe.

Venture to either side of the boulevard and you'll discover the most splendid collection of summer houses found on the Jersey Shore. In communities like Ship Bottom and Surf City are streets and lanes of white-washed cottages and boxy beach bungalows. Down in Beach Haven and up in Barnegat Light, Victorian mansions remain from a century ago. In Harvey Cedars and Loveladies, you'll come across the dazzling assortment of luxurious, contemporary ocean and bay front homes. Most of them were constructed after the 1962 March storm, which decimated much of the island. All of these poststorm homes were built on pilings to prevent in the future the millions of dollars in flood damages suffered during that memorable storm.

In between all this, two cultures coexist side by side, much like they do, once again, in Cape Cod. The most obvious of the two is the beach culture, which permeates every aspect of day-to-day Long Beach Island living. People come to Long Beach Island, first and foremost, to enjoy its excellent beaches and the activities that revolve around them.

In July and August everyone sports a golden tan on Long Beach Island because a sunny day doesn't go by in which *some* time isn't spent on or near the beach. Long Beach Island has more than its share of sun bums. But it also supports very hearty surfing, bodysurfing, windsurfing, water ski, jet ski, and sailing crowds. And after the sun has gone down, surf fishermen, beachwalkers, and beachcombers armed with metal detectors take over the beach as do kite-fliers when there's a decent breeze.

Over on the bay side of Long Beach Island is just as much activity. Some of the best clamming and crabbing waters north of Chesapeake Bay lie between the island and mainland towns like Tuckerton, Manahawkin, Barnegat and Waretown. Lower Barnegat Bay and Little Egg Harbor (which, together, are often known simply as "the bay") are dotted with tiny green islands that provide shelter and nesting areas for waterfowl and migratory birds.

Because of the bay's shallow waters, boat navigation can, at times, prove tricky. There are a number of hidden shoals. But these don't prevent all sorts of pleasure craft and their crews from enjoying the bay's waters in spring, summer and fall. Charter and party boats are docked up and down the bay side of Long Beach Island, and the sails of windsurfers and sailboats fill out the scenery with their color. Water-skiers and jet skiers zip across the water's surface at a fast clip, negotiating the fishermen, crabbers and clammers in their rowboats. It all makes for a very busy bay.

The beach culture of Long Beach Island extends itself away from the water's edge, too. Surf shops, shell shops, bait and tackle shops, and a wide range of seafood restaurants can be found practically anywhere on the island. Clothing boutiques feature the latest surf 'n' sail fashions. Virtually every store, be it a grocery store or pharmacy, sells beach chairs, suntan lotion, bellyboards and children's sandpails. Even the names of the streets—Lagoon Drive, Beachview Street, Bay View Avenue, Nautilus Drive, Marina Boulevard, Sand Dune Drive—reflect the "beachiness" of those who summer on Long Beach Island.

But another culture thrives on the island in the summer, too. It's a bit less obvious than the island's beach culture and more refined and urban-influenced. It's one that enables such Long Beach Island institutions as Beach Haven's Surflight Summer Theatre, which stages musicals and comedies throughout the season, and the unusually large number of art galleries to do more than simply survive.

Long Beach Island possesses museums, historical societies and cultural groups that sponsor lectures and seminars on island legend and lore, weekly outdoor concerts, poetry readings, art and sculpture instruction and dance classes. Artists show and discuss their work at the Long Beach Island Foundation of the Arts and Sciences. In short, the availability of beach alternatives makes Long Beach Island more than just an island of sun, surf and sand.

During the off-season, Long Beach Island is not nearly as busy or as crowded as it is during the summer. But it's just as inviting. Like anywhere on the Jersey Shore, September is an excellent time to visit Long Beach Island. The weather is usually gorgeous—warm days and cool, sweater nights—and the water temperature in the ocean is the warmest of the year. It's not unusual to swim in 75-degree water in early autumn on Long Beach Island.

Many restaurants, guesthouses and bed and breakfasts remain open throughout the fall. This is the time to go surf fishing, beachwalking and surfing. Bird-watchers make a point of getting down to Holgate National Wildlife Refuge at least once during the fall. It's also a good time to visit the island's antique shops and other specialty shops, as many of them offer solid bargains on merchandise left over from the summer season.

Activity on the island slows down to a trickle in winter, but, by mid-March, summer is on many people's minds. Boaters are busy readying their boats for summer. Summer home owners are patching roofs and painting porches. Families from Philadelphia and West and North Jersey begin their search for a bungalow to rent once June rolls around. This continues until Memorial Day when many islanders settle in for the summer.

The easiest way to get to Long Beach Island is via the Garden State Parkway (Exit 63) and Route 72 East. Once you leave the Parkway and get on Route 72, you'll pass through Manahawkin and drive over a causeway. This will take you over the lower reach of Barnegat Bay and Cedar Bonnet and Bonnet Islands. If you look to your left (north) as you ride over the causeway and Manahawkin Bay Bridge, you'll get a view of the Barnegat National Wildlife Refuge and the many tiny islands and marshland coves that comprise it.

The first thing you should do before beginning your visit or vacation on Long Beach Island is to stop at the Information Center, located on Ninth Street in Ship Bottom, just a few hundred yards from the Manahawkin Bridge. It's open seven days a week, year-round. Here, you can get up-to-the-minute information on lodging and a calendar of events that will list times and places for such things as fishing tournaments, fairs, surfing contests and lifeguard competitions. Also available are copies of Long Beach Island's three weekly newspapers. The *Sandpiper, Beachcomber* and *Summer Times* are all free and provide really excellent coverage of island life and activities.

You can also pick up information on weekly and season beach badge fees. Badges, however, are not sold at the Information Center. Instead, they're available at the municipal offices of the towns of Long Beach Island. Prices for beach badges on the island are quite cheap, especially when compared to the prices of badges sold at other Jersey beach resorts. Expect to pay less than $10 for a full season badge, no matter what municipality you purchase it from. Badges are not required for children under 12, and some Long Beach Island towns offer special discounts to senior citizens. Badges are good only in the town where they are purchased.

Once you get your bearings (don't forget to pick up a free map of the island at the Information Center), you'll have to decide what part of Long Beach Island you plan to explore first. The town of Ship Bottom sits almost in the middle of the island. If you make a left on Long Beach Boulevard, you'll head north and go toward Barnegat Light State Park and such beach communities as Harvey Cedars and Loveladies. A right turn on the boulevard will take you in the direction of Beach Haven and the Holgate National Wildlife Refuge Area.

A Short History of Long Beach Island

The Dutch were the first Europeans to sight and then settle on the spit of land that came to be known as Long Beach Island. But it was

New England whalers who were the first to exploit the island's chief natural resource, namely, its close proximity to migratory whale routes. As a result, whaling was the first real industry begun on Long Beach Island.

There were three known whaling stations on the island. With crews on land ready to launch whaleboats from the beach the moment a whale was sighted, and other crews aboard whaling ships offshore, the whaling industry was a thriving one. Most people living on the island in the eighteenth century were connected to whaling in one way or another.

Whaling, however, began to die out on Long Beach Island in the early part of the nineteenth century. What essentially followed was the growth of tourism, which, today, is still the island's number one source of revenue. Hunters began frequenting Long Beach Island in search of ducks and birds, and fishermen caught plenty of fish, both in the shallows of the bay and in the ocean's surf. The earliest Long Beach Island guesthouse, built at the beginning of the 1800s, was for hunters and fishermen. Another one was built in 1822. Known as the Mansion of Health, it stood on land in what is today Surf City.

By the mid-1800s, a stagecoach route was begun by enterprising Philadelphians to bring outdoorsmen and their families from the city of Brotherly Love and nearby Camden to the bay town of Tuckerton. From there, island-bound visitors were taken across the bay in a boat.

Tourism picked up substantially when a railroad bridge was completed across Barnegat Bay. A rail line was also established in Beach Haven; it ran north to Barnegat Light and was a main means of transportation on the island for years. During this time people stayed at the Harvey Cedars Hotel, the Engleside and the Spray Beach Hotel. By the end of the century, Beach Haven established itself as the island's main tourist town. In addition to staying in hotels there, people began building Victorian summer homes and seaside cottages and stayed the summer.

While tourism was being developed on Long Beach Island, there was another, shall we say, "alternative" means of making a living, at least according to local legend. Those involved were known as Barnegat Pirates or "wreckers" and "mooncussers," as David J. Seibold and Charles Adams III tell it in their delightful little book, *Legends of Long Beach Island*.

According to the authors (who also wrote *Shipwrecks Near Barnegat Inlet*, another book dealing with Long Beach Island history and lore), "The wreckers waited until a moonless night ... the lights of the ships offshore were visible, as they sailed the busy shipping lanes north and south of New York. These ships tried to cut their sailing time and distance by coasting as close to the shore as possible, avoiding any of the navigational hazards that could bring a voyage to an abrupt and tragic halt."

The Barnegat Pirates knew all about such shortcuts. Accordingly, these shady characters would tie a lantern to a mule or ox and walk it up and down the shoreline. Occasionally a passing sea captain would spot it and think the light to be from a nearby ship. He might have ordered his ship toward it, hoping to get a better view of it and gain a route even closer to the shore. It was too late when he realized the dastardly trick that was played on him. Usually the ship was wrecked on the shoals, or else broken into pieces by waves and ultimately beached. The pirates then looted the ship, which most likely carried valuable cargo.

There's little to prove convincingly that such acts of piracy and sometimes murder did indeed occur, as Seibold and Adams carefully point out. Chances are, however, some of this did go on. Similar stories circulate of pirates performing the same evil deeds on Cape Cod and Cape Hatteras. And there have been a *lot* of shipwrecks off Long Beach Island. But until more research is done on the subject, the truth about the Barnegat Pirates will remain shrouded in mystery.

Despite such grim tales, Long Beach Island continued to prosper as a summer tourist resort. The Barnegat Lighthouse, affectionately known as Old Barney, became increasingly popular with visitors. Bird-watchers and boaters enjoyed the bay side of the island. By the 1950s sunbathers and swimmers filled the island's beaches.

But it was the construction of the Manahawkin Bay Bridge and the completion of the Garden State Parkway that brought even more people to Long Beach Island in the summer. These two factors, coupled with the widespread reputation the island possessed (and still does) for its all-around beauty, today make Long Beach Island one of the Shore's most prized possessions.

BARNEGAT LIGHT STATE PARK

At the northern tip of Long Beach Island lies Barnegat Light State Park, home of **Old Barney**, the famous lighthouse. Barnegat Light is New Jersey's smallest state park; it consists of only 36 acres. Nonetheless, it's a very popular park, mostly because of the lighthouse, which is easily Long Beach Island's most noted landmark. Over the years Old Barney has become one of the most photographed and painted lighthouses in America.

Old Barney, though, isn't the original lighthouse to beam a light from the top of Long Beach Island. The first was quite smaller than Old Barney and much less sturdy. It was constructed in 1834; in 1856 it collapsed after a storm.

Old Barney was begun in 1857 and completed a year later. Designed by Gen. George Gordon Meade, the Yankee Civil War hero known for his victory at Gettysburg, the new lighthouse was built to last. Meade constructed it so that its stability was "nine times stronger than is required to resist the maximum force of the wind," that element of nature that helped cause the destruction of the original lighthouse.

Old Barney's white beam, derived from a kerosene lamp of 16,000 candlepower, could be seen nearly 30 miles out at sea. It provided a reliable point of reference for ships offshore and remained in operation for 69 years. In 1927, a lightship stationed off the coast forced it into retirement. But then during World War II, Old Barney was taken over by the U.S. Coast Guard. It was used as a lookout tower for surfacing

German U-boats. The vigil staged by the Coast Guard atop the lighthouse wasn't entirely successful, however. In 1942, two tankers were sunk off Barnegat Light by German torpedos.

Visitors are permitted to climb the 217 steps that lead to the top of the lighthouse. The lens, however, is no longer there. It's on display at the Barnegat Light Historical Museum, located a mile south of the park on Central Avenue in the town of Barnegat Light. Still, the climb to the top is well worth the effort. From there one is treated to a sweeping view of Barnegat Bay, Island Beach State Park and virtually all of Long Beach Island.

Enter the park on Broadway Avenue. In the summer there is a small admission charge. The park is open year-round, although the lighthouse closes sometime in October.

Things to Do

Climb Old Barney. One doesn't have to climb all the way to the top to enjoy the vista. Small rest areas on the stairwell have portholes. But climbing to the second and third porthole will give the visitor a pretty good idea of just how narrow Long Beach Island really is. Along with Twin Lights and Mount Mitchill in Highlands, Old Barney offers the best bird's-eye view on the Jersey Shore.

Go Swimming. Out front of the lighthouse is a small beach area. Due to the shifting nature of sand, a small, dry sandbar was formed during a recent winter storm, which makes the water wonderfully calm—perfect for small children and senior citizens. Lifeguards are on duty during the summer. Bathhouses, showers and lockers are available.

Have a Picnic. Picnic tables are situated on the rim of Barnegat Inlet. The view is that of Barnegat Bay and neighboring Island Beach State Park.

Boat Watch. During the summer and on weekends in the spring and fall, Barnegat Inlet is filled with boats. You'll see both pleasure craft and commercial fishing boats. Despite its popularity, the inlet is one of the most dangerous inlets to navigate on the coast. In bad weather it's downright dangerous to pass through due to its many shoals and strong currents.

Beach Walk. You're not apt to find anything unusual on a July weekend, save a few odd pieces of driftwood. But after a storm, all sorts of things wash ashore here.

Go Fishing. Anglers have the choice of fishing from the inlet jetty where weakfish and occasional stripers are hooked, or from the beach where fluke, bass and bluefish are commonly caught.

BARNEGAT LIGHT

Directly below Barnegat Light State Park is the town of Barnegat Light. Known as Barnegat City until 1948, it has some of Long Beach Island's best beaches, a number of old Victorian homes, some of which were once owned by local sea captains, one of the island's two museums, and a large portion of the area's commercial fishing industry.

Barnegat Light's main historical significance, of course, is its connection to Old Barney. But an incident in the Revolutionary War occurred here in 1782 that has also secured Barnegat Light a place in New Jersey history. In what has been labeled the Long Beach Massacre, Capt. Andrew Steel and his band of men, who slept on the beach after taking ashore cargo from a grounded British vessel raided by American privateers, were murdered by Tory sympathizer John Bacon and his men. Twenty-one American patriots were killed in the darkness, and the mass murder has haunted the island's history ever since. A plaque commemorating the event and honoring the Americans killed is in Barnegat Light State Park.

There are only two main thoroughfares in Barnegat Light. One is Long Beach Boulevard (called Central Avenue in Barnegat Light), which leads visitors to the entrance of the park. The other is Bay View Boulevard, which meanders along the bay side of Barnegat Light. After a visit to Old Barney and the park, a drive along Bay View Boulevard is recommended. It's here where the town's string of small marinas can be found. Docked in them are charter fishing boats, private craft and small boats that can be rented by the day. **Kubel's Bar** on Seventh Street and Bay View is a favorite hangout for local anglers, commercial and amateur alike, and a great place to trade fishing information.

Farther south on Bay View, past the Barnegat Coast Guard Station, is Viking Village, home of Barnegat Light's tile fishing fleet. Barnegat Light is called the Tile Fish Capital of the World. The reason? The bright-colored, speckled bottom fish, which tastes something akin to red snapper or grouper (some even say lobster, but that's stretching it a bit) and used to go by the name leopard fish, was brought back into fish markets by local fisherman Lou Puskas. Almost singlehandedly, he resparked a demand for the fish that had disappeared years ago.

Some of the world's prime tile fishing grounds are located in the huge underwater canyons (Hudson, Veatch and Oceanographer) that lie off the Mid-Atlantic coast of the United States and within reach of Barnegat Light fishermen. Puskas, and later other local fishermen, began bringing in tile fish after Russian fishing trawlers practically destroyed the living they made fishing for cod. Hauling their tile fish catch up to New York's Fulton Fish Market, the demand for the fish grew and grew in the 1970s.

You can purchase fresh tile fish at **Cassidy's Viking Village Fish Market** (18th Avenue and Bay View Boulevard), which buys the fish directly from the dozen or so tile fish boats that call Viking Village home.

Also in Viking Village is a small group of shanties where nautical items, antiques, beach bric-a-brac and paintings are sold.

Over on Central Avenue is the **Barnegat Light Historical Museum** (5th and Central avenues). The former one-room schoolhouse is a small museum, but those interested in local history will find a visit rewarding.

An exhibit depicts life from Long Beach Island's Victorian past, and a number of old photographs show the island's Life Saving Service crew in action. But the museum's biggest attraction is the original lens of Old Barney. Also, a number of relics, photographs and documents trace the history of the lighthouse and the museum's attempt to track down and obtain the lens after it was removed from the structure some years ago.

The **Edith Duff Gwinn Gardens** are located behind the museum and cared for by friends of the fondly remembered local environmentalist and botanist. No admission is charged to either the museum or gardens, although the former has a very limited schedule in the summer and fall and is not open in the winter or spring. Check with the Information Center in Ship Bottom for opening and closing times, or else call (609) 494-3407.

LOVELADIES

Most people who visit Long Beach Island are amused by the peculiar names of some of its towns. The name Loveladies is indeed unusual. But unlike Ship Bottom, which has as unusual a story of how the town was so named as the name itself, Loveladies was simply named after a hunter, Thomas Lovelady, who used to hunt ducks in the area.

Loveladies possesses an altogether different type of charm than her neighbor, Barnegat Light. Because the town took such a large part of Mother Nature's wrath in the 1962 storm, virtually all traces of Loveladies' past were swept away by the ocean. Residents and newcomers to the town rebuilt it, and in Loveladies today you will see the most thorough display of contemporary seashore summer homes found anywhere on the Jersey Shore.

Most of these summer homes are examples of bold, even spectacular architectural design. The shapes and sizes of the structures vary tremendously. Some are truly grand and most beautiful to look at with their strange angles, extraordinary curvatures and sweeping views of the ocean. Others could only be described as extreme, depending, of course, on one's taste and architectural fancy.

Loveladies is mostly residential; there are really no places for the weekend visitor, for example, to rent a room. Those wishing to stay in the Loveladies area will have to look in Barnegat Light or Surf City and Ship Bottom for lodging.

While visiting or merely passing through Loveladies, a stop at the **Long Beach Foundation of the Arts and Sciences** (120 Long Beach Boulevard) is recommended. The foundation is the hub of cultural activity on the northern part of the island. Aside from the various courses in art, yoga and even marine biology that are open to summer and year-round residents, exhibits and lectures are also presented as well as an annual Seashore Open House Tour that is especially popular. Many of the events and activities sponsored by the foundation have fees, but they are quite reasonable. Stop by the foundation office for a calendar of events; you'll notice that something's going on practically every day.

HARVEY CEDARS

Today, the name Harvey Cedars is a misnomer. No red cedars are left, although in the nineteenth century, many of these trees stood tall on this part of the island. That explains at least where the *Cedars* part of the town's name comes from. As for *Harvey*, the town was originally known as Harvey's Whaling Station, or Harvey's Whaling Quarters. Legend has it that a cave dweller named Daniel Harvey was one of the area's first inhabitants.

Some of Long Beach Island's earliest settlers—whalers from New England—settled here. From the shore, whales would be spotted by lookouts and the hunt would begin. Unfortunately, very little remains in Harvey Cedars that recalls its whaling heritage. (Some relics and tools can be found, however, in the Long Beach Island Historical Museum in Beach Haven.) Storms accounted for much of the area's destruction over the years.

About the only prominent building that remains from those days is the Harvey Cedars Hotel, located on the bay side of town. Today it's known as the **Harvey Cedars Bible Conference Center**. Another old building, the headquarters of the Long Beach Island Fishing Club, was once a Life Saving Service Station. It's located on Long Beach Boulevard.

SURF CITY

No, the Beach Boys' Brian Wilson didn't compose the classic 1960s pop song, "Surf City," for singers Jan and Dean with this Long Beach Island town in mind. He could have, though. Surf City reflects all the elements of a surf town Jan Berry and Dean Torrence sang about, with the possible exception of "two girls for every boy."

Surf City possesses a whaling history as strong as Harvey Cedars, but once again, due to storms, few reminders of its past can be found except what's in the Long Beach Island Historical Museum. Originally, the area where Surf City now sits was known as the Great Swamp. Its name was then changed to Long Beach City and finally, Surf City. The term *City*, though, is really misleading. Fewer than 500 residents live in Surf City year round, although the population bulges to perhaps 10 or 15 times that during the summer.

A small shopping area in Surf City caters to those who summer on the north part of Long Beach Island. Stores carry a full line of beach essentials, and there's also lodging and a number of places to eat here. Most everything is located on or very near Long Beach Boulevard.

Not only does Surf City have excellent beaches on the ocean, but there's a delightful bay beach at the end of 16th Street that is just right for small children. The water there is shallow and calm and the beach filled with families. It's also a great place to watch the sun set each evening as well as boat watch on the bay.

Treasure Hunting

Beachcombing, or "treasure hunting," as it's also called, has become increasingly popular over the past few years. By slowly skimming sections of the beach with a metal detector, treasure hunters often find coins, rings, bracelets and other pieces of jewelry, plus silverware and other valuable trinkets buried beneath the sand. They also find bottlecaps, nails and an assortment of other useless pieces of metallic junk. As any treasure hunter will admit, "you take the good with the bad."

Few beachcombers or treasure hunters expect to strike it rich. But it's the thrill of possibly discovering that diamond ring or sixteenth-century Spanish coin, in addition to the relaxation and gentle form of exercise that accompanies it, that makes treasure hunting so popular at the Jersey Shore.

What You'll Need: A metal detector (prices range from $100 to as high as $700) plus accessories, such as headphones, a sand scoop, sifter, prober and patience.

How To Do It: Locate a section of the beach where crowds normally congregate. Turn on the metal detector and walk across the sand, moving it in a slow, wand-like manner. Plan out the area you intend to beachcomb so as to be sure the same stretch of beach isn't covered twice. When you hear a beep, or if your meter indicates something metallic underneath your metal detector, scoop up the sand, let it filter through your sifter, and see what you've found. Experienced treasure hunters might simply stick their prober into the sand and determine whether or not the object is worth scooping out.

When To Go: The best time to treasure hunt with a metal detector is immediately after a storm or after an unusually high tide, if you're most interested in finding things that wash up onshore. Those looking for lost jewelry and money should wait until late afternoon or dusk after the beach has emptied. Weekends are better than weekdays. Longtime treasure hunters like to take out their metal detectors just after sudden thunderstorms when people scurry from the beach seeking cover from rain and lightning. They're not as apt to be careful packing up their belongings, and they often drop into the sand things of value.

SHIP BOTTOM

Ship Bottom, one of the largest year-round communities on Long Beach Island, is also the commercial center of the island. As already noted, the legend behind the name Ship Bottom is a strange one. It seems that sometime in the early 1800s, a bottom-up boat washed ashore, a victim of the dreaded Barnegat Shoals. When islanders went to investigate the shipwreck, they heard a frantic knocking from within the hull. Immediately they broke a hole through it and found a beautiful Spanish-speaking woman inside, the ship's only survivor.

One of the more popular Ship Bottom specialty shops is **Ron Jon Hatchcover Furniture** (9th and Central avenues), which sells tables made from the hatchcovers of World War II Liberty ships. The covers have iron bands strapped around their edges and handwells; the look of the cover is that of weathered driftwood. Ron Jon adds coffee-table legs to the hatchcovers after they've been sanded and lacquered. They make excellent pieces of furniture and look particularly attractive in homes with a nautical decor.

Since the Liberty Ship is now part of Americana and maritime history, few original hatchcovers are left. Ron Jon purports to be the world's largest hatchcover shop. One thing is for certain: it undoubtedly has the best selection of the covers on the Jersey Shore.

BEACH HAVEN

The southern half of Long Beach Island is dominated by Beach Haven. It is the busiest beach town on the island during the summer because it contains the most accommodations, the island's only amusement area, lots of restaurants, a few nightclubs and fine beaches.

A balanced blend of old and new exists in Beach Haven; the town boasts a historical district in which you'll find the bulk of its remaining Victorian seashore homes as well as its bed and breakfasts and guesthouses. Yet, there are also a number of newer homes and commercial establishments in town and a definite commitment to tourism.

Like all other Long Beach Island towns, Long Beach Boulevard is Beach Haven's principal thoroughfare, although it's called Bay Avenue in Beach Haven. On it can be found many of the town's shops and restaurants, plus **Fantasy Island Amusement Park** and the **Pier 18 Mall**. Centre Street and Engleside Avenue are important streets, too. They intersect Bay Avenue in the town's center. The east or ocean side of these two streets contains much of the Beach Haven historical district. These streets and those adjoining them are delightfully kept; many of them have lawns and white picket fences and possess a quality not unlike what you'll find in Bay Head on the Barnegat Peninsula (see chapter 4).

It's also in this section where you'll find the **Long Beach Island Historical Museum**, the **Surflight Summer Theatre**, **Bicentennial Park** and some of Beach Haven's excellent beaches. There are bicycle lanes on Bay Avenue and Atlantic Avenue. By renting a bike or riding your own, you'll be able to get much more than a glimpse of the nicest section of Beach Haven.

Beach Haven's beaches have sand that is clean and quite fine in texture. The size of the town's beaches, however, like the size of all the ocean beaches on Long Beach Island, varies considerably during the course of the summer. Because Long Beach Island is a barrier island, storms, currents, tides and erosion force the beaches here into a continual state of flux.

Things to Do

Visit the Long Beach Island Historical Museum. Housed in an old church, a number of fine exhibits pertain to Victorian Long Beach Island, its commercial fishing industry and the golden age of whaling. But what seems to capture the attention of most visitors to the museum is the collection of photographs and charts that vividly tell the story of the March 1962 storm. Aerial photographs show the astonishing amount of beach erosion that occurred and the of homes that were washed away by waves and high tides. There are even photos of two naval warships grounded on the beach. On a rainy or cloudy day expect to find the museum fairly crowded. Young children can play in a special hands-on, kiddie corner where they can learn a bit about island history at the same time. The museum is located on Engleside and Beach avenues and has an admission charge. For museum hours, call (609) 492-0700.

Take a Walking Tour of the Victorian Historical District. After visiting the Long Beach Historical Museum, purchase the pamphlet, *Walking Tour of Beach Haven,* available at the curator's desk. The museum sits smack in the center of the historical district; therefore, the tour begins right outside the museum. Actually, there are two walking tours to choose from. One includes 16 homes; the other, 27. All the homes on both tours were built prior to 1900 and are fine examples of Victorian and traditional seashore colonial homes. Because all the houses are privately owned, the tour doesn't include entrance into any of them. However, each Fourth of July, Beach Haven sponsors a Victorian Days Weekend. Local merchants, members of civic groups and private citizens turn back the clock and don Victorian era costumes. Many of the Victorian homes are then open for visitors to inspect. Some owners conduct full house tours. Other town-sponsored, Victorian related events fill out the weekend.

Homes of particular interest on the walking tour include the island's first **Life Saving Service Station**, built in 1848 in Harvey Cedars and later brought down to its present location at 509 Old Dock Road; the only **salt box home** on Long Beach Island at 114 Second Street; and the **Magnolia House** at 215 Centre Street, one of the island's oldest boarding houses and presently a bed and breakfast.

Attend a Historical/Cultural Lecture. Each summer the Long Beach Island Historical Association sponsors a number of superb programs that do much to keep the Shore's culture and heritage alive as well as to entertain vacationers and year-round residents alike. Lectures such as "Spooks, Ghoulies, and Things that Make Noise in the Night," "The History of the Life Saving Service," and "The Wreck of the Fortuna" attract enthusiastic crowds. Most of the presentations are free and occur during the evening. The association also sponsors a Victorian Porch Party, a Garden party, craft shows and flea markets. For complete information on this summer's programs, contact the Historical Association at P.O. Box 232, Ship Bottom 08008.

Attend a Play at the Surflight Summer Theatre. The Surflight Summer Theatre is a Long Beach Island institution. Its official name is the **Joseph P. Hayes Surflight Summer Theatre.** Hayes founded the theater nearly 40 years ago (He died in 1976) in a converted mechanic's garage; it's still there. It was Hayes's intention to bring first-rate theatrical entertainment to Long Beach Island during the summer, and almost from the beginning, he succeeded beyond his expectations. Today, the Surflight is one of the very few summer theaters in the United States that still produces a different show each week. The Surflight actors and actresses perform on the theater's stage at night and practice their parts for the following week's production in the day. Walk past the theater parking lot on any given afternoon and you're sure to find actors and actresses wrestling with new lines and song lyrics. The players who perform at the Surflight are selected through a number of channels. Drama students, upcoming actors from the regional play circuit and even New York City actors and actresses compete for a spot in the summer cast. They reside in Beach Haven for the entre summer and perform in every play the Surflight presents during the season. The Surflight is located at 211 Engleside Avenue. For information on plays and tickets, call (609) 492-9477.

Attend an Outdoor Summer Concert. Every Saturday evening, weather permitting, the Beach Haven Bicentennial Park Association sponsors a free concert in **Bicentennial Park** (Beach Avenue, between Engleside and Amber streets). Dixieland jazz, big band, orchestral music and Pine Barrens folk music are usually heard from the bandshell throughout the season. The concerts run from mid-June through the end of August.

Take the Kids to Fantasy Island. Long Beach Island's only amusement area is small and aimed at kids under 12. The park boasts a dozen amusement rides, a casino arcade, a miniature golf course, some wheels of chance, and a Victorian Ice Cream Parlour. Next to Fantasy Island is the **Thundering Surf Water Slide**, also a popular attraction for kids. There is no admission charge to Fantasy Island, though there is, of course, for Thundering Surf (located at Bay Avenue and W. 7th Street).

Go Shopping in the Pier 18 Mall. Located on the corner of Bay Avenue and Third Street, the Pier 18 Mall contains more than 50 shops and fast food stands. You can buy anything from a hot dog smothered in onions to fresh cherrystone clams on the half shell. You can also purchase clothes, beach accessories, nautical knick-knacks and much, much more. A great place to spend a rainy summer afternoon.

Take a Boat Trip to Atlantic City. One of the more popular attractions on the bay side of Beach Haven is to step aboard a party boat called the *Black Whale II* for a fun ride to and from Harrah's Marina Hotel Casino in Atlantic City. There you can spend the day playing blackjack or stuffing nickels or quarters into slot machines or just plain stroll the famous Atlantic City boardwalk. The *Black Whale*

II is moored at the Beach Haven Fishing Center. Reservations are highly encouraged.

Tucker's Island

Tucker's Island *used* to be an island; today it is under the Atlantic Ocean, as good an example of the unpredictable nature of barrier islands as you're apt to find. Back in the late 1800s, Tucker's Island, also known as Sea Haven, Short Beach and Tucker's Beach, played an important role in the rescue of hundreds of people from the frequent shipwrecks that occurred off Long Beach Island.

The island was inhabited by members of the U.S. Life Saving Service and their families. The Tucker's Island crew performed rescue operations for some 200 shipwrecks between 1869 and 1915. There was a 50-foot lighthouse at the Life Saving Service Station, which with Old Barney on the north end of the island provided valuable beacons for ships passing in the night.

There was a time when Tucker's Island was actually part of Long Beach Island. But nor'easters gradually created what is today known as Beach Haven Inlet, and Tucker's Beach became Tucker's Island. From that point on it was just a matter of time before the ocean began eating away the island. By the turn of the century, beach erosion was so great that the inhabitants were forced to leave and resettle on the mainland. One by one, the buildings on Tucker's Island fell into the sea. In 1935, the life saving station, which was the last building standing on Tucker's Island, was destroyed by storm waves. In 1955 the whole island disappeared under the Atlantic.

DID YOU KNOW THAT ... TUCKER'S ISLAND IS FREQUENTLY CALLED THE JERSEY SHORE'S ATLANTIS?

Holgate National Wildlife Refuge

Part of the **Edwin B. Forsythe National Wildlife Refuge Area**, this 2½-mile stretch of barrier beach and tidal saltmarsh sits at the southern tip of Long Beach Island. Along with a portion of Barnegat Light State Park, Holgate possesses the only undeveloped barrier beach tract on the island.

Because it's designated primarily for the survival of wildlife, there are no basic amenities like bathrooms or a visitor's center, even though the public *is* encouraged to visit Holgate. U.S. Fish and Wildlife rangers patrol the beach in four wheel drive jeeps, will hand out brochures that explain the delicate ecosystem of Holgate and answer any questions you might have about Holgate. They will also hand out a summons to anyone who disobeys rules that prohibit walking on the sand dunes and disrupting the nesting sites of birds.

Things to Do

Bird-watch. Three birds on New Jersey's Endangered Species List—the piping plover, the black skimmer and the least tern—nest at Holgate and can be seen during the summer. Many other migratory birds use Holgate as a rest and feed stop in the fall and then later in the spring. Other birds one might see during the summer: the snowy egret, peregrine falcon, great blue heron, American oystercatcher, glossy ibis and great black-backed gull. For a complete list of birds that frequent Holgate, stop at the visitor's center of the Edwin B. Forsythe National Wildlife Refuge Area one mile east of Route 9 in Oceanville.

Walk the Beach. A walk from one end of Holgate to the other will undoubtedly tire most people's legs; it is, after all, a five-mile round trip in soft sand. But for those who enjoy early morning beachwalks or walks at dusk, Holgate is the very best place to walk, and you don't have to walk *all* the way to the end of the refuge.

Treasure Hunt. A number of Spanish coins have been found on the beach here over the years. There are tales of buried treasure, but it's more likely that the coins are from sunken Spanish galleons off the coast. The best time to sift the sand is immediately after a storm.

Go Surfing. Some of the best waves found on Long Beach Island are at Holgate. Be advised, however, that there are no lifeguards on the beach and currents can be a problem. Swimming is not recommended here for the very same reason, although experienced bodysurfers do go into the water at their own risk.

Go Windsurfing. When the wind is right, boardsailors find Holgate quite exciting, especially if there is a small swell running which allows for wave jumping and wave riding.

Take a Ride in a Dune Buggy. Dune buggies and four wheel drive vehicles are allowed on the Holgate beach providing the driver has a permit. Permits are available at the Long Beach Township municipal office.

Go Fishing. Most vehicles you'll see on the beach belong to fishermen who ride down to Beach Haven Inlet where they catch bluefish, flounder, fluke and striped bass.

Some Recommended Restaurants
on Long Beach Island

Bayberry Inn
13th Street and Long Beach Boulevard
Ship Bottom
(609) 494-8848
Price Code: Moderate
Menu: International
Certainly one of the more popular restaurants on Long Beach Island. Especially enticing are the crab and lobster dishes.

Charles Seafood Garden
8611 Long Beach Boulevard
Beach Haven Crest
(609) 492-8340

Price Code: Moderate/Expensive
Menu: Seafood

There are many seafood restaurants on Long Beach Island; many of them are quite good. Charles seems a cut above the rest because of its creativity. The standards like stuffed flounder and bluefish aren't really standards at Charles.

Crane's Surf City Hotel
Eighth Street and Long Beach Boulevard
Surf City
(609) 494-7281
Price Code: Moderate/Expensive
Menu: Mostly seafood

The stuffed mussels are out of this world; most other dishes on the menu quite good also.

Dutchman's Brauhaus
Long Beach Island Causeway
Ship Bottom
(609) 494-8909
Price Code: Moderate
Menu: German

Enjoy pigs knuckles? Weiner schnitzel? There are but a few German restaurants on the Jersey Shore. Fortunately, those that are there are quite good. Dutchman's Brauhaus is no exception.

Gourmet's Mooring
9th and Bay avenues
Beach Haven
(609) 492-2828
Price Code: Moderate/Expensive
Menu: Italian and seafood

If you like tile fish, you'll certainly want to try the Gourmet's Mooring's tile fish salad. An excellent place for a late night dinner; romantic setting on the bay.

Harvey Cedars Shellfish Company
7904 Long Beach Boulevard
Harvey Cedars
(609) 494-7112
Price Code: Moderate
Menu: Seafood

More than one Long Beach Islander will tell you this is the island's best restaurant, seafood and otherwise. Informal dining, large portions, everything delicious. Perhaps it *is* the best restaurant on the island.

Howard's
33rd and Baltic avenues
Beach Haven Terrace
(609) 492-2319
Price Code: Moderate
Menu: Seafood, beef

When you eat at Howard's you order fried lobster, although other seafood and also beef dishes are up to par. Eat before 5:45 p.m. and save 10 percent on your bill.

Mike's of Mexico
1715 Long Beach Boulevard
Surf City
(609) 494-9009
Price Code: Moderate
Menu: Mexican

Order the Chicken Mexicali or the Steak Aztec and you won't be sorry. Interesting menu and house specials.

Octopus's Garden
414 Long Beach Boulevard
Surf City
(609) 494-7205
Price Code: Moderate
Menu: International

Another of Long Beach Island's very popular restaurants. The flounder tempura is quite good, so are the shrimp dishes.

Owl Tree
7908 Long Beach Boulevard
Harvey Cedars
(609) 494-8191
Price Code: Moderate
Menu: Mostly seafood

Seems to be popular with the locals. Menu goes beyond the typical. Live entertainment on weekends.

Panzone's Pizza
1100 N. Bay Boulevard
Beach Haven
(609) 492-5103
Price Code: Inexpensive
Menu: Pizza

When in the mood for pizza, Panzone's is the place. There are three Panzone's on the island. They're all good. The one in Beach Haven is the best, though. Tasty dough, spicy tomato sauce; one of the Jersey Shore's best pizzas.

Polish Peasant
122 North Bay Ave.
Beach Haven
(609) 492-0134
Price Code: Moderate
Menu: Polish/East European

The stuffed cabbage at the Polish Peasant will make you a regular visitor. Everything on the menu is wonderfully prepared. A Long Beach Island favorite.

6. THE PINE BARRENS

It's a vast area; it covers nearly 25 percent of New Jersey. Much of it includes the last remaining true wilderness area on the Atlantic coast between New Hampshire and Virginia. It's an area of great green forests and swampy marshlands, of amber-tinted rivers and streams, of rich folklore and legends. People call the area the Pinelands or simply the Pines, although it's most commonly called the Pine Barrens. Unfortunately, it's also the most inappropriate name of the three.

How can an area that is the heart of New Jersey's agricultural industry, where the harvest of blueberries and cranberries is one of the largest in the nation, and where one can find 54 threatened plant species and 35 threatened wildlife species in thousands and thousands of acres of wilderness forest be called barren? There *is* a logical reason. The term *Pine Barrens* goes all the way back to the area's original settlers who found the sandy soil unsuitable for farming. The Pinelands were "barren" to them. And the name stuck.

But it certainly shouldn't be considered barren today—especially for the vacationer or visitor looking for the perfect alternative to the beach and boardwalk and the madness that grips the rest of the Jersey Shore each summer. It's here in the Pine Barrens where hikers can spend not hours, but *days* in the forest and not see another soul, where canoeists can paddle some of the East Coast's most scenic and mysterious rivers, and where New Jersey campers can come to truly understand the meaning of "wilderness" without leaving their state. It's also here in the Pine Barrens where history comes alive in the form of a restored nineteenth-century bog iron community like Batsto and where bird-watchers and naturalists delight in the sights and sounds of waterfowl and migratory birds as they take refuge in the marshlands that lie between the ocean and the forest.

Far too many Shore visitors, it's true, underestimate the excitement of exploring the Pine Barrens. From Toms River to Atlantic City and points further south, the ride on the Parkway is, all too often, a swift, direct one. There are rest areas with picnic tables, toll booths, exit ramps—and little else. Or so they think. But beyond the guard rails on either side of the highway lies an uncomplicated, unspoiled forest area practically the size of Yellowstone National Park that can make a man marvel at its beauty and intrigue in this, the nation's most densely populated state.

A few interesting facts about the Pine Barrens. Underneath the thick forest is a 17-trillion gallon lake called the Cohansey Aquifer, a vital

---

DID YOU KNOW THAT ... IF THE COHANSEY AQUIFER WERE
DRAINED, IT WOULD COVER THE ENTIRE STATE OF NEW JER-
SEY WITH TEN FEET OF WATER?

---

drinking water supply for New Jersey residents. The sand that separates
the aquifer from the surface is porous. There's been more than one
threat to the water's purity due to pollution seepage on the outlying
edges of the Pine Barrens.

Legislators certainly had this in mind when they made the Pine
Barrens America's first national reserve. The difference between a
national park and a national reserve is that park land is federally owned,
but reserve land is owned by local, state and federal agencies as well as
private individuals. The land included in the Pinelands National
Reserve is protected from indiscriminate development and unwise use
of the land, the kind that would harm the delicate ecological balance
there.

Interestingly enough, in the eighteenth and part of the nineteenth
century the Pine Barrens was the industrial center of New Jersey. Towns
like Batsto, Weymouth, Atsion, Washington and Speedwell were bustling bog iron communities which supplied iron and iron products for
the developing nation. Little of this era remains in the Pine Barrens,
except at Batsto in Wharton State Forest (see below) where one can
step back in time and learn how this area played a critical role in the
American Revolution.

Finally, the Pine Barrens is the birthplace and home of that infamous
creature, the Jersey Devil. This horned, half human and half animal,
with batlike wings and a demon's tail, has been roaming the Pinelands
for more than two centuries. It continues to terrorize residents, kill
livestock and perpetuate a legend that seems to grow a bit larger with
each passing year. Actually, the Pine Barrens are filled with tales and
stories that will make any night under the stars there a spooky one.
Stories about Sam Giberson and his fiddle, the Rabbit Woman and
Captain Kidd still float around the Pine Barrens. These and others are
celebrated in song—Piney folk music—and by word of mouth. No
other part of the Jersey Shore possesses more colorful legends and tales
of days gone by.

If the Pine Barrens, because of its wilderness descriptions, seems
inaccessible, it isn't. And that's what makes a visit even more appealing.
The Parkway will get you to the Pine Barrens; Routes 70, 72, 539 and
563 crisscross the area, enabling the visitor to get to most points of
interest, hiking trails and canoe launches with little problem. There
are few places to stay in the Pine Barrens, however. Most visitors who
plan to spend more than a day there, camp.

Not all of what is generally considered the Pine Barrens territory is
wild and uninhabited. Tiny towns of fewer than 50 residents can still
be found thick in the heart of the Pines. Toms River is a large, historically

significant community that sits in the northeast corner of the area. The stretch along Barnegat and the smaller bays to the south is dotted with old towns and villages that seemed to have been passed by when tourism came of age on the Jersey Shore. Places like Forked River, Waretown and Barnegat have retained much of their Pineland and bay heritage, despite the presence of nudging residential developments and shopping malls. Further down you'll find wetlands and barrier islands that fill the void between forest and ocean and are frequented by bird-watchers year round.

One could write an entire book on the Pine Barrens. Some, like John McPhee, already have. His book, *The Pine Barrens*, is an acknowledged classic and anyone interested in Pine Barrens culture should read this absorbing work before exploring it. This chapter then, is meant as an introduction to the Pine Barrens, especially that area of it closest to the coast. The Pine Barrens extend far beyond the Jersey Shore, so to keep within the boundaries of this book, I've concentrated on points of interest and things to do well within an hour's drive of the Parkway.

Toms River

Set back on the banks of the Toms River, the town of Toms River is the principal community in Ocean County (also the county seat) and the site of an important Revolutionary War battle. It was here in March, 1782 that Capt. Joshua Huddy and his men were set upon by British regulars and Tory sympathizers. Huddy's militiamen were ordered to defend the Toms River Block House and the nearby salt warehouses. (Salt was vital in munitions making and the preservation of meat and fish.) Huddy's men held out, despite being outnumbered more than four to one, until they ran out of gunpowder. Huddy fled, but was captured by the British. Later he was hung in Highlands (see chapter 1).

The British forces destroyed the salt warehouses, something they had set out to do twice before, but failed. Nevertheless, Toms River continued to play a part in the war effort until its conclusion a year later. Privateers continued to harass British shipping by attacking and plundering supply ships. In all, there were 77 recorded naval skirmishes off the Jersey Shore during the Revolutionary War. Many of the privateer ships engaged in such skirmishes were out of port town such as Toms River, Tuckerton and Little Egg Harbor.

Things to Do

Visit the Toms River Block House. Located at the intersection of Water Street and Route 166 in downtown Toms River is a replica of the Toms River Block House. The original block house was a crude log fort with no entrance way; one had to scale the wall using a ladder to gain entry. Inside the block house was a log barracks and an underground room where ammunition and gunpowder were stored. The original block house was built in 1776 to protect the port and the local saltworks. The British destroyed it in 1782.

Visit the Toms River Maritime Museum. Run by the Toms River Seaport Society, the Maritime Museum is housed in an old carriage house overlooking the Toms River. The museum is noted for its collection and restoration of old Barnegat Sneakbox boats, used by outdoorsmen on Barnegat Bay earlier this century. There are also photographs of other old boats indigenous to the area, boat models, sea chests and old sailing paraphernalia. The Maritime Museum, located at 78 Water Street, is open Saturdays 10 a.m.–noon. Appointments can be made for visits during the week, however. Call (201) 349-9209 or (201) 240-3873 for more information.

Visit the Ocean County Historical Museum. To get a proper perspective on the history of Toms River and the rest of Ocean County, spend part of an afternoon at this fine museum. It's located at 26 Hadley Avenue in a house built sometime in the 1840s and is decorated with mostly Victorian furnishings. A guide will lead you on a tour of the house, which includes a Victorian parlor, dining room and kitchen, complete with mannequins dressed in original period clothes and household items on display. All of this gives the visitor a good indication of what day-to-day living during the Victorian Era might have been like. Upstairs is a "one room school," furnished with material used in various Ocean County schools some 75 years ago. Downstairs in the basement are numerous Indian artifacts, fossils found locally and memorabilia of the Lighter Than Air Era, namely the years between World Wars I and II when dirigibles dotted the sky. Remnants of the most famous dirigible, the *Hindenberg*, which exploded and burned at the Lakehurst Naval Air Station some ten miles northwest of Toms River in 1937, are on display. (This is the only area museum where one can find exhibits pertaining to dirigibles, particularly the *Hindenberg*. Contrary to popular belief, the Lakehurst Naval Air Station does not have a dirigible museum, although Hangar No. 1, where the *Hindenberg* was serviced and stored, is a national historic landmark.) The museum is open on Tuesdays and Thursdays 1–3 p.m. and on Saturday from 10 a.m. until noon. Call (201) 341-1880 for details and information on special exhibits.

CATTUS ISLAND COUNTY PARK

Perhaps because it's a fairly new park (established in 1980), or perhaps because it's nearly surrounded by a sprawling residential area rarely frequented by tourists, Cattus Island is one of the Jersey Shore's best kept secrets. This 500-acre natural preserve of salt and tidal marshes, white cedar swamp, pitch pine forest and coastal lowlands is a nature lover's delight. The six miles of marked trails and views of both Silver and Barnegat bays make for fine hiking. But it's the Cooper Environmental Center and its numerous nature programs that make Cattus

Island a "must" stop for Jersey Shore nature lovers, especially those with young children.

The Cooper Environmental Center, named after local environmentalists A. Morton Cooper and Elizabeth Cooper, is a nature learning resource center filled with hands-on displays, wildlife games and quizzes, and theme exhibits that pertain not only to the Cattus Island ecosystem, but all the ecosystems found in Ocean County. Much of this is aimed at young people. Naturalists, however, conduct all kinds of special programs designed to stimulate and educate young and old alike, and do so in an area that is mere minutes from the southern half of the Barnegat Peninsula and downtown Toms River.

On a map, Cattus Island appears to be a peninsula; it separates Silver Bay from the much larger Barnegat Bay. Yet Cattus Island is referred to as an island because during high tide, the saltmarsh floods and water surrounds Cattus on all four sides. Cattus Island County Park is on Fischer Boulevard, which is off Route 37. The entrance to the park is two miles north of the Route 37–Fischer Boulevard intersection. No admission charge. (201) 270-6960.

Twelve Tips For Beginning Birdwatchers

1. Purchase a copy of Roger Tory Peterson's *A Field Guide to the Birds East of the Rockies*. Thumb through it before you go into the field. This way you'll become familiar enough with the way birds are described and the various sections of the guide to be able to use it effectively when it counts most—in the field.
2. Purchase a good pair of binoculars. Nikon and Bushnell are reputable names in binoculars and have midpriced models that are worth the $200 or so you can expect to spend on them.
3. Join a local bird-watchers' club and/or the New Jersey Audubon Society to meet and work with other "birders," as they're often called. It's also a great way to learn where the really good bird-watching spots are.
4. If you begin bird-watching on the Jersey Shore, start with shore birds. They're quite common and fairly easy to identify. Along with the Edwin B. Forsythe Wildlife Refuge, Sandy Hook, Stone Harbor and Cape May are also excellent places to sight birds.
5. Whenever possible, go bird-watching with an experienced bird-watcher. He or she will provide not only company, but will teach you things about bird-watching that might take you months to learn.
6. Don't wear loud colors; browns and greens are best.
7. Move slowly. Don't talk and don't smoke. Whenever possible, stay in your car. Birds are afraid of people; they're not usually frightened by cars.
8. Never feel intimidated by other bird-watchers in the field who seem to be able to spot every bird in the vicinity and never have to open up their guidebooks. Bird-watching should be a pleasant, relaxing experience. As a novice, enjoy the sport within your capabilities.
9. Listen as well as look. You'll get just as much enjoyment out of identifying a bird by his whistle as by his coloring and markings.

10. If you plan to stay out in the field more than an hour or two, bring a snack and perhaps something to drink. Also, dress appropriately. A good pair of rubber shoes is a wise investment.

11. Keep track of your sightings by way of a "life list." If you become a serious bird-watcher, you'll be amazed at how many birds you spot each year.

12. Appreciate the joys that bird-watching brings, and support laws that seek to increase wildlife acreage in addition to protecting those already in existence.

Things to Do

Go on a Naturalist-Led Nature Walk. There is much to experience on the Cattus Island hiking trails. To walk with someone whose knowledge of the ecology there is more thorough than yours makes for an interesting learning experience. Two-hour nature walks usually begin at 2 p.m. and occur Sundays year-round. Rarely is there more than a handful of walkers, which allows better interaction among walkers and naturalist. Naturalists also conduct boat tours in the summer, but on a less frequent basis. Ask at the Cooper Environmental Center for details.

Go Seining Off the Cattus Island Bay Beaches. Who knows what kind of marine life will be trapped in your net for inspection as you wade through the shallow bay waters? Because it juts out into the water, Cattus Island is one of the best places on the Barnegat to seine any time of the year, except, of course, the winter, when it's too cold to be in the water.

Bike the Cattus Island Fire Road. Trail bikes are better than ten-speeds as the road is not paved. The fat trail bike tires make for easier peddling and a smoother ride. The road is four miles long, which makes for a pleasant eight-mile roundtrip. Bring your lunch or a snack and eat it as you admire the splendid view of Silver Bay and the Barnegat Peninsula at the end of the road. A good time to bicycle Cattus Island is during October when the weather is cool, the mosquitos are gone (hopefully), and the change in foliage is at its peak.

ISLAND HEIGHTS

Island Heights, set snugly on the northern bank of the Toms River, has much in common with Ocean Grove (see chapter 2). Both began as Methodist camp meeting towns in the late nineteenth century, both are still dry towns today, meaning no liquor can be bought or served except in the privacy of one's own home, and both possess an extraordinary amount of beautiful Victorian homes, most of which have been meticulously restored. There are more than 100 Victorian structures in Island Heights. Unlike Ocean Grove or Cape May, however, Island Heights has not welcomed tourism in a grand way. There are no museums, no homes to visit and no true Victorian selling points except the architecture of the homes. Be sure to drive along the Toms River on River Road—the homes that face the water are quite impressive.

Island Heights is located off Route 37, between Toms River and Barnegat Bay. Take the exit marked Island Heights and proceed down to the Toms River where your auto tour of the town should begin.

DOUBLE TROUBLE STATE PARK

Few people realize there's a state park called Double Trouble. That's because though it's open to the public, it's not *officially* open. Located in Berkeley Township (Parkway, Exit 80) on Double Trouble Road West, the park's historic cranberry village is still very much in the restoration stages. State officials say they don't advertise Double Trouble the way they do other state parks in New Jersey because it has no parking or restroom facilities.

Don't let this stop you from visiting Double Trouble State Park, however. The caretaker will let you walk around the village homes, which once housed workers who worked the nearby cranberry bogs. Also, walk the 1½-mile hiking trail that begins at the packing house.

> DID YOU KNOW THAT ... NEW JERSEY IS THE THIRD HIGHEST CRANBERRY PRODUCING STATE, AFTER MASSACHUSETTS AND WISCONSIN?

Double Trouble comprises 4000 acres of prime Pine Barrens; a walk on the trail is especially recommended for those wishing to experience a bit of Pine Barrens forest without having to drive as far south as Wharton State Forest (see below).

The sawmill that is currently being restored is said to have been built in the mideighteenth century. According to local legend, the Double Trouble area got its name because of a beaver who first built one dam and then another, causing the water that ran the mill to trickle and the mill operator to run into "double trouble."

Once Double Trouble is fully restored, it's a sure bet it will become one of New Jersey's most interesting state parks, taking its place next to Allaire and Batsto as important historical sites in the Pine Barrens section of the Jersey Shore.

THE BAY TOWNS

The best way to gain an appreciation of the small towns that sit on the western shore of Barnegat Bay is to drive along Route 9 rather than the Garden State Parkway. The Parkway is quicker and perhaps more direct if your destination is, say, the Edwin B. Forsythe Wildlife Refuge, or the Historic Village of Batsto in Wharton State Forest. But you're certain to miss much of the Barnegat Bay tradition that seems to reveal itself in the oddest places. Case in point: You'll find no better example of Barnegat Bay and Pine Barrens culture than in the voices and guitar chords that echo each Saturday night out of Albert Hall in Waretown.

It's the home of the Pinelands Cultural Society (see below), a home, by the way, that's located at the rear of a building that contains a Route 9 auto body shop.

As you ride up or down Route 9, you'll pass through such towns as Ocean Gate, Bayville, Lanoka Harbor, Forked River, Waretown and Barnegat. Individually, none of these old towns contains what one might call "must" places to visit, although some of them have interesting historical sections and local museums, and these are listed and described below. Rather, it's the Barnegat Bay ambiance, which is found in these communities, that makes a ride through them inviting.

As with so many places on the Jersey Shore, contrast is the rule of thumb. You'll see numerous residential developments and small shopping centers side by side with homes and churches 100 and 200 years old and cemeteries that contain the remains of the Barnegat Bay area's original settlers. Unfortunately, many of these old structures have not been restored and there they sit, full of faded memories and little else.

Blocked by the Barnegat Peninsula and Long Beach Island, these communities have no beaches, save those on the bay—which aren't nearly as nice or as spacious as those on the ocean. Because of this, activity revolves exclusively around the bay's excellent fishing, clamming, crabbing and boating. Marinas abound in this area.

But there are no amusement areas here, no boardwalks, little nightlife and few good restaurants. For most, these are more than enough reasons to continue south to Atlantic City or the resorts on the South Jersey Shore, or to the North Jersey Shore in the opposite direction. Yet, a stop in Barnegat to browse through a few antique shops or a Saturday night visit to Albert Hall for an old-timey Piney hootenanny should certainly be considered.

Going Clamming? Here's How.

When to Go: The summer and fall are the best times of the year to clam since you will be wading in water. However, ardent clammers clam the year round. Boots and warm clothing are obvious necessities, then. Bear in mind it is illegal to clam at night or on Sundays. The best tide to clam is low tide.

Where to Go: Barnegat Bay, Little Egg Harbor and Reed's Bay are good places, although certain areas in each of the three bays are off limits to clammers. To be certain you're not clamming in condemned areas, adhere to the "Condemned Areas Clamming Chart," which can be obtained at Marine Police stations or by writing to the New Jersey Department of Environmental Protection, Division of Water Resources, Bureau of Shellfish Control, Stoney Hill Road, Leed's Point, Star Route, Absecon 08021. Experienced clammers point to the waters around Waretown and Forked River as being fairly rich in clams.

What to Bring: You'll need a clamming license available from the New Jersey Division of Fish, Game and Wildlife or from a reputable sporting goods store on the Jersey Shore. You'll also need a clamming rake, gloves, a wooden peach basket placed in an inner tube with a piece of rope attached to it and you to prevent it from floating away.

Put the clams that you find in the basket. Clam tongs and clam forks are also good tools to have with you.

How to Do It: Scrape the clam rake along the sandy bottom of the bay as you move backwards. Move and scrape slowly until you feel the shell of a clam. Quickly dig under the clam and dislodge it from the bed. Rake in a recognizable pattern to avoid raking the same area twice. Clamming is hard, often backbreaking work. Be prepared to sweat a little. The rewards, though, are worth it, especially when you taste that first mouthful of homemade Jersey Shore clam chowder.

Each year regulations are posted concerning the size of clams you're allowed to keep as well as the number. Check these out in advance. If you ignore such regulations or are ignorant of them, you'll pay a steep fine if you're found disobeying them.

FORKED RIVER

The **Forked River State Marina** is the second of three state-owned and operated boat basins on the Jersey Shore. (The northernmost state marina is located in Leonardo, see chapter 1. The southernmost is the Senator Frank S. Farley Marina in Atlantic City, see chapter 7.)

Unlike Leonardo, though, Forked River does not have a boat launch, which makes it less useful to the day visitor. But with so many other marinas in the area, the visiting boater will have little difficulty getting his boat in the bay. Forked River State Marina does possess 110 berths and reserves 2 of them for boaters wishing to moor their craft for one night only. Like Leonardo, there is a waiting list for the other 108 berths. The wait at Forked River is approximately one to two years, depending on the size of the boat. The marina is located at 311 South Main Street. For more information, call (609) 693-5044.

WARETOWN

The music begins promptly at eight o'clock each Saturday night, and it doesn't wind down until near midnight. In the summer, when the air is thick with humidity, the picking and singing lasts much longer than that. Although the lights in **Albert Hall** are turned off and the doors locked, many of the musicians move outside to the parking lot where the "Sounds of the Jersey Pines" continue under the stars until the last singer is too tired to call out another tune.

The stage at Albert Hall is set to resemble the old lodge in the Pines where members of the Pinelands Cultural Society first gathered to pick and sing. The place was Joe and George Albert's secluded hunting cabin. When folks started bringing their friends to listen in, it was decided a bigger place was needed. Today, Albert Hall, named in honor of the Alberts, is located behind Monari Auto Body in Waretown Plaza on Route 9.

What you'll hear at Albert Hall are home-bred, self-taught groups of musicians and singers who blend interesting slices of traditional American folk, country and bluegrass with Pine Barrens and Barnegat

Bay themes. It's a sound that's as indigenous to the Jersey Shore as Bruce Springsteen's and Southside Johnny's brand of rock 'n' roll further north (see chapter 2).

The Saturday night lineup is filled with both regulars and newcomers. Each performer gets 20 minutes up on the stage. No one gets paid. Everyone has a grand ol' time. A small admission charge goes into the fund currently being raised to build a new Albert Hall somewhere in the Pine Barrens. Those interested in obtaining information about becoming a member of the Pinelands Cultural Society should write to the organization at P.O. Box 657, Waretown 08758.

BARNEGAT

Of all the towns on the bay, Barnegat is the one that has strived the hardest to preserve its past. The Barnegat Historical Society has a small museum on East Bay Street and a collection of old, semirestored buildings that have been spared destruction. The **Lippencott Falkinburg House** (circa 1800) is an excellent example of the types of homes built nearly 200 years ago on Barnegat Bay. Found next to the Lippencott Falkinburg House are buildings built in Barnegat more than a century ago and moved to this location for preservation. One of the most interesting is the old barbershop, a place where hair was cut and town politics discussed.

Much of Barnegat's historical preservation work began in 1976 during our nation's bicentennial. Since then, however, funds for local preservation projects have practically dried up, leaving much of the work unfinished. Because of limited funds, the Barnegat Historical Society Museum and related historical buildings are only open from June 1 to September 15, on Fridays and Saturdays from 2 to 4 p.m. No admission charge.

Before visiting the museum, antique lovers might want to browse through the group of shops at the intersection of Bay Avenue and Route 9. **First National Antiques** (708 West Bay Avenue), **Elegant Odds and Ends** (696 East Bay Avenue), **Creative Clutter** (694 East Bay Avenue) and **By-Gone Antiques** (Route 9 and Bay Avenue) have a wide selection of interesting pieces, many of which are local in nature. Also check out **Yellow Bird Antiques** (Route 9 and Cedar Street), two blocks north of Bay Avenue on Route 9. Very good deals can be found in this cluster of shops.

After you've had your fill of antiques, one must stop at the **Hurricane House** on 688 East Bay Avenue, located smack in the middle of the Barnegat antique center for an old-fashioned ice cream treat. The Hurricane House is Ocean County's oldest ice cream parlor, initially established in 1920. Sip a malted on the shop's original ice cream counter, or perhaps take a booth and feast on a scumptious chocolate ice cream sundae. You'll find few other ice cream parlors like the Hurricane House on the Shore.

If one continues down East Bay Avenue, past the Barnegat Historical Society Museum and historic buildings, you'll come to Barnegat Bay. To your right (south) is the Barnegat Wildlife Sanctuary. East Bay Avenue eventually turns into Bayshore Drive, which loops around back to Route 9. It's on Bayshore where the town's marinas can be found, along with its municipal dock, public swimming beach and a sweeping view of Barnegat Bay and Long Beach Island. A careful look on a clear day will provide the visitor with a view of Old Barney, the Barnegat Lighthouse at the northernmost tip of Long Beach Island. There is also a public boat launch here as well as fishing and crabbing facilities. Crabbing can be quite good in Barnegat as can clamming, although a clamming license is needed (see below).

Canoeing in the Pine Barrens

One of the most pleasant ways to explore and fully appreciate the natural, unspoiled beauty of the Pine Barrens is by canoe. So much of the best that the Pine Barrens has to offer is inaccessible by car. Therefore, traveling along an inland river with nothing but the calls of catbirds and warblers and the easy swoosh of the cedar-stained water to break the soft silence is surely the best way to go.

Some of the state's best canoeing can be found in the Pine Barrens. But that doesn't mean you'll find raging rapids and foaming white water. On the contrary. Most of the navigable rivers aren't really rivers at all, but quiet, lazy streams. Some are so quiet that it's possible to paddle upstream with little effort. That's good news for those unable to get someone to pick them up at the end of their journey.

Canoeing the Pine Barrens is considered so good because of the magnificent scenery more than anything else. The Pines possesses a plethora of unusual plantlife and vegetation on the banks of its streams and rivers. Some species can be found only in Pine Barrens and nowhere else.

You'll see towering cedar and pine trees and sandy beaches, marshland, swamps and cranberry bogs. You might spot beavers busily working on dams and deer nibbling on the riverbank vegetation. You'll do lots of twisting and turning on some Pine Barrens rivers, which, at times, might require the skill of a seasoned canoeist. You'll also do lots of head-ducking as the vegetation gets quite thick in some areas.

Four excellent rivers for canoeing, the Oswego, Wading, Mullica and Batsto rivers, wind through Wharton State Forest and adjoining forest areas. These rivers provide canoeists with an unhurried, up-close look at the Pine Barrens, while at the same time allowing them to experience the serenity of the forest one only finds far from urban sprawl.

Oswego River Tour

The Oswego River, also known as the East Branch of the Wading River, is not recommended for first-time canoeists. There are simply too many difficult turns in the journey, which combined with the narrowness of the river can make canoeing a bit too challenging for some novices. The Oswego River tour, however, is the shortest of the four described here. One should get from Lake Oswego at the edge of Penn State Forest on the Route 563 Spur, your starting point, to

Harrisville Pond, also on the Route 563 Spur, in approximately three hours.

This river tour is excellent for those wishing to see perhaps the biggest cedar trees in the Pine Barrens and also many of the wildflowers the area is noted for. Bring a wildflower field guide with you to help in identification.

The Wading River Tour

This is a better tour for novice paddlers because, except for the earliest part of the journey where the river is narrow, the Wading River is quite wide and thus easy to navigate. Launch your canoe at Speedwell on Route 563. Approximately five hours later you'll come to Evans Bridge, your destination. For a longer version of the tour, continue past Evans Bridge and paddle on to Bodine Field, also on Route 563. Be advised, however, that the Wading River can get rather congested during the summer because it's the most popular Pine Barrens river to canoe.

The Mullica River Tour

The Mullica River is nearly as popular with canoeists as the Wading River. Good for beginners as well as more experienced canoeists, the river winds through savannah marshes and clumps of cedar tree forest. It also provides the best possibility to see wildlife other than beaver, say veteran Pine Barrens river paddlers. Begin your journey on the shores of Atsion Lake and paddle to Pleasant Mills, just across from Batsto. It should take you approximately six hours to get there.

The Batsto River Tour

If you want wilderness canoeing, the Batsto River Tour is for you. The river is quite inaccessible, which discourages all but the most determined canoests. It also can be difficult paddling across Batsto Lake if you're going against a headwind. You'll encounter a more varied riverbank than on any of the other tours. Virtually all the ecosystems of the Pine Barrens can be experienced and viewed on the Batsto River. Put in at Hampton Furnace and canoe to the end of Batsto Lake. It should take you about five hours.

For more detailed information on canoeing the Pine Barrens, pick up a copy of Robert Parnes' superb book, *Canoeing the Jersey Pine Barrens*. No other book on the market gives so much material on the rivers, their history and vegetation, and the Pine Barrens's ecology that canoeists will paddle by than this one. Highly recommended.

Privately Owned Canoe Rentals

Adams Canoe Rental
Lake Drive, Atsion
R.D. #2, Vincetown 08088
(609) 268-0189
Bel Haven Lake
Route 542, Green Bank
R.D. #2, Egg Harbor 08215
(609) 965-2031
Mick's Canoe Rental
Route 563, Jenkins

Chatsworth 08019
(609) 726-1380
Paradise Lakes Campground
Route 206, P.O. Box 46
Hammonton 08037
(609) 561-7095
Pic-A-Lilli Canoe Rental
Lake Road, Atsion
R.D. #2, Vincentown 08088
(609) 268-9831

Mullica River Boat Basin
Green Bank, R.D. #2
Egg Harbor 08215
(609) 965-2120

Mullica River Marina
R.D. #1, Weekstown Rd.
Sweetwater 08037
(609) 561-4337

Pine Barrens Canoe Rental
Route 563, Box 27, Jenkins
Chatsworth 08019
(609) 726-1515

Wading Pines Campground
Route 563, Jenkins
Chatsworth 08019
(609) 726-1313

Historic Towne of Smithville

Two hundred years ago James Baremore opened the Smithville Inn to weary South Jersey travelers. Because it was built on a stagecoach route, which connected Cooper's Landing in Camden to nearby Leed's Point, and because it served uncommonly good grub, the inn's popularity grew until the advent of the railroad, which made the stagecoach in these parts diminish in importance. The Inn closed and fell into disrepair, until, in 1949, the Noyes family restored it and reopened it as a restaurant. To attract diners, old South Jersey buildings from the nineteenth century were moved to Smithville and also restored. At its peak, Smithville had more than 25 historic structures, which gave a good indication of what a South Jersey Pine Barrens town might have looked like in the nineteenth century. Craftspeople demonstrated the traditional skills of rugbraiding, soapmaking, and woodcarving, and brought to life a way of living that had been all but forgotten.

A second set of buildings was constructed in Smithville to capitalize on the influx of visitors. Replicas of old country stores were filled with crafts, clothes, candles, antiques and other merchandise. Today, these buildings make up virtually all there is to see, as the historic part of Smithville—known as the Old Village—has suffered from lack of loving care and the funds necessary for proper upkeep. The sailing ship in the harbor is half sunk and vandals have left their ugly mark on many of the structures. As of this writing, Smithville's Old Village was in desperate need of a facelift.

Nevertheless, Smithville is still very much worth a visit as the shops are quite fun to browse through and sell crafts and other goods of the highest caliber. Some of the shops are not in replica buildings, but original historic structures, brought to Smithville when those in the Old Village were brought there. The **Country Place**, for instance, which sells mostly country antiques, is located in an old gristmill. Built in the 1790s in Sharpstown, its workers ground such grains as wheat, buckwheat and rye in it for local consumption. The waterwheel on the side of the building still turns the water of Lake Meone.

Other shops that sit along the cobblestone paths of Smithville include the **Brower House**, which sells expertly crafted Early American reproduction furniture; the **Gourmet Pantry**, where you'll find imported cheese, meat, tea and spices; the **Tomasello Winery**, where one can sample and purchase wines and champagnes made by one of South Jersey's leading wine families (see chapter 8); and the **Lil' Brass Duck Shoppe**, which offers brass lamps, weather vanes, bedposts and door knockers, among other items. Smithville has more than 30 shops in all.

Be sure to have lunch or dinner at the **Smithville Inn**, where the food is good and the atmosphere distinctively colonial. In addition, you'll get a receipt that entitles you to $10 worth of coins at Harrah's Marina Casino in Atlantic City.

Smithville is at its best during May and October, when the May Fest and October Fest occur, respectively. Arts and crafts shows, music, food sampling and other special activities make these annual events quite popular. For more information, call (609) 652-7775. Smithville is located on Route 9, 12 miles north of Atlantic City. Take Exit 48 for those coming via the Parkway.

OCEANVILLE

Noyes Museum. The Noyes Museum is the Jersey Shore's largest fine arts museum, and one of two found in the area. (The other is on the Atlantic City Boardwalk. It's called the Atlantic City Arts Center. See chapter 7.) Opened in 1983, the Noyes Museum sits in a rustic, serene setting amid tall pine trees on the shore of Lily Lake and adjacent to the Edwin B. Forsythe Wildlife Refuge (see below). Located just off Route 9 on Lily Lake Road, and less than ten minutes south of Smithville, the museum regularly displays the work of some of New Jersey's most talented artists.

The museum, established by Fred W. Noyes and his wife, Ethel Noyes, has five galleries; one is devoted entirely to waterfowl and shore bird decoys. A resident woodcarver on the premises demonstrates the art of woodcarving to the public. Fred Noyes was once an avid decoy collector, and many of the finest pieces of his personal collection can be found here.

The remaining four galleries offer exhibits that change approximately every three months. At least two of the four galleries are usually dedicated to paintings; the other two often feature the work of sculptors and furniture makers.

The Noyes Museum is open Wednesday through Saturday 11 a.m.–4 p.m. On Sundays, doors open at noon and close at 4 p.m. A small admission is charged. For information on current exhibits, call (609) 652-8848. The museum is usually closed in January and February.

Edwin B. Forsythe National Wildlife Refuge. Formerly known as Brigantine National Wildlife Refuge, this 34,000-acre coastal salt marsh and wetlands preserve was initially established to protect a critical stopover for migrating waterfowl on their way south or north, depending on the season. The refuge is on the Atlantic Flyway, and more than 250 species of birds visit the marsh area each year. Needless to say, the Forsythe Refuge is a prime location for bird-watching. Nowhere on the

Jersey Shore is it easier to spot birds in such large numbers or to photograph them.

It's possible to see loons, pelicans, cormorants, herons, swans, geese, ducks, vultures, falcons (including the peregrine falcon), grouse, quail, cranes, plovers, gulls, terns, finches, sandpipers, larks, swallows and woodpeckers among other birds. One can ask for a pamphlet entitled *Birds of Edwin B. Forsythe National Wildlife Refuge* at the Visitor's Center; it contains a bird checklist, plus information on what season you're most apt to see them and average number of yearly sightings.

Of course you don't need to be an avid bird-watcher to appreciate or enjoy the Forsythe Refuge. The mere sight of so many birds in their natural environment is interesting and quite special, even for those who can't tell a wren from a warbler. The best time to view birds is in the fall during their annual migration south. Spring is also a good time, although birds don't usually linger in the marshland there as much during this season as they do in the fall. Those bent on viewing the arrival of ducks and snow geese, which number close to 100,000 each year, should visit the refuge in November and early December. It's at this time that one is also apt to catch a glimpse of a bald eagle.

Visitors will find the self-guided Auto Tour, an eight-mile loop road on elevated ground, an ideal and comfortable way to view the birds. The backdrop is the Atlantic City skyline and Great Bay, while just below you is the patchwork of tiny islands and marshland where birds rest and feed. Binoculars aren't a must, but they're highly recommended.

The Auto Tour has 14 stops and takes about 90 minutes to complete it, although one can easily spend the better part of a day observing and photographing the birds. Many do just that. You'll see automobile license plates from states all around the country as the Forsythe Refuge is very well known among bird-watchers and naturalists everywhere. To enhance your tour of the refuge, the Visitor's Center has another free pamphlet, this one called simply, *The Auto Tour of the Edwin B. Forsythe Natural Wildlife Refuge*, which is good to read in order to fully appreciate what you'll see out on the loop.

Bird-watching, of course, is the overriding attraction at the Forsythe Refuge. Those who wish to get closer to the birds and have more personal contact with the land they inhabit than what you get sitting in a car, can walk the Auto Tour, or else walk the Leeds Eco Trail and/or People's Trail.

The former is just a half mile long, but it winds through a wonderfully scenic area of the refuge and the place where the infamous Jersey Devil is said to roam. You'll walk by greenbriar and honeysuckle, red cedar and black cherry trees, salt marshes and shrubs, and that seemingly ubiquitous plant, poison ivy. In addition to birds, you might catch a glimpse or two of white-tailed deer, a mink or fox, snapping or box turtles, rabbits or fiddler crabs.

The People's Trail is only a quarter mile long. It enables walkers to see nearly the same vegetation and possibilities of wildlife that the Leeds Trail offers, but in a shorter distance. Both hikes are made more enjoyable if you use the guide pamphlets available at the Visitor's Center.

Speaking of the Visitor's Center, take time to view the wildlife exhibits there and perhaps view one of the numerous nature slide shows shown in the auditorium. A ranger or volunteer is available to answer questions and pass out guides and brochures. Often asked of rangers is whether boating is permitted in the channels and waterways surrounding the marshland islands. The answer is no simply because such activity is apt to disturb the birds and the refuge's exceedingly delicate, yet complex ecosystem. One can, however, enjoy hours of boating on Great Bay as well as excellent fishing. Great Bay is the largest body of water in the area. It lies to the north of the refuge and contains the mouth of the Mullica River. On the south side of the Forsythe Refuge is Reed's Bay. Boaters venturing north or south on the Inland Waterway are permitted to pass through certain confines of the refuge.

As for hunting, it is permitted during hunting season in specially designated areas of the refuge, providing one possesses a valid New Jersey hunting license and follows the refuge's rules and regulations. The Edwin B. Forsythe Wildlife Refuge is open year-round, from dawn to dusk. It can be reached via Route 9 and Lily Road, where the Noyes Museum is located. The entrance to the refuge is just beyond the museum. Admission is free.

The Jersey Devil

There are as many stories that seek to explain the origins of the Jersey Devil as there are descriptions of the notorious creature who has prowled the Pine Barrens since people can remember. Most accounts attribute the birth of the demon to a Mrs. Leeds of Estelville sometime in the early eighteenth century, perhaps 1735. Apparently Mother Leeds already had 12 children, and when she found out she was expecting yet one more time, she cried out in rage, "Not another child! I hope this one's a devil, then!"

Her wish was granted if you believe in the Jersey Devil. On the night of its birth, local midwives gathered at Mrs. Leeds' house and helped her along with her labor. At the point of delivery they were horrified to learn that the child wasn't really a child at all, but a grotesque, horned, winged creature with the face of a horse, and the tail of a devil. The demon either flew up the chimney or out the window and into the Pines. And from that time on, he became known by a number of names, but the Jersey Devil was the one passed from generation to generation.

Other stories differ significantly from the one mentioned above. According to one interpretation, Mrs. Leeds didn't curse her unborn child, a sorcerer did. Another interpretation has the Jersey Devil the product of a steamy extramarital affair Mrs. Leeds had with a young British army officer. There are also discrepancies as to where the Jersey Devil was born. Some people claim he was born in Estelville; others say he was born in Leed's Point, the small town in the middle of the Edwin B. Forsythe Wildlife Refuge, where many sightings of the Jersey Devil have occurred.

Descriptions of the Jersey Devil are just as diverse as the stories pertaining to his origins. Perhaps James F. McCloy and Ray Miller, Jr., in their fine book, *The Jersey Devil*, give the best description: "His size varies from eighteen inches to twenty feet. He has the body of a kangaroo, the head of a dog, the face of a horse, the wings of a bat, the feet of a pig, and a forked tail."

As for his dastardly deeds, the Jersey Devil has been accused of killing farm animals; causing forest fires, even wars; causing crops and good luck to fail; being the cause of unexplained events; and terrorizing Pineys and travelers alike. The Jersey Devil has also been linked in one way or another to the infamous pirate, Captain Kidd; the American naval hero, Como. Stephen Decatur; and Joseph Bonaparte, the brother of Napolean Bonaparte.

One thing about the Jersey Devil *is* absolutely certain. In Pine Barrens folklore, he lives! The area is brimming with all sorts of legends and tales, but none is so well-known or more believed than the Jersey Devil. It doesn't matter that people can't agree on what he is, where he came from, what he looks like and what he's responsible for. Ask any Piney about the Jersey Devil and he'll tell you he's indeed alive and well. Why, just the other day a neighbor of his . . .

DID YOU KNOW THAT . . . THERE IS A SOUTH NEW JERSEY COCKTAIL CALLED THE JERSEY DEVIL? THE DRINK IS MADE FROM CRANBERRY JUICE, APPLEJACK AND RUM. LOCALS SAY THAT IF YOU DRINK TOO MUCH OF IT, YOU'RE BOUND TO SEE ONE OR TWO OR THREE JERSEY DEVILS AS YOU STAGGER OFF.

CHATSWORTH

Set at the crossroads of Routes 532 and 563, between Lebanon and Wharton state forests, Chatsworth is often called the capital of the Pine Barrens. It's here at Buzby's General Store, made famous by John McPhee's wonderful depiction of it in his book, *The Pine Barrens*, where you'll find Pineys sipping soda pop and trading local gossip. Chatsworth is also the home of the area's largest and most popular cranberry festival. Held each fall, usually on the third weekend in October, everything and anything relating to cranberries is on display. You can pick up all sorts of cranberry recipes, plus the tastiest cranberry juice you've ever tasted, and watch local cranberry farmers determine who has the largest cranberry in the Pine Barrens. There's also an arts and crafts sale and music by the Pinelands Cultural Society. For information on this year's Chatsworth Cranberry Festival, call (609) 859-9701.

WHARTON STATE FOREST

Wharton State Forest is New Jersey's largest state forest and the hub of virtually all Pine Barrens outdoors activity for the Shore visitor.

Located off Route 542, less than 13 miles west of the Parkway (Exit 50 or 52), Wharton sits in the heart of the Pine Barrens. It encompasses thousands of acres of tall pine trees, cedar swamps, yellow rivers and streams, and some of the best camping areas, hiking trails and canoeing in the mid-Atlantic region, along with over 400 miles of sand roads, which provide fairly easy access to nearly all reaches of Wharton with a four wheel drive vehicle.

Despite Wharton's vast natural wealth, its most popular attraction is the historic village of Batsto, once South Jersey's leading bog iron producer. Today, there are more than 25 restored iron workers' homes, barns and stables, and buildings such as the General Store, sawmill and iron master's mansion to visit, plus a visitor's center, which also includes a small, but excellent museum. Like Allaire Village in Allaire State Park (see chapter 3), Batsto is well preserved and provides visitors with a chance to step back to the days when bog iron furnaces burned bright and hot in the New Jersey heartland, furnaces which helped build America.

The Batsto Iron Works began operations in 1766. Its owner, Charles Read of Burlington, chose the site because of the availability of water power, the accessibility of the Atlantic Ocean via the Mullica River, which would enable ships to transport iron products made at Batsto to ports along the Eastern seaboard, and, finally, close proximity of bogs and riverbeds rich in ore from which iron was extracted. (Ore is formed from decayed plant matter after it has blended with iron salts in rivers and swamps.)

In 1773, a Philadelphian named John Cox bought the Batsto Iron Works from Read. Cox was an ardent patriot, and once America claimed its independence from England, he and those employed at Batsto began making cannonballs and other munitions for the Continental Army. So important was the military significance of Batsto, that those who worked there were exempt from serving in the army.

Only once during the Revolutionary War was Batsto threatened by the British. That was in the fall of 1778 when redcoats attacked Chestnut Neck on the Mullica River, the largest seaport in southern New Jersey during the Colonial Era and a haven for American privateers. The British destroyed Chestnut Neck and planned to proceed up the Mullica River to destroy Batsto. But news of the arrival of Gen. Casimir Pulaski's troops and a brief engagement with some of them prompted the British to turn back.

In addition to making cannonballs and munitions, Batsto also produced domestic iron products such as pots and kettles, stoves, even ducts from which fresh water was carried to citizens of some colonial cities. In 1812, Batsto was again called upon to make munitions for the American army, once more engaged in conflict with the British.

Like Allaire, Batsto thrived as a bog iron community until the 1830s when coal was discovered in Pennsylvania as well as new iron ore deposits. The Richards family sought to revive Batsto by turning to the production of glass. The fine white sand of the Pine Barrens seemed perfect for the making of glassware, thus the Batsto Glassworks was created in 1846. But due to mismanagement and continuing financial woes, the Glassworks at Batsto survived only until 1867. Then in 1874, more than half the village was destroyed by fire, and Batsto was abandoned.

Two years later, Joseph Wharton bought the Batsto property along with other tracts of land in the Pine Barrens. Wharton, a shrewd investor and entrepreneur, realized the immense value of the Pine Barrens' underground aquifer and planned to sell the pure water to the city of Philadelphia. Things looked bright for Wharton and his water-selling scheme, until New Jersey legislators passed a law that prohibited the export of water from the state. Batsto and the Wharton Tract, as it became known, sat idle until 1954 when New Jersey purchased it and made it into a state forest for use as a recreational area, natural preserve and historic site.

Wharton State Forest is open year-round. An admission fee is charged on weekends and holidays, from Memorial Day to Labor Day. For more information, call (609) 561-0024 or write Wharton State Forest, Batsto R.D. #4, Hammonton 08037.

Things to Do

Tour the Historic Village of Batsto. Your first stop in Wharton State Forest should be the Visitor's Center, just outside the Batsto village. Here, you'll be able to pick up all the detailed information you need on current activities and special events in the park, plus gain a good understanding of the historical significance of the Batsto Iron Works before touring the village that evolved from it. It is also a good idea to purchase a ticket for the iron master's mansion tour at this time, since only a limited number of tickets are sold each day, and they go very quickly. You cannot enter the mansion unless you are part of one of the guided tours which run a few times each day.

The Visitor's Center is bright and modern, and full of exhibits that pertain to the Pine Barrens, the bog iron industry in New Jersey in the eighteenth and nineteenth centuries, glassmaking, and, of course, Batsto, plus remnants of items excavated by archeologists who have conducted extensive digs in the Batsto area.

After the Visitor's Center, a walk through the village is in order. Immediately outside it is an ore boat that was found at the bottom of Batsto Lake. It was used to haul raw iron ore to the Batsto furnace. An interesting display nearby explains the hows and whys of burning charcoal in the furnace. Continue walking toward the iron master's mansion. In its vicinity you'll see the General Store and post office, various barns and worksheds, and the remains of the furnace. Many of the buildings are open to the public. In the craft houses, for instance, you'll find craftspeople demonstrating such things as the art of quilt-making, weaving and candlemaking. A blacksmith is usually on the premises, too, and you might see a miller in the gristmill.

It is the iron master's mansion, however, that draws the most attention. The largest building in the village, it is certainly the most interesting, architecturally speaking. The mansion has been remodeled several times, so it contains a variety of architectural styles. Inside are furnishings from various periods. Tastefully decorated and renovated, the iron master's or Richards' Mansion, as it is also called in honor of Jesse Richards, the bog iron baron who owned Batsto during its last heyday, is the pride of Wharton State Forest.

Hike the Batona Trail. With the exception of the Appalachian Trail, there is no better hiking trail in New Jersey than the Pine Barrens' Batona Trail. The 41-mile trail cuts through some of the most scenic sections of the Pine Barrens and much of what is deemed "wilderness." It begins at Ongs Hat on Route 72 in Lebanon State Forest and ends at Evans Bridge on Route 563 in Wharton State Forest, if you're hiking north to south. Experienced hikers will want to walk the entire trail, taking a few days to do so. There are wilderness campsites at Lower Forge Camp and Batona Camp in Wharton, and one at the "300 Area" for summer hikers and Butler Place for winter hikers in Lebanon State Forest. To camp in any of these areas, however, requires a camping permit.

The length of the Batona Trail should not discourage novices from enjoying a day's walk on the trail, or even for a couple of hours. The terrain is mostly flat and easy to traverse, and the trail is well marked with pink markers, which are simple to follow providing you don't wander off the path. Pick up a map of Batona Trail at Wharton's Visitor's Center, and with the help of a ranger there, select a specific section within Wharton to walk.

A good choice for a day's worth of hiking might be to walk the last part of the trail, from Batsto to Evans Bridge, which is approximately ten miles long. A lesser distance walk might be from Batsto to Quaker Bridge, where two sand roads meet. The distance is approximately six miles. Those wishing for anything less should settle for the short nature trails, which begin and end near Wharton's Annie Carter Nature Center (see below).

Along the Batona Trail you'll walk through mostly pitch pine forest that's sprinkled with hardwood trees, cedar swamps, bogs and streams. All around you will be the remarkable sights and sounds of the Pine Barrens. You'll come across blueberry and huckleberry patches, lush green carpets of forest ferns, and wildflowers. As for wildlife, there's a good chance you'll spot some white-tailed deer, and if you're particularly lucky, a fox, mink, otter or a beaver. Many types of birds and reptiles wander here, including box and snapping turtles and the rare Pine Barrens tree frog, of which a glimpse would make any hiker's day who has a special appreciation of endangered wildlife.

To guarantee solitude and minimum exposure to other hikers, a

DID YOU KNOW THAT ... THE PINE BARRENS IS HOME TO SEVERAL SPECIES OF CARNIVOROUS PLANTS? PLANTS SUCH AS THE NORTHERN PITCHER AND SUNDEW EAT INSECTS. PITCHER PLANTS BLOOM IN EARLY MAY; SUNDEWS BLOOM IN EARLY SUMMER.

winter or late fall trek on Batona Trail is recommended. But winter hiking and camping should be done only by experienced woodsmen and walkers. This *is* a wilderness area, remember. Spring and fall are excellent times to hike Batona Trail, too. In the spring and early summer, you'll find the blueberries and huckleberries in season, which make for delicious trail treats. Summer is when Batona Trail is most crowded. But even then, the trail is long enough to accommodate large numbers of hikers. If you hike any time other than winter, don't forget insect repellent.

Go Camping. Wharton State Forest has nine camping areas, including the two that lie on Batona Trail. **Atsion Lake Camp** is on the north shore of Atsion Lake, just off Route 206. It's a good summer camping area because of swimming in Atsion Lake. **Batona Camp** is on the Batona Trail. **Bodine Field** is the largest of the Wharton camping areas; it holds some 500 people comfortably. You'll find many large groups camping here, which can make it quite noisy at night. It's located off the Route 563 Spur, behind the Harrisville ruins on the Wading River. **Buttonwood Hill Camp** is the smallest camping area in Wharton. It's located on Route 542 near the Mullica River. **Godfrey Bridge Camp** is on the west branch of the Wading River. Canoeists camp here often. It's located off Route 563. **Goshen Pond Camp**, off Route 206, is on the Mullica River, but close enough to Atsion Lake where swimming can be enjoyed. **Hawkin Bridge Camp** is another favorite camping area with canoeists; it's also located on the west branch of the Wading River. **Lower Forge Camp**, like Batona Camp, is on the Batona Trail. Here, you'll camp with many of the trail's hikers. The **Mullica Camp** on the Mullica River does not permit motor vehicles and, therefore, is a favorite camping area for those wishing truly to escape civilization for a few days.

No matter where you camp, you must have a camping permit. Permits are obtained at the Visitor's Center. Because Wharton is so large and possesses so many camping areas, you'll almost always find a place to pitch a tent, even in the peak of the summer season. No other state park or state forest along the Jersey Shore offers as many areas or such a variety of sites as Wharton.

Visit the Annie Carter Nature Center and Auditorium. Set back behind the Batsto Village is the Annie Carter Nature Center and Auditorium, which contains numerous ecological exhibits and hands-on displays. You'll see, for instance, a 52-pound shell of a snapping turtle found in the Pine Barrens some years ago, plus stuffed birds and other forms of wildlife whose natural habitat is the pine forests of

Wharton. A naturalist is usually on the premises to answer all your questions. Kids especially enjoy the nature center and auditorium where slide shows depict the natural history of the area. The center and auditorium are open in the summer, from Memorial Day to Labor Day.

Near the center is the Batsto Lake Nature Trail, which in less than an hour's time gives one an interesting firsthand overview of Pine Barrens ecology. You'll walk through a portion of pine forest, see a cedar swamp, and perhaps spot some wildlife. Take any of the trail spurs that lead down to the lake. Walk quietly and you might see a snapping turtle or box turtle on the shore. The ground is often wet and muddy. Wear rubber shoes.

Have a Picnic. Many people who visit Wharton State Forest, especially Batsto Village, bring their lunch and picnic in the grove nearby. A concession stand is there, but its menu is quite limited. Also, there are few, if any, places to eat near the entrance to the village area.

Go Freshwater Fishing. Three lakes offer fishing in Wharton State Forest and vicinity. Harrisville, Oswego and Batsto lakes have pike, perch, pickerel and some largemouth bass. Spring is the best time to fish these bodies of water. During the summer fish stay in the deeper areas where the water is cooler. But during the spring you'll have good luck using light tackle and minnows for bait, especially if you're after pickerel. The Wharton State Forest rivers provide fishing, too, and some regular anglers insist the fishing is much better in them than in the lakes. All anglers must have a valid New Jersey fishing license.

Go Deer Hunting. Deer hunting is very good during the season in the specified hunting areas of Wharton State Forest. One hunting area is west of Quaker Bridge and the Mullica River. The other area is near the Pine Barrens town of Friendship in the thick of the forest. A New Jersey hunting license is mandatory. Check with a park ranger for rules and regulations regarding hunting areas.

Go Horseback Riding. In addition to hiking, another excellent way to enjoy Wharton State Forest and the Pine Barrens is on a horse. Although Wharton does not have horses for hire, visitors can bring their own or else rent them from nearby stables. The southeast and northwest sections of the park offer particularly good riding, and horses are permitted in all but three camping areas (Atsion Lake, Buttonwood Hill and Godfrey Bridge). A ranger at the Visitor's Center will tell you where to park your car and trailer.

Wharton State Forest Special Events. Each year Wharton sponsors at least five annual events that attract thousands of visitors. In June and July woodcarvers bring their duck decoys to display and sell at Batsto. July is also a month of music as the Wharton State Forest Music Festival features some of New Jersey's finest folksingers, bluegrass pickers and songwriters. Then in September, there's an art show, and in October, the Country Living Fair, which celebrates what else, but the art of country living. You'll see basket-making, spinning and weaving exhibits, needlework, stained glass and quilt-making displays, pick up cranberry recipes, learn how to repair a canoe, and watch a woodcarver in action. For information on these events, including this year's dates, call (609) 561-3262.

Some Recommended Restaurants in the Pine Barrens and Barnegat Bay Areas

Allen's Clam Bar
Route 9 (New York Road)
New Gretna
(609) 296-4106
Price Code: Inexpensive
Menu: Seafood

Allen's could very well be the Shore's best clam bar. Oyster stew and clam fritters are the tastiest on the coast. Casual atmosphere. Everything fresh and wonderfully delicious.

Captain's Inn
Lacey Road
Forked River
(609) 693-3351
Price Code: Moderate
Menu: Seafood, some beef

Looking for a harbor setting in which to enjoy your seafood dish? The Captain's Inn doesn't disappoint. Standard menu, good-sized portions.

Carla and Ezio's
1450 Route 88 West
Bricktown
(201) 458-5411
Price Code: Expensive
Menu: Italian

Bricktown isn't exactly in the Pine Barrens region, though it's close. Yet Carla and Ezio's must be mentioned somewhere. Absolutely mouth-watering Northern Italian dishes and salads. Small dining area, bland atmosphere, but the food makes up for it in a big way.

Clayton's Log Cabin
Route 72
Barnegat
(609) 698-4407
Price Code: Moderate/Expensive
Menu: German-American

Set in a real log cabin, the German dishes are quite good. Lunch menu is as tempting as the dinner menu.

Forked River House
Route 9
Forked River

(609) 693-2310
Price Code: Moderate/Expensive
Menu: Seafood, beef

Dining area overlooks Forked River; the restaurant has long been a Barnegat Bay area standard. Seafood combination platter is a wise choice.

Joe Italiano's Maplewood Inn
470 White Horse Pike
Hammonton
(609) 561-9621
Price Code: Moderate
Menu: Italian

Virtually all the South Jersey restaurant critics agree that it's impossible to find a better plate of spaghetti than what you get at Joe Italiano's Maplewood Inn. Homemade pasta. Terrific sauces.

Joe's Place
Route 9
Smithville
(609) 652-8819
Price Code: Moderate/Expensive
Menu: International

Select Joe's Place instead of the Smithville Inn or Prima's if you want to try something unusual like Mexican Pizza. Good food, chic setting.

Oyster Creek Inn
Leeds Point Road
Leeds Point
(609) 652-9871
Price Code: Moderate
Menu: Seafood

Classic Jersey Shore/Pine Barrens ambiance and delicious clam dishes. A favorite with locals.

Prima's
(Located in Quail Hill Inn)
Route 9
Smithville
(609) 652-8814
Price Code: Moderate/Expensive
Menu: Italian

Surprisingly good Italian seafood dishes and not necessarily the usual ones that appear on Jersey Shore menus.

Ram's Head Inn
9 White Horse Pike
Absecon (Galloway Township)
(609) 652-1700
Price Code: Expensive
Menu: Seafood, beef, Continental

One of *New Jersey Monthly*'s three top restaurants in the state. Talk about atmosphere. An excellent place to have dinner when you're celebrating something truly special.

Smithville Inn
Route 9
Smithville
(609) 652-7777
Price Code: Moderate/Expensive
Menu: Traditional American and seafood

Most popular of the Smithville restaurants; very good menu, nice setting. Expect a wait if you go on a weekend.

7. ATLANTIC CITY

Atlantic City is the crown jewel of the Jersey Shore. Within a few short years after New Jersey legalized gambling there in 1976 and the first casino, Resorts International, opened in 1978, Atlantic City has come to overshadow America's other glitzy and glamorous gambling resort, Las Vegas. Today, Atlantic City has even gone a step further. It's now the number one vacation city in the entire country and an internationally known, year-round playground for the world's rich and famous.

They call it the Queen of Resorts, the City-by-the-Sea, Casino City, the Gay Dowager. Whatever, it is indeed a city of endless activity. Enter into any one of Atlantic City's 11 casinos (and more are being built), and you're instantly transformed into a world seemingly oblivious to everything but excitement, pleasure and pampering. Such things come in many forms and cater to all five senses. There are blinking bright lights, the perpetual patter of the slot machines, and sexy cocktail waitresses clad in seductive outfits at your service. Down the corridor, away from the betting action, are elevators that take you to plush hotel suites, spas, convention rooms, exquisite restaurants, and expensive shops for those wishing to spend what they've won.

Men in tuxedos, women in evening gowns. High rollers and Slot Machine Sallys. World-class entertainment: performers like Frank Sinatra, Dionne Warwick, Bob Hope, Eddie Murphy and Racquel Welch grace Atlantic City stages nightly. World-class sporting events such as championship boxing matches and top-notch tennis tournaments are held there regularly. Atlantic City offers, as one writer put it, "the feeling of having *been* somewhere."

And where, exactly, is that? On Absecon Island, an eight-mile long barrier island, seven miles off the mainland, which also includes the Atlantic City suburbs of Ventnor, Margate and Longport. The city sits just south of the Edwin B. Forsythe National Wildlife Refuge, and just north of Ocean City and the rest of the South Jersey Shore. Surrounded by marshland and twisting, shallow waterways, it would seem to be the last place a city of such fame, fortune and fabulous entertainment would be located.

You can get to Atlantic City by bus; literally hundreds pull into and out of the city each day and night. It's the cheapest way to go, because on your arrival, you'll receive as much as $20 in quarters to get you started in slot machine mania. You'll also get meal tickets and drink discounts. Call the casino of your choice for information on bus lines that leave from your area. (See below for toll-free casino telephone numbers and other information pertaining to the casinos, hotel reservations, and such.)

You can arrive by car, but if you do, expect monumental parking problems. Some casinos offer free parking. If you drive, take that into *serious* consideration. There are three ways to drive into Atlantic City: the Atlantic City Expressway, which goes from Philadelphia and cuts right across the state, leaving you in downtown Atlantic City; the White Horse Pike, which is actually Route 30 and in the city, Absecon Boulevard, which connects with Route 9 and points north; and the Black Horse Pike, in the city, Albany Avenue, which connects with Routes 40 and 322 as well as Route 9 and points south. All three eventually link up with the Garden State Parkway. By car, Atlantic City is an hour from Philadelphia and 2½ hours from New York City.

You can also arrive in Atlantic City by plane. Bader Field Airport has shuttle and charter service from Philadelphia, Washington and other cities. You can even take a helicopter; consult your travel agent for flight times and airfare, or call the casinos and request information on package deals.

Finally, you can also arrive by boat. Beach Haven, on Long Beach Island, for instance, has daily boat excursions to and from **Harrah's Marina Casino** (see chapter 5). Other resorts and beach towns near Atlantic City are doing the same. In the future you'll even be able to arrive by train. Plans are currently being completed to restore the rail link to Philadelphia and construct a new terminal in Atlantic City. There's even talk of a monorail hookup to New York City. Anything seems possible.

When should you come to Atlantic City? Because it is truly a year-round resort, unlike many of the other resorts on the Jersey Shore, anytime is the right time. However, as might be expected, summer is peak season and hotel rooms are at a premium. The more budget-minded might consider coming in midwinter—January through March—when almost all of the hotel-casino complexes offer outstanding deals and discounts, and the facilities in town are much less crowded. It might be a bit too cold for some (but not all) to stroll Atlantic City's famous boardwalk, but much of the city's excitement is indoors, no matter what season it is.

And what if you're not a gambler? Are there things for you to do in Atlantic City? Absolutely. For starters, there's the beach and the Boardwalk. Both are free and both can mean hours of fun and entertainment. Atlantic City also boasts, and rightfully so, the best collection of first-class, four-star restaurants on the Jersey Shore. Many are located in the casino complexes, but more and more are popping up away from the Boardwalk. As already noted, Atlantic City's stage entertainment has few rivals; a night of Sinatra or Pavarotti is what some people consider the ultimate in evening entertainment. Also, small clubs in the city have nightly jazz, pop, piano bar and disco

---

DID YOU KNOW THAT ... THE GREAT AMERICAN PARLOR GAME, MONOPOLY, DEVISED BY PHILADELPHIAN CHARLES DARROW AND PRESENTED TO THE AMERICAN PUBLIC BY PARKER BROTHERS IN 1935, IS A GAME ABOUT BUYING AND SELLING REAL ESTATE IN ATLANTIC CITY?

DID YOU ALSO KNOW THAT ... MARVIN GARDENS IS THE ONLY NON-ATLANTIC CITY PROPERTY ON THE MONOPOLY GAME-BOARD? IT'S LOCATED IN NEARBY MARGATE AND, IN THE GAME, IS MISSPELLED. IT'S REALLY MARVEN GARDENS.

---

entertainment. It's here where you'll find many of the casino workers as they unwind after their shift on the casino floor.

There are also such things as shopping and sightseeing to enjoy, too. Ocean One, the huge mall on the Boardwalk, has many shops and eateries; Gardner's Basin, Absecon Lighthouse, Lucy the Elephant (in Margate) and the Atlantic City Art Center are all worthy of a visit. Finally, you don't have to bet, but you can watch others do so. Walking around the casinos, especially in the evening when the action is hot, is also entertainment. Thousand dollar bets go on a roll of the dice. Tension, excitement, jubilation or devastation are the highs and lows felt every minute where millions change hands each day. It's all enough to dazzle participants and observers alike.

Unfortunately, not all of Atlantic City glitters. As you enter the city and approach the Boardwalk and casino area, you'll be surprised, some even shocked, at the poverty and blight that encompasses most of Atlantic City. It's a sad, sorry sight. Here live welfare families in ghettolike conditions, while a mere mile or less away, on the very same street, millions are being wagered in the name of entertainment.

Government officials and proponents of further casino expansion in Atlantic City say eventually all of the city's residents will profit from the incredible inundation of money, big money, here. Perhaps *someday* they will. Already derelict buildings on Absecon Inlet are being torn down and condominiums constructed. But any overnight transition of the "other" Atlantic City is simply, er, not in the cards. Visitors should therefore be prepared, for the gap between rich and poor is indeed a big one.

THE BOARDWALK

Long before the casinos changed the skyline of Atlantic City, it was the Boardwalk that attracted tourists. Boardwalk is spelled with a capital "B" in Atlantic City because it's a legitimate "street" on the city map, and perhaps also, as some insist, out of honor. The very first boardwalk in the world, you see, was constructed in Atlantic City in 1870.

The story behind its creation is a story of practicality. A conductor on the Camden & Atlantic Railroad named Alexander Boardman was fed up with passengers tracking sand into his rail car after a visit to the Atlantic City beach. He thought hard about how people might enjoy the sand without bringing it onto the train and came up with the idea of a collapsible footpath made of wooden planks or boards.

Boardman took his idea to local hotel owners who were also tired of sand in their lobbies. With the city's support, a boardwalk 10 feet wide was built 1½ feet above the sand. The 12-foot sections would simply be picked up whenever there were unusually high tides or storms, and then permanently packed away for the winter. The Boardwalk was such a success that people came from all over to walk on it. The original Boardwalk gave way to a second Boardwalk, this one built on pilings; it extended some two miles along the beach. Also, it was 20 feet wide instead of 10.

After an 1889 hurricane did much damage to the Boardwalk's structural support, it was agreed by city officials to reconstruct it on steel pilings rather than wood, make it 24 feet wide, and increase it to four miles in length. Today's version of the Boardwalk is 60 feet wide and six miles long, and although it has seen better days, the Boardwalk is still a major Atlantic City attraction. It also remains the longest and most popular boardwalk in the world.

Prior to World War II, when Atlantic City experienced its first Golden Age, the Boardwalk had a number of piers attached to it that contained amusement rides, side shows, dance halls and restaurants. The Steel Pier grew to be Atlantic City's most famous pier. But due to storms, fires and general neglect, the piers lost their charm; some became eyesores. Today renovation is under way to restore the piers. The Garden Pier, for instance, is now the home of the Atlantic City Art Center (see below). Formerly the Million Dollar Pier, Ocean One juts out into the ocean in the form of a huge ocean liner. Located on the Boardwalk at Arkansas Avenue, it has over 150 shops and boutiques, fast food parlors and ocean view dining on its upper decks. Resembling more a large, sprawling suburban mall than a classic Atlantic City pier, it contains stores that are pretty standard. But some shops carry quality clothing and women's accessories, including jewelry, while the others are simply places to spend money won at the blackjack table or slot machine.

Another part of Atlantic City's past is coming back into vogue. Hand-pushed "Rolling Chairs," a leisurely and nostalgic form of Boardwalk transportation, first appeared on the Boardwalk in 1887. Today these canopied wicker chairs on wheels can be hired to get from one point on the Boardwalk to another. There are also "Boardwalk Rolling Chair Tours" during the summer. For information and reservations, call (609) 347-7148. Finally, motorized trams ride up and down the Boardwalk, a fine alternative to walking. Trams run from Albany Avenue to the Garden Pier; they're in service 10 a.m.–9 p.m on weekdays and to midnight on weekends and throughout the summer.

The Atlantic City Boardwalk differs from all other major boardwalks on the Jersey Shore not only because of its long tradition, but because it's minus amusement rides and wheels of chance, although some rides can be found on Steeplechase and Central piers (refurbishing plans, however, may result in the relocation of these rides). There are fast food outlets and tacky T-shirt stands, but generally what you'll find on the Boardwalk here is a higher standard shop, even stores that sell clothes, fashionable beach apparel, hats, and ladies' handbags and footwear.

An excellent selection of fudge and taffy awaits you at **Fralinger's** (1325 Boardwalk), where in 1885 Joseph Fralinger made his first tasty batch of Atlantic City saltwater taffy (see below). You can purchase 16 different flavors of the chewy stuff, including chocolate-dipped taffy, as well as peanut butter chews, almond macaroons and sea foam fudge. It's virtually impossible to pass Fralinger's without stopping. The same holds true for **James' Candy** (1101 and 1519 Boardwalk), **Steel's Fudge** (1112, 1633 and 2719 Boardwalk) and the **Peanut Shoppe** (2633 Boardwalk).

Irene's Souvenirs & Gifts (1239 Boardwalk) is Atlantic City's oldest gift shop; if you're looking for that Atlantic City novelty item to take home with you (T-shirt, sweatshirt, ashtray, mug), you'll probably find it here. For more unusual Atlantic City novelties, try **Rainbow's End Gift Shop** (1409 and 2215 Boardwalk). And at **Ol' Times** (1639 Boardwalk) you can buy custom-blended tobacco, snuff and imported cigars.

Undoubtedly the most noted Boardwalk landmark is Atlantic City's **Convention Hall**. This 532,800 square foot arena is the largest convention and exposition hall in the Northeast, and the home of Atlantic City's most famous event, the Miss America Pageant. Located on the Boardwalk between Mississippi and Florida avenues, Convention Hall is in the final stages of a $23 million renovation. The extensive facelift is in preparation for the dramatic increase in conventions that city officials say will occur in the next five years. There are also plans to stage more sporting events there, such as championship boxing and tennis matches.

In addition to Convention Hall, there are plans for a brand new convention center in Atlantic City. To be built on the site of the former rail terminal at the entrance to the Atlantic City Expressway, this new convention center will stand beside a new rail terminal and share the convention and sporting event business with Convention Hall.

The Short and Long of Saltwater Taffy

Saltwater taffy is made with saltwater, true or false. If you answered false, you're correct. The only salt that is found in saltwater taffy recipes is salt used in *any* candy recipe. It seems that the idea of calling the first taffy made and sold in Atlantic City "saltwater" taffy was more gimmick than anything else. One legend has it that the taffy became "saltwater" taffy after seawater soaked the supply of a taffy vendor named David Bradley in an 1883 summer storm. He jokingly referred to the candy as "saltwater" taffy, and the name stuck.

But it wasn't Bradley who *invented* taffy, as some people believe. No one knows for certain who was responsible for the sweet, sticky stuff that tastes delicious. Once again legend has it that it was created by the Ritchie Brothers and Windle Hollis in 1880. But taffy historians (there are such people) claim that taffy was being sold at Midwest county fairs that same year. So, although the Ritchie Brothers and Mr. Hollis were the first to make the candy in Atlantic City, they may or may not have been the candy's true creators.

One thing is certain, though. It was Joseph Fralinger who popularized saltwater taffy and became Atlantic City's first Saltwater Taffy King. Fralinger not only realized the potential of selling candy to bathers and boardwalkers, but he also figured there was a market for taking home taffy as an Atlantic City souvenir. He boxed some of the candy as an experiment and quickly sold out.

Like with all good marketing ideas, competition sprouted quickly. Fralinger's biggest rival was confectioner Enoch James and his sons; they had heard about the taffy hoopla going on in Atlantic City out in the Midwest and moved to the Jersey Shore to set up shop just down the boardwalk from Fralinger's. Supposedly, James added vegetable oil to his brand of taffy in order to lessen the chances of it pulling out dentures, and he cut his candy "to fit the mouth." Fralinger's, on the other hand, had taffy that was long and slender rather than rectangular, and Atlantic City's first taffy war was on. To this day, Fralinger's and James' taffy stores are in keen competition with each other.

Others joined in the fray, so by the mid-1920s, when saltwater taffy was at the height of its popularity, more than 450 companies were making and selling saltwater taffy. Despite the fact that it was sold all over, Atlantic City remained the saltwater taffy capital of the world, and the candy is still synonymous with the boardwalk here.

THE CASINOS

RESORTS INTERNATIONAL
(North Carolina Avenue and the Boardwalk)

There's no larger casino in town than what's found at the Resorts International hotel/casino complex. Nearly the size of two football fields, the mammoth gambling mecca is, according to Atlantic City regulars, the top of the line in casino comfort and elegance. The swirling, dazzling display of lights, glass and chandeliers is enough to make any gambler feel as if he is truly a preferred customer here.

Resorts International was the very first casino to open in Atlantic City. That was in May 1978; since then, Resorts has invested nearly $300 million in its expansive complex and plans to be at the half billion mark by 1988. In addition to the casino, which boasts 60,000 square feet of 1750 slot machines, 82 blackjack tables, 20 craps tables, 14 roulette tables, 4 big six tables and 3 baccarat tables, the complex also includes the celebrated **Superstar Theatre** where nationally televised sporting events occur as well as performances by such show business names as Johnny Mathis, Liberace, Tom Jones and Peter Allen, among many more. Then there's also the **Rendezvous Lounge** and the **Carousel Cabaret** where musical revues and stage shows entertain guests nightly.

As with all the casino complexes in Atlantic City, the best dining and shopping can be found mere steps away from the betting tables. Resorts has seven quality restaurants under its roof. The most noted are **Le Palais**, which offers French cuisine; **Camelot**, which is distinc- tively English; **Capriccio Italiano**, which features dishes from both northern and southern Italy; and the **House of Kyoto**, which is truly one of the best Japanese restaurants on the Jersey Shore. Some of the more exclusive shops under the Resorts roof include **Andrew Geller Footwear, Brittany Jewels, Abel's Antiquarium Antiques** and **Pierre Gerard** (men's clothes).

Rates for a room at Resorts International begin at $90. A number of excellent package deals are offered by the complex during the winter, however, which include reduced rates plus discounts or free admission to floor shows, the Resorts Health Spa and some of the eateries on the premises. Most of the 686 rooms are located in the Resorts' main wing, although some are in the North Tower. All of the rooms are tastefully decorated and quite spacious. For reservations, call 1-800-GET RICH or write Resorts International Casino Hotel, North Carolina Avenue and the Boardwalk, Atlantic City 08404.

Resorts International also operates RIA, a helicopter airline that links Manhattan with Atlantic City. For a $79 one-way fare, New Yorkers can be in Atlantic City in less than an hour. Departure points are at the West 30th Street, East 34th Street and Battery Park heliports in Manhattan and the Steel Pier in Atlantic City. There are three daily roundtrips. Call (212) 972-4444 in New York, (201) 865-4100 or (609) 344-0833 in New Jersey for more information.

CAESAR'S ATLANTIC CITY
(Arkansas Avenue and the Boardwalk)

The theme at Caesar's Atlantic City is decidedly Roman, as you might expect. The bold, lusty motif of reds and purples coupled with marble columns and staircases is only enhanced by the reproduction of famous works of Italian art, including Michelangelo's classic sculpture of David. You'll also see toga-clad waiters and wine servers and feel a festive, often bacchanalian spirit, which permeates much of the complex. Formerly the Howard Johnson Regency, Caesar's was originally called Caesar's Boardwalk Regency. It was the second casino to open in Atlantic City, taking its first bet in June 1979.

Aside from its lavish casino, Caesar's is also noted for its 1100-seat luxury **Circus Maximus Theater.** The Circus Maximus in Rome was a huge amphitheater built for contests where gladiators fought to the death and chariots raced recklessly around the track. This Circus Maximus, located on the second level of the hotel and adjacent to the Appian Way Mall, is more suited for boxing matches, floor shows and internationally known singers and entertainers. Columns and marble floors grace the theater. The 78 velvet-upholstered banquettes have superb views of the stage.

For added entertainment try the **Electric Company Amusement Arcade**, rooftop tennis, two swimming pools, a health spa and beach club privileges, or browse through such elegant shops as **Gucci, Tiberius, Talk of the Walk,** and **Frobbiani Shoes.**

Caesar's Casino ranks among the largest in Atlantic City. It has 72 blackjack, 24 crap, 10 roulette, 4 baccarat and 4 big six tables, plus almost 1600 nickel, quarter and dollar slot machines. For a great view of the casino action, go up to the fourth floor chrome and glass skylight and peer down at the excitement.

There are eight restaurants in the Caesar's complex, including the sinfully satisfying **Bacchanal**, where wine servers gently massage the temples and necks of each of their gentlemen guests; the **Primavera**, which offers its famous Fettucine Primavera; and **LePosh**, where a continental cuisine is served by waiters who wear white gloves and where the tables have white linen coverings.

Caesar's Hotel contains 645 units; 427 rooms and 16 suites are in the 12-story Regency Tower, and another 150 suites are in the 19-story Boardwalk Tower. Rates range from $95 to $710 per night. (The latter is for the penthouse suite.) For reservations, call 1-800-257-8555. In New Jersey call 1-800-582-7600, or write to Caesar's Atlantic City, On the Boardwalk at Arkansas Avenue, P.O. Box 389, Atlantic City 08404.

Tickets for shows at Circus Maximus are available at Caesar's Box Office, Second Floor, Appian Way Mall, or via Ticketron and Teletron. For show information, call (609) 348-4411.

BALLY'S PARK PLACE
(Park Place and the Boardwalk)

When you walk into Bally's Park Place Casino, you can't help but be taken by the cascading waterfalls on both sides of the large escalator, which transports visitors to the Restaurant Promenade level. On the way up, be sure to check the sweeping, stunning view of the casino floor. The Bally's "tree" logo can be found throughout the complex as can flowers, plants and general greenery, which provides an interesting juxtaposition of nature and neon. Bally's has 117 table games: 76 blackjack, 22 craps and 3 baccarat tables, plus 12 roulette and 4 big six wheels. There are also nearly 1600 slot machines.

Bally's opened in December 1979 as Atlantic City's third casino/ resort. To make way for it, the Marlborough and Blenheim hotels were demolished. However, many of the gargoyles and ornaments from these old structures were preserved and can be seen throughout the complex. A third old hotel, the Dennis, was renovated and became part of the resort. Bally's Park Place Casino Hotel has 510 guest rooms, including 42 suites. No two guest rooms have identical layouts and some bathrooms are equipped with oversized tubs plus telephones. The suites are done in one of four decors: Oriental, Contemporary, Louis XIV or Art Deco. Two suites were created from the former ballroom of the Dennis Hotel at a cost of one million dollars. For reservations call 1-800-225-5977. Rates are from $115 to $135.

The menus of Bally's best restaurants are supposedly revised at least three times a year. **By the Sea** is steeped in an atmosphere that recalls the grandest of luxury cruise liners; the cuisine is French. **Prime Place Steak House** features classic American dishes. Try **Sundae's** for sumptuous ice cream treats and **Jib's Oyster Bar** for mouth-watering fresh clams, oysters, mussels and shrimp.

For entertainment other than gambling, **Bally's Park Cabaret**, although small in comparison to, say, Caesar's Circus Maximum, nevertheless features first-class entertainment. The more intimate setting (325 seats as opposed to over 1000 in Circus Maximus) is perfect for comedy and solo performances. Call (609) 340-2709 for a schedule of events and ticket information. **Billy's Pub**, the former jazz lounge, now features Top 40 bands. Finally, shops such as the **Park Place Boutique**, the **Reese Palley Gallery**, and **Shooze** carry top-of-the-line merchandise and are fun whether you browse or buy.

THE SANDS
(Indiana Avenue and Brighton Park)

The Sands is located on the Brighton Park Mall, which also includes the Claridge and Bally's, and is the hub of casino activity in Atlantic City. Formerly the Brighton, Atlantic City's fourth casino, the Pratt Hotel Corporation purchased the practically bankrupt casino and took over operations in 1981. Since then business has improved dramatically, thanks to better management and a $26 million expansion project that saw the addition of a two-story food court/shopping mall and an additional 12,000 square feet of casino space. Today, the Sands Casino has 47 blackjack tables, 21 craps tables, 12 roulette wheels, 2 big six wheels and 2 baccarat tables along with 1460 slot machines.

The Sands offers much in the way of special concepts and amenities. For example, nearby **Greate Bay Country Club** in Somers Point is part of the Sands facilities. There, guests can play golf on a par 72 championship course or tennis on any of the club's beautifully maintained courts. Transportation to and from Greate Bay is provided by the Sands. There is also **The Plaza Club**, "a private world of entertainment, exceptional luxury, hospitality, and convenience," designed for the Sands's most prestigious customers. The V.I.P. treatment, say insiders, is unparalleled. And last but not least is The Food Court at the Sands, an atrium plaza that offers the widest selection of eateries in any of the Atlantic City casinos. Most of it is fast-food dining, but it's of the highest quality. You can get a corned beef sandwich at the **Carnegie Delicatessen**, a Coney Island frank at **Nathan's**, a South Philly cheese steak at **Pat's**, pan pizza at **Boston Pizza** and gourmet popcorn at **Jack's Corn Crib**.

The Sands doesn't offer just fast food, however. At **Mes Amis** you can order locally raised pheasant or New England venison, while the **Brighton Steak House** is noted for its exceptionally tender steaks.

For live entertainment, it's the Sands **Copa Room**, complete with deep red banquettes, elegant carpeting, high ceilings and a superb sound system. The Copa Room seats 850. For ticket reservations, call (609) 441-4100. The room is fast becoming known for its world-class boxing bouts. Michael Spinks, Ray "Boom Boom" Mancini, Aaron Pryor, Alexis Arguello and Trevor Berbick have all fought here.

The Sands Hotel has 501 guest rooms and suites. Rates range from $95 to $125. Cable TV is found in some rooms. Some suites have jacuzzi tubs. For reservations, call 1-800-257-8580.

HARRAH'S MARINA
(Brigantine Boulevard)

Not all of Atlantic City's casinos are situated on or just off the Boardwalk. Harrah's Marina (along with Trump's Castle, see below) is located on Absecon Inlet across from the Frank S. Farley State Marina. At first this might seem a bit inconvenient, especially for those who wish to gamble and visit more than one casino. But Harrah's is just two miles away from the Boardwalk and is easily connected to the other casinos at Brighton Park by jitneys that transport people back and forth free of charge.

A few other factors also make Harrah's a bit different from the other casino/hotel complexes in Atlantic City and, therefore, worth visiting. Harrah's seems to pay special attention to families. While parents gamble in the casino or socialize in, perhaps, the **Promenade Lounge**, teens and children are entertained, too. **Lucy's Marina Fun Center** on the third floor of the complex is the largest of its kind in any of the other casinos. Supervised by hotel personnel, kids can enjoy such games as air hockey, bumper pool and pinball, or else play a variety of video games. Nursery and baby-sitting services are also available.

Being on the water, Harrah's also pays special attention to boaters. Over 107 slips are available for customers' use, and, as already mentioned, visitors can arrive by boat from other Shore resort towns that sponsor excursions to the casino. Harrah's even has its own boardwalk. It's called the Baywalk and it wraps around the bay side of the complex. And finally, an interesting selection of classic antique cars is usually on display. These come from Harrah's magnificent collection in Reno, Nevada.

Harrah's Casino has 99 table games: blackjack, 60; craps, 22; roulette, 12; big six, 3; baccarat, 2; as well as over 1300 slot machines. It was here where one of the most incredible slot machine payoffs took place. Here's how the publicity explains it: "A man won $1.25 million on a progressive slot machine. During a press conference the next day, the man returned to the exact machine for publicity photos. Asking a woman who was playing to step aside for a moment, the lucky winner deposited his coins, pulled the handle, and hit for another $11,000. Harrah's also paid the woman who had so graciously given up her spot."

Those who wish to dine in elegance before or after gambling or after attending a show at the **Broadway By The Bay Theatre** need not leave the Harrah's complex. **The Steakhouse** has wonderfully tender New York, porterhouse and filet mignon steaks, **The Meadows** features gourmet French specialties, and **Andreotti's Ristorante** serves meticulously prepared Northern Italian dishes.

As for accommodations, there are more than 500 rooms and suites in the Harbour and Atrium Towers. There are special family plans, children's rates and package deals. Rates range from $90 to $155. Call 1-800-242-7724 for reservations.

THE GOLDEN NUGGET
(Boston Avenue and the Boardwalk)

Of all the Atlantic City casino Chairmen of the Board, perhaps none is as familiar to the public as the Golden Nugget's Steve Wynn. It is Wynn with whom Kenny Rodgers and Frank Sinatra toy on the casino's TV commercials. Wynn is the one to whom Sinatra throws an added tip for the extra towels—all in jest, of course. Wynn is a genius when it comes to marketing an image and running a casino. Therefore, it really comes as no surprise that the Golden Nugget is one of the most elegant, image-conscious casinos in Atlantic City.

> DID YOU KNOW THAT ... HARRAH'S IS THE ONLY GAMING CORPORATION WITH PROPERTIES IN ALL MAJOR UNITED STATES GAMING LOCATIONS: RENO, LAS VEGAS, LAKE TAHOE AND ATLANTIC CITY?

Presently, the theme is Victoriana, much like the theme of the Golden Nugget in Las Vegas. Gold is the dominant color in the casino. You can see it in the lavish lobby, on the ceilings, in the mirror frames, even on the brass-trimmed tables and the slot machine handles. However, the Golden Nugget plans major decorative alterations in the near future. One casino executive says the Golden Nugget will have a more "contemporary Californian ambience." As it stands, the Golden Nugget has 95 table games: 61 blackjack; 18 craps; 10 roulette; 4 big six; and 2 baccarat. There are over 1200 slot machines. Not an especially large casino—40,717 square feet—the Golden Nugget appears much larger due to its elegant motif and clever floor plan.

If a room with an ocean view is important to you while vacationing in Atlantic City, the Golden Nuggett is your best bet. The reason? *All* 522 guest rooms have an ocean view. And all of them are decorated in Victorian decor. High atop the 23-story hotel is the two-bedroom Regency Suite that is usually where the newly crowned Miss America spends her first night. Room rates begin at $110 per night. For reservations, call 1-800-582-5977, in New Jersey 1-800-257-8677, or write Golden Nugget Reservations Dept., P.O. Box 1827, Atlantic City 08404.

For entertainment there's the **Opera House**, a 524-seat theater that is small enough so everyone in the house has a good seat. And for dining, try **Victoria's** if you appreciate truly fine French dishes, **Lillie Langtry's** if you prefer Cantonese cuisine, or the **Cornucopia Cafe** for something less exquisite yet thoroughly satisfying. The eggs Benedict are quite delicious.

ELSINORE'S ATLANTIS
(Florida Avenue and the Boardwalk)

The Atlantis casino is unique in Atlantic City. Instead of one massive casino, the Atlantis offers three smaller casinos, each on a different level in the complex, each with its own theme and decor, and each specifically aimed at a certain type of gambler. The first level houses the **Riverboat** casino. Decorated as if Atlantis were in the heart of Dixie, perhaps rolling down the Mississippi River, this casino attracts the average gambler, not the high roller. He would take the escalator to the third level where the **Salon Privé** offers special, personalized service to big bettors. Beautiful chandeliers and marble and glass elegance set the mood for truly big stakes. The mid-level casino, the **Shangri-La**, is for the gambler who falls in between the other two. In all, there are 1300 slot machines and 92 table games: 60 blackjack, 16 craps, 11 roulette; 3 baccarat; and 2 big six.

Formerly the Playboy Hotel and Casino, the Atlantis was purchased by the Elsinore Corporation in early 1984 and renamed shortly thereafter. Since then, much renovation has occurred. The complex has three very good restaurants: the **Chat Noir** offers French decor and continental dining; at the **Empress** one can order classic Szechuan and Hunan dishes; while at the **Golden Steer**, thick, juicy steaks and Maine lobster are the recommended entrees. If something lighter than a full gourmet meal is more to your liking, try the **Garden State Cafe** and a crisp vegetable salad or tempting deli sandwich.

The Atlantis **Cabaret** is where big name entertainers perform; not as lavish as other casino showrooms, the Cabaret does possess a rich, warm atmosphere and virtually all of the 850 seats are good ones. Call (609) 441-2888 for ticket information. If shopping is more your idea of entertainment, the **London Arcade** is where you'll find gift shops and boutiques.

The Atlantis Hotel usually receives high marks from its guests. Service is quite good, and the rooms are large and comfortable. Rates are comparable with the other casinos; they range from $80 to $140. The more expensive rooms are the ones with an ocean view. Call 1-800-257-8672 for reservations.

THE CLARIDGE
(Indiana Avenue and the Boardwalk)

Despite being the smallest casino in Atlantic City (34,000 square feet as opposed to 60,000 at Resorts, Trump Plaza, Caesar's), the Claridge still has much to offer. The 64 table games are blackjack, 40; craps, 12; roulette, 8; big six, 2; baccarat, 2; and there are 1000 slot machines. A refined, even chivalrous ambiance is found throughout the Claridge. Much of this is due to the European and English decor. There is a deliberate downplay of bright, gaudy ornaments and designs, which often clash with the senses. The Claridge is a bit more subdued than the other casinos. Some gamblers enjoy that very much; others opt for more spectacle and eventually wind up betting at Caesar's or one of the other larger casinos.

The same can be said about Claridge's **Palace Theater.** Intimacy more than extravagance is the general rule of thumb here. The color scheme is quite British, the sound system quite good, and the entertainment generally top-notch. For ticket information, call the Palace Theater Box Office at (609) 340-3700. Before or after the show visit the **London Pavilion Lounge** where the music and lighting are both soft and where one can enjoy the Claridge's best dining. If it's more lively surroundings you prefer, try the **HiHo Lounge.** And for a less formal meal, **Hyde Park** is a good choice as is the **Half Shell,** which offers tasty clams and clam chowder among other seafood specialties.

The Claridge Hotel has 504 rooms with city, bay or ocean views in the wonderfully restored 26-story building that has been part of the Atlantic City skyline for many years. Room rates start at $75. The Claridge offers a fine selection of package deals. Potential guests should inquire about them if they plan to visit during the winter season. For reservations and information on packages, call 1-800-257-8585. In New Jersey call 1-800-582-7676.

TROPICANA
(Iowa Avenue and the Boardwalk)

It seems the Tropicana goes out of its way for the mid-range gambler more than any other casino in Atlantic City. For slot machine players, that part of the casino called **Slot City** contains nearly 1500 slot machines. The rows of machines are named Big Bertha Boulevard, Jackpot Lane, Royal Flush Court and Million Dollar Drive. It was on Million Dollar Drive that a patron won $2,202,482 in December 1984. Slot machine regulars also find the Trop's "Slot Market" a gambling gimmick that really does pay off. By playing one dollar slots, gamblers collect Exchange Notes. Accrue 30 of them and your portfolio is complete. Gamblers can then cash in their portfolios for a Silver Certificate that is good for five dollars in cash.

For blackjack bettors, the presentation of the Trop Gold Card at specially designated blackjack tables gets you special treatment and

---

DID YOU KNOW THAT ... THE AVERAGE DAILY TOTAL WIN IN ATLANTIC CITY'S CASINOS IS MORE THAN FIVE MILLION DOLLARS?

discounts. The more you play the more points you attain, which adds up to Trop Gold Dividend Dollars. These are as good as cash in all Tropicana restaurants, bars, showroom performances and the **Tropicana Gift Shop**.

More serious, less budget-minded bettors are treated equally special. First-rate service and individualized pampering are routine for high rollers. They can bet their money on some 76 blackjack, 25 craps, 13 roulette, 3 big six, and 3 baccarat tables.

In keeping with the discount programs, the Tropicana Hotel offers a number of truly excellent package deals in the winter, spring and fall. These should be investigated by anyone thinking of coming to Atlantic City during these three seasons. Room rates are otherwise comparable with other Atlantic City hotels. For information on current rates and package deals, call 1-800-228-2828. There are 515 guest rooms in all, including 46 theme suites that go from Traditional English to Oriental.

While at the Trop, be sure to dine in one of the complex's highly rated gourmet restaurants. **Les Paris** is French, **Il Verdi** features Northern Italian cuisine, and the **Regent Court** is a top steak house. For entertainment Tropicana's **Showroom** has the largest seating capacity—1700 seats—of any casino hotel theater in the United States. Tuesday night boxing is a regular feature. Call (609) 340-4020 for ticket information.

TRUMP CASINO HOTEL
(Mississippi Avenue and the Boardwalk)

The Trump Casino Hotel, also known as Trump's Plaza, is situated next to Atlantic City's Convention Hall. An enclosed overhead skywalk connects the hotel/casino complex with the huge arena. Such proximity and accessibility make rooms at the Trump Casino Hotel much in demand when special events like the Miss America Pageant and business conventions are held in Convention Hall. Perhaps that's why the Trump Casino Hotel, at 39 stories, is the tallest casino hotel in Atlantic City. There are 614 rooms, 83 of which are suites, and all have ocean views. For information on rates and reservations, call 1-800-441-0909.

The Trump complex has seven restaurants and six lounges. Most noted are **Ivana's**, which features candlelight dining, a tuxedoed pianist and extraordinary French Nouvelle entrees; **Maximilian's**, where the prime rib is supreme; and **Le Grand Buffet**, which offers a fabulous selection of food and a very popular Sunday brunch. For a sumptuous snack, visit **Scoops** and treat yourself to a Haagen Dazs hot fudge sundae.

Located on the third floor of the complex is the Trump casino. There are 125 table games in all: 52 blackjack; 22 craps; 12 roulette; 6 big six; 3 baccarat; and more than 1700 slots. The **Baccarat Salon** might be the most plush of any found in Atlantic City. Crystal chandeliers, beveled glass and magnificent marble columns reflect the big money that regularly changes hands here.

Those who come to Atlantic City for the first-class entertainment in addition to the gambling experience, will find **Trump's Theatre** much to their liking. The 750-seat showroom features headliners such as Bill Cosby, Sammy Davis and Loretta Lynn as well as Las Vegas-styled stage shows and revues. Call (609) 441-6158 for ticket reservations.

Some Things to Remember when Gambling

1. The axiom, "Bet with your head, not over it," is a good one and worth keeping in mind whenever you walk into an Atlantic City casino.
2. Betting schemes don't work. No matter how elaborate yours is, your fortune (or misfortune) rides on your luck.
3. You must be 21 years old to gamble in Atlantic City.
4. Before you enter a casino, set a limit on how much you can lose *before* it starts to hurt—and stick to it.
5. Gambling should be fun, not a make-or-break situation.
6. Atlantic City casinos open at 10 a.m. and close at 4 a.m. on weekdays and 6 a.m. on weekends and holidays.
7. Know the rules of the games you play. You can pick up a pamphlet called *Rules of the Game* at most casino security booths.
8. Taking photographs in the casinos is not allowed.
9. The Casino Control Commission of New Jersey states that all slot machines must be designed to return a minimum of 83 percent to bettors.
10. Cheating in the form of marked cards, weighted dice and diversionary tactics don't work. Undercover security men, pit bosses and state police detectives are always on the floor.
11. The smartest bettor stops betting while he's ahead.

TRUMP'S CASTLE
(Huron Avenue and Brigantine Boulevard)

They say that a pot of gold can be found at the end of every rainbow. That's the theme at Trump's Castle. High atop the 26th floor of the hotel is a huge, five-color rainbow. As the color wheel turns, the fiber optics strands respond so that the colors—red, orange, yellow, green and blue—dazzle the viewer and, hopefully, bring him good fortune.

Formerly the Atlantic City Hilton, Trump's Castle is the second of two casinos on Absecon Inlet directly overlooking the Frank S. Farley State Marina (the other is Harrah's Marina). It's also the second casino that real estate baron and owner of the New Jersey Generals of the United States Football League, Donald Trump, has invested here in Atlantic City; the other, of course, is Trump's Casino Hotel on the Boardwalk. The 605 rooms in the Castle offer sweeping views of the Atlantic City skyline or the adjacent Edwin B. Forsythe National Wildlife Refuge, and they possess an art deco decor. Room rates range from $75 to $150. Call 1-800-441-5551 for reservations.

The casino is located on the third floor of the complex. One of its regal attractions is the five "Pot O' Gold" dollar slot machines, each with a jackpot that builds to a cool million dollars. You'll recognize these potentially very rich slots by their computer-controlled flashing rainbows. Enjoy a total of 1684 slot machines, plus 117 table games: blackjack, 74; craps, 24; roulette, 13; big six, 3; baccarat, 3.

Other attractions at Trump's Castle include two very fine restaurants: **Delfino's**, which serves Continental specialties in an atmosphere that brings to Atlantic City the splendor of the romantic Mediterranean, and the **Beef Baron**, which offers choice cuts of steak, plus duck, venison and even wild boar. The **King's Court Theatre** seats 454 and features Las Vegas–styled entertainment. *City Lites* is the theater's ongoing revue; it's a musical extravaganza with wonderful dancing and ice skating. There are two shows, six days a week. For ticket reservations, call (609) 441-8300.

AROUND ATLANTIC CITY

Things to Do

Visit the Atlantic City Art Center. Located on Garden Pier (Boardwalk and New Jersey Avenue), paintings, photographs and pieces of sculpture exhibited here feature the talents of Art Center members, plus those artists from outside the fold whose work is on special display. Along with the Noyes Museum in nearby Oceanville (see chapter 6), the Atlantic City Art Center provides visitors the opportunity to view the work of some of South Jersey's best artists. The center also offers art classes and occasional seminars and is open daily 9 a.m.–4 p.m. Call (609) 347-5844 for information on the latest exhibits. Admission is free.

Visit the Atlantic City Historical Museum. Also located on Garden Pier adjacent to the Atlantic City Art Center is the Atlantic City Historical Museum. It should be considered a must for those fond of nostalgia. Few American cities have undergone such a rapid and profound change in their overall makeup as Atlantic City. Here at the museum you will get a good idea of what Atlantic City B.C. (Before Casinos) was like. See the displays and exhibits on the city's old theaters and cabarets, memorabilia pertaining to the Boardwalk's Golden Age as well as photographs of the beach and piers and the slew of special events and promotional stunts that seemed to keep Atlantic City in the news during the 1930s and 1940s. For those interested in absorbing themselves further into Atlantic City history and culture, pick up a copy of *Atlantic City: 125 Years of Ocean Madness* by Vicki Gold Levi and Lee Eisenberg. It is much of Levi's memorabilia that is on display in the museum. Open daily from 9 a.m. to 4 p.m. Admission is free. Call (609) 927-5218 for more information.

Visit the Absecon Lighthouse. Like Old Barney on Long Beach Island, Old Ab was designed and built by Gen. George Gordon Meade in 1857 and for a long time was an Atlantic City symbol and trademark. Today, Absecon Lighthouse is a symbol of yesteryear as it stands on a barren lot surrounded by urban renewal and urban blight. Located on Pacific and Rhode Island avenues, the lighthouse is open to the public during the summer from 10 a.m. to 5 p.m. Visit the tiny museum at the base of the lighthouse for a small admission charge.

Visit Gardner's Basin. It was to this cove off Absecon Inlet where pirates and privateers retreated when they weren't confronting merchant vessels off the Jersey coast in the eighteenth century. It was also here, later on, that whalers and whaling boats created much activity on the docks during the height of the hunting season. Today the basin is home to a historic maritime village that contains old, restored buildings moved from various parts of South Jersey and brought here for preservation. There are exhibits to see and sightseeing boat trips, which leave the basin at various times during the day. Of special interest is the *Young America*, a 130-foot, nineteenth century–styled, two-masted ship that embarks on two cruises a day. Call (609) 348-2880 for this season's schedule. On display nearby is a two-man research submarine that was designed to assist in the underwater salvaging effort of sunken ships. Gardner's Basin is located at North New Hampshire Avenue and the Inlet. Admission is free, although there is a charge for the sightseeing excursions.

Boat Watch at Senator Frank S. Farley State Marina. Located on Clam Creek just across from Trump's Castle and near Harrah's Marina, the Frank S. Farley State Marina has berths for 432 craft and is the center of boat activity in Atlantic City. Looking to crew on a sailboat? Dockside here at the Farley Marina is a good place to start inquiring what boat is in need of an extra mate. There are big yachts here, small fishing skiffs and annual fishing tournaments; it's the best place in the area to boat watch and mingle with sailors. For information on mooring privileges and berths, call (609) 348-2292 or write Senator Frank S. Farley State Marina, 600 Huron Avenue, Atlantic City 08401.

Take a Peek Inside Lucy the Elephant. Lucy is a 65-foot-high, 90-ton pachyderm that was built in 1881 by a Philadelphia real estate developer to lure prospective land buyers to South Atlantic City or what is today the Atlantic City suburb of Margate. Blessed with a tin skin and the loving care of the Save Lucy Committee, which raised thousands of dollars to restore the elephant, the architectural oddity is a favorite with both kids and adults. Now listed as a National Historic Landmark, Lucy sits at the intersection of Atlantic and Decatur avenues. Guides take tourists inside the giant elephant's belly by ascending a flight of stairs inside its hind legs. A small museum houses exhibits pertaining to Lucy's 100-year history. Visitors are also able to peer out Lucy's eyes and check the view from the observation deck atop the elephant, which is in the form of a howdah, or Indian-styled traveling basket designed to carry prominent citizens.

During the summer, free weekly concerts are held at Lucy Park next to the elephant; big band, Dixie and country music usually comprise the schedule of musical entertainment. Nearby is a Lucy gift shop where you can buy Lucy T-shirts, stuffed elephants and knick-knacks. All proceeds go toward the continued upkeep and restoration of the elephant. There is an admission charge to tour Lucy. Open daily in the summer from 10 a.m. to 4:30 p.m. and on weekends through October.

Visit the Atlantic City Race Course. If there's not enough betting action for you in the casinos, or if blackjack, craps or slot machines just aren't your style, what about thoroughbred racing? Take the Atlantic City Expressway to Exit 12, or head west on the Black Horse Pike to McKee City, 15 miles outside of town, for yet another form of gambling and entertainment. The racing season runs from June to September. Post time is 7:30 p.m. Call (609) 641-2190 for the latest racing information.

Some Recommended Restaurants in Atlantic City

(Note: Because mention has already been made of the excellent restaurants found in the hotel/casino complexes, the following are some of the best restaurants found in Atlantic City proper.)

Angelo's Fairmount Tavern
2300 Fairmount Avenue
(609) 344-2439
Price Code: Moderate
Menu: Italian

Nobody serves better meatballs. Many other homemade specialties. A big favorite with locals.

Cafe Orleans
Lincoln Place and Boardwalk
(609) 347-0400
Price Code: Expensive
Menu: New Orleans

Spicy sauces, delicious fish entrees, a real treat for those who truly appreciate New Orleans cuisine.

Dock's Oyster House
2405 Atlantic Avenue
(609) 345-0092
Price Code: Expensive
Menu: Seafood

A popular Atlantic City restaurant for years. Oyster dishes, especially the oyster stew, are heartily recommended.

Herman's Place
2 South New York Avenue
(609) 344-9410
Price Code: Inexpensive
Menu: Chili

Atlantic City's best chili can be found here. Sausage sandwiches are worth raving about, too. Bar atmosphere, nothing fancy.

Johan's
3209 Fairmount Avenue
(609) 344-5733
Price Code: Expensive
Menu: French/Flemish

Gourmet dining all the way; expensive, but worth it. Reservations are essential.

Knife and Fork Inn
Atlantic and Pacific avenues
(609) 344-1133
Price Code: Expensive
Menu: Seafood, steaks

An Atlantic City tradition. Swordfish is absolutely delicious. Routinely receives raves from the critics.

Los Amigos
1926 Atlantic Avenue
(609) 344-2293
Price Code: Inexpensive/Moderate
Menu: Mexican

Best bet: burritos. Do try the margaritas and Mexican pizza.

Peking Duck House
Iowa and Atlantic avenues
(609) 344-9090
Price Code: Moderate/Expensive
Menu: Chinese

Szechuan, Mandarin and Cantonese cuisine. The house specialty is what else, but Peking Duck. Formal atmosphere.

Shumsky's
2319 Pacific Avenue
(609) 344-0415
Price Code: Moderate/Expensive
Menu: Jewish

Delicious Jewish dishes such as beef tongue keep the tables filled with regularly returning customers.

White House Sub Shop
2301 Arctic Avenue
(609) 345-1564
Price Code: Inexpensive
Menu: Submarine sandwiches

No question about it—South Jersey Shore's best subs are made at the White House Sub Shop. The right place for lunch when you're hungry and feel like a hoagie.

8. THE SOUTH JERSEY SHORE

The South Jersey Shore sits comfortably between New Jersey's largest and most popular resorts: Atlantic City to the north and Cape May to the south. It is an area of striking beauty in the form of more than 150 tiny islands; wide, sandy beaches; bays, both big and small; marshlands; nature preserves; bird sanctuaries; and summer resort towns. It is a place that, for years, resisted the often uncontrolled development and the hurried, hectic pace found farther north along the coast.

Strangely enough, the charm of the South Jersey Shore was first discovered by wealthy Philadelphians and southerners from cities such as Baltimore and Washington, D.C. Before they arrived, the area was inhabited by fishermen, whalers and shipbuilders. They came from New England to exploit the area's excellent fishing grounds, its proximity to migratory whale routes, and its cedar swamps, which provided wood to build some of the finest ocean vessels of the nineteenth century.

Philadelphians came to the South Jersey Shore to escape the city summer heat and humidity. They arrived by coach, train and steamboat. The word spread south that New Jersey's beaches were the best in the mid-Atlantic and Upper South regions, and eventually wealthy southerners were making the trek north to bathe in the South Jersey Shore's warm ocean waters and to sail in its back bays. Few realize it, but much of the South Jersey Shore lies below the Mason–Dixon Line, including Atlantic City. And although New Jersey was most definitely a Yankee state during the Civil War, there were some southern sympathies on the South Jersey Shore.

Today, the area is still dominated by vacationers from Pennsylvania, Delaware, Maryland and, believe it or not, Canada. In Quebec, for instance, the Jersey Shore is regarded as an ideal summer retreat. Walk along the streets of Ocean City or Stone Harbor—two popular South Jersey beach resort towns—and you'll probably find more out-of-state license plates on cars parked there than you will cars with New Jersey plates. It's a fact that Baltimore is closer to the South Jersey Shore than New York or even parts of North Jersey. And, of course, Philadelphia is closest of all. With the Cape May–Lewes, Delaware Ferry bringing visitors from the Upper South to the South Jersey Shore (see chapter 9), and with the Atlantic City Expressway providing an excellent link to Philadelphia, it's no wonder that the area is as popular as it is with out-of-staters. Add to that the lure of Atlantic City with its casinos and legalized gambling, and the thousands of visitors from New York and northern New Jersey who are exploring the South Jersey Shore for the first time, and you have an area along the Jersey coast whose popularity is growing in leaps and bounds.

In addition to its superb beaches, most of which are wider, cleaner and prettier than what you'll find anywhere else in New Jersey, the South Jersey Shore provides visitors with the opportunity to make day or evening runs into Atlantic City and Cape May. And for those wanting to enjoy the beaches, yet who are not fond of hotels or motels, South Jersey is the state's major camping area. There are many camp-grounds to choose from; some sites are primitive and situated deep in a state forest, others have almost all the conveniences of home. Most of the campgrounds are within fairly easy access of the beaches and resort towns.

Once you arrive at the South Jersey Shore and wish to get around, there are three different routes to consider. The Parkway is the main artery and is usually the quickest route to get from one point to another. But those wishing to experience a sample of the small towns and lowland countryside situated in the vicinity of the beach area should opt for Route 9. It is a two-lane road and local traffic often meanders along. But you'll come across farms, picturesque towns, roadside vegetable stands, antique dealers, old homes that date back as far as two centuries, quiet rivers, wetlands and places to camp and go horseback riding.

The most popular route, however, and one that is also highly recommended, is Scenic Ocean Drive, which extends from Absecon Inlet at the northern tip of Atlantic City, to the edge of Cape May Point. Going from north to south the route is approximately 40 miles long and weaves through the marshland and beach towns of the South Jersey Shore. As you follow the "Flight of the Gull" signs, you'll drive through Atlantic City and the suburban towns of Ventnor, Margate and Longport, pass over the Ocean City-Longport Bridge, into and through Ocean City, down through Corson's Inlet State Park where the Corson's Inlet Bridge connects it to Strathmere and Sea Isle City. From there you'll pass over Townsend's Inlet Bridge and onto Seven Mile Beach, where Avalon and Stone Harbor are located. Grassy Sound Bridge takes you over Hereford Inlet and onto Five Mile Beach. Here, you'll drive through the Wildwoods—North Wildwood, Wildwood and Wildwood Crest. Finally, you'll come to the Middle Thorofare Bridge, bypass the U.S. Coast Guard Receiving Station, and head into historic Cape May.

Along the way you'll see some of the East Coast's most valued marsh and wetlands and get an excellent idea of what the South Jersey Shore has to offer. Be advised, though, that on weekends and holidays during the summer, traffic can be rather heavy along Ocean Drive, as all the bridges are toll bridges.

OCEAN CITY

Ocean City proudly proclaims itself "America's Greatest Family Resort." You see the slogan all over the South Jersey beach city: on billboards and welcoming signs, on postcards and tourist booklets, on the boardwalk and even on the beach. Ocean City doesn't want visitors to forget where they are or why they came.

Such a bold claim would be considered little more than hot air or perhaps a clever publicity gimmick if Ocean City did not actively work to make such a statement as valid as possible. Few people on vacation in Ocean City can cry boredom during the summer. Literally dozens of activities are sponsored each month by the city—most of them free—that encourage participation from all age groups. Everything from sand sculpturing contests to free concerts, from a baby parade to a Miss Crustacean Contest, from a hermit crab race to a half marathon, from a Bike-A-Thon to a Big Band Dance and Banjo Bash, from an art show to a sun tanning tournament, from a crafts show to a variety show. And the list goes on.

Then there's the calendar of events sponsored by the Ocean City Recreation Department. Ocean City's playgrounds and ball fields are manned by counselors every day during the summer. There's basketball, tennis, volleyball, softball, gymnastics, shuffleboard and much more.

Next, there's the boardwalk and the beach, the amusement rides and the fine restaurants, the marinas and the sailing, the bay and the ocean, the warm weather and the sun. Is there anything, one might ask, that Ocean City doesn't offer vacationers?

Yes, there is. Ocean City does not have, nor does it care to have, a nightlife, other than what's found on the boardwalk. It is, always was, and if some people have their way, always will be a dry town. That means no public drinking, no bars, no nightclubs. Ocean City is a family resort with an accent on family. You can be sure that anything that might tarnish Ocean City's rather polished image will be frowned on at the very least.

The reason why Ocean City is a dry town, much like Ocean Grove and Island Heights to the north, is that it was settled more than a hundred years ago by three Methodist minister brothers: Samuel, James and Ezra Lake. Their aim was to establish a summer community where families could not only come and pray, but do so in an environment free from vices such as liquor and gambling. And they did just that. The three signed a covenant in 1879 under a large cedar tree near what is now North Street which provided the framework for Ocean City's growth as a religious retreat.

Yet, it is rather amazing that Ocean City's blue laws have remained in effect all these years. Unlike Ocean Grove (which is a sealed community, actually enclosed with natural and man-made impediments, and which has kept its religious commitment far above any commitment to tourism), Ocean City covets summer visitors and tourists—just as long as they remain within the confines of propriety and decency.

Given all this, it's not surprising then, that Ocean City calls itself America's Greatest Family Resort. Certainly enough people believe it, for the beach city continues to attract hordes of visitors and vacationers during the summer. Ocean City's year-round population is somewhere in the neighborhood of 18,000. In the summer, some city officials say the population balloons to 150,000. Without a doubt, Ocean City is an extremely popular South Jersey resort, ranking behind only Atlantic City in sheer numbers, and regularly entertaining visitors from as far west as Ohio, as far south as Virginia and as far north as Canada.

Ocean City lies less than ten miles south of Atlantic City on a barrier island that sits between Great Egg Harbor and the ocean. The best way to get to Ocean City is to take the Garden State Parkway to Exit 30; you'll then approach Ocean City via Route 52 East, and thus will be able to stop at the Information Center just prior to entering town.

It is not advisable to come to Ocean City in the summer without lodging reservations. But if you do, the Information Center, which is open year-round, has a computerized telephone access board sponsored by the Ocean City Guest and Apartment House Association that will give you free, up-to-the-minute information on the guesthouse or apartment of your choice. The center is also staffed by very knowledgeable and helpful guides who will give you all the information you need to make your stay in Ocean City an enjoyable one. There are information centers at the old municipal building on 46th Street and West Avenue and at the Music Pier on the boardwalk, too. The latter is only open during the summer. Ocean City also has two toll-free telephone numbers to call for accommodations. Call before your vacation or visit. It's a good idea to call and request a copy of the Ocean City Vacation Guide; it will help you select the best place to stay, given your budget. In New Jersey call 1-800-624-3746; in Pennsylvania it's 1-800-225-0252.

Ocean City's main attraction is its eight-mile-long beach. Beach badges are mandatory. Seasonal, weekly and daily badges are available; if you purchase yours prior to the start of the summer season, you'll receive a discount. Call the Information Center (the above number) for current rates and information on when badges go on sale. Badges can be obtained at the Music Pier Information Center, the City Clerk's office (Municipal Hall), the Information Center on 46th Street and West Avenue, the Information Center on Route 52, or any of the small booths on the boardwalk located at the entrances to the beach.

You'll find Ocean City much more than a standard summer resort. It has a fine year-round downtown shopping section, which boasts a number of fine stores and restaurants. For world renowned entertainment, Atlantic City is only minutes away. Corson's Inlet, where fishing, windsurfing, bicycling and bird-watching are favorites, lies just south of Ocean City. It too is mere minutes away.

In many ways Ocean City resembles Long Beach Island. People who summer at Ocean City usually do so year after year. Many eventually buy summer homes there. There's much interaction between neighbors and there's a strong sense of civic pride even though many will leave Ocean City on Labor Day Weekend. You'll find more than one regular summer visitor who will heartily agree that if Ocean City isn't America's greatest family resort, then it's got to be a mighty close second.

Common Sense in the Sun

1. Respect the sun. Its rays are stronger than you think.
2. Respect your skin. It's more delicate than you think.
3. Don't attempt a summer's worth of sun the first day on the beach. Limit your first couple of outings to approximately 30 minutes and gradually build up your exposure time.
4. If you burn easily, use a sunscreen or sunblock. Sunscreen diminishes the amount of ultraviolet rays, which not only cause sunburn but can also wrinkle your skin prematurely and, worse, cause skin cancer. Note the initials SPF on sunscreens. The letters stand for sun protection factor. The greater the SPF, the greater the protection from the sun.
5. Sunblocks are stronger than sunscreens. Sunblocks literally block out the sun's untraviolet rays, whereas sunscreens simply screen out some of the rays.
6. Use a suntan oil or lotion if you tan easily. You'll acquire a deeper, darker tan if you do. Be careful, however, not to overdo it. Too much sunning with oil or lotion is apt to leave your skin leathery in appearance.
7. Always use a moisturizer after a day at the beach. Regular use will cut down on peeling and drying.
8. If you do get a sunburn, treat it with Aloe Vera, a natural moisturizer.
9. Also, drink plenty of liquids. Gatorade is a good choice. Take Tylenol or aspirin for pain. Cool, wet dressings will take the sting out of the sunburned area.
10. If your body temperature reaches 101 degrees and you become nause-ated, see a doctor.
11. If someone you're with vomits and seems confused or dopey due to too much sun, call a doctor immediately. The person could very well be suffering from heat stroke, a life-threatening situation.
12. On the beach, wear sunglasses that filter out ultraviolet rays. If you plan to be out in the sun all day, wear white, cotton clothing.

Things to Do

Stroll the Boardwalk. There are three true boardwalks on the South Jersey Shore: Atlantic City, Wildwood and Ocean City. The Atlantic City Boardwalk is, of course, the granddaddy of *all* boardwalks, and a stroll on it is something every visitor to the South Jersey Shore ought to do at least once. Wildwood is the thrills and chills boardwalk; no boardwalk in New Jersey, or anywhere else for that matter, has the sheer number of rides that Wildwood does. Geared especially toward the 14–24-year-old age group, the pace on the boards there is fast and lively. Ocean City is the family boardwalk. There are amusement rides, but not an impossible number of them. There are specialty shops and a shopping area known as **The Flanders** (11th Street and Boardwalk) that has wonderful men and women's apparel shops. What you won't find are a plethora of shops selling T-shirts with the last bawdy slogans on them ("Party Naked," "I'm Hot for U," "Party Animal," and "Sex is my Mission"), the kind that seem to overwhelm Wildwood and Seaside Heights up north.

Gillian's Wonderland Pier and Playland are where the amusement rides are located. If you plan to eat on the boardwalk, try **T. R. Fenwick's Breakfast and Dinner Buffet**, especially if you've worked up a sizable appetite. Reasonably priced, it's all you can eat. A steak sandwich at **Del's** is also a good bet. To quench a sunbaked thirst, try a delicious orange drink at **Tittere's** or **Kohr's**. And for snacking, **Shriver's** is the best place on the boardwalk to get saltwater taffy and fudge; it's the oldest candy shop in Ocean City.

Enjoy the Beach. You'll find less crowded beaches further south in towns such as Avalon and Stone Harbor. But Ocean City's beaches are nonetheless nice; they're also guarded by some of the best lifeguard crews on the South Jersey Shore. Due to offshore sandbars, the waves gently approach the shore, which makes swimming and frolicking in the water a delight for youngsters.

Attend a Concert on Music Pier. Throughout the summer there are a number of concerts and musical programs on the Music Pier at the north end of the boardwalk. The Ocean City Pops Orchestra is a regular attraction, although most types of music, including rock, jazz and religious are well represented. You can pick up a calendar of events for the entire summer at any of Ocean City's information centers.

Visit the Ocean City Arts Center. Housed in an old school building (409 Wesley Avenue), the Ocean City Arts Center consists of the Ocean City Historical Museum (downstairs) and an art gallery and work room (upstairs). The museum is one of the better museums on the South Jersey Shore. Each room has a theme: the *Sindia* Room contains artifacts, cargo, photographs and sailing papers of the ship, *Sindia*, a four-masted barque that sunk during a storm off Ocean City in 1901. As you'll find out, the *Sindia* was carrying approximately three thousand cases of fine china on board. One thousand cases were removed; the rest remain trapped inside the ship's hull.

There's also a Fashion Room where visitors will find Victorian costumes and period furniture, all nicely presented; a wonderful doll collection, and memorabilia pertaining to Ocean City's history. Admission is free, although donations are encouraged. Open all year. Summer schedule: Monday through Saturday, 10 a.m.–4 p.m. Winter schedule: Tuesday through Saturday, 1–4 p.m. For more information, call (609) 399-1801.

After viewing the exhibits in the museum, walk upstairs to the art gallery. Here, you'll find paintings done by some of the area's most talented artists as well as an occasional special exhibit that presents the work of more established painters. A big part of the Art Center's appeal is the drawing, sculpturing and painting classes that are held each summer. For information on classes, call (609) 399-7628. The Arts Center also sponsors a Boardwalk Art Show each summer and in the fall a Boardwalk Crafts Show. Both draw people who come not only to browse and admire the work of the many artists and craftspeople, but to buy, too.

See the Remains of the *Sindia*. There isn't really much left to see of the *Sindia*, save the rudder post and tiller. But Ocean City has adopted the sunken ship as you'll see "Sindia this" and "Sindia that" throughout the resort. Make the pilgrimage to 16th Street and the boardwalk like most who visit Ocean City eventually do.

Visit the Discovery Seashell Museum. The family that runs the Seashell Museum has amassed a most unusual and thorough collection of seashells from around the world. The museum, for instance, claims to have the only Siamese twin helmet shell ever found. About ten thousand varieties of seashells are on exhibit. In addition, crates of shells are for sale as well as hermit crabs, carved shells and beachy bric-a-brac. A must for beachcombers and shell collectors. Free admission. Located at 2717 Asbury Avenue. The telephone number is (609) 398-2316.

Visit the Ocean City Tabernacle. The current structure was built in 1957, but it stands on the site of Ocean City's first church, which was constructed in 1881. Located between 5th and 6th streets and Wesley and Asbury avenues.

View the Birds on Cowpens Island. Located west of Ocean City, south of the 9th Street Bridge, and quite near the Information Center on Route 52 is the Cowpens Island Bird Sanctuary. Go there with your binoculars at dusk and you'll probably get to see your share of egrets, herons and perhaps a glossy ibis or two.

Play Golf. Ocean City even boasts its own golf course. Located at 26th Street and Bay Avenue, the Ocean City Golf Course is a 12-hole course. Not for the seasoned pro, but a good alternative to sunbathing on the beach. And what good would a golf course be in Ocean City without golf tournaments? Yes, there are city-sponsored tournaments throughout the summer. Call (609) 399-6111, extension 219, for further information. The golf course is open seven days a week during the summer; discounts are available.

Ride the Ocean City Trolley. A good way to get a feel for Ocean City is to take a ride on one of the trolleys; they run every 25 minutes from 8:30 a.m. to midnight. The most popular route extends from 59th Street on Central Avenue to 23rd Street. It then follows along Wesley Avenue up to 15th Street, Ocean Avenue to 9th Street, then Atlantic Avenue along Battersea to the Longport Bridge. It returns via the same route. Pick up a free map of Ocean City and further information on the trolleys at any of the information centers. Discounts for senior citizens and children.

Cruise to Harrah's in Atlantic City. Why drive to Atlantic City when you can step aboard the *Casino Challenger* and go by boat? The early trip (9 a.m.) is via the Intracoastal Waterway. The evening trip (6 p.m.) is by way of the ocean. The *Casino Challenger* sails from Sampson Brothers Marina, 228 Bay Avenue. Very popular, and a good bargain, too. Call (609) 399-3111 for details.

See a Parade. Mark your calendar for two of Ocean City's biggest and most popular summer events. The **Annual Baby Parade**, which takes place on the boardwalk, draws thousands of spectators. You'll see dressed-up, made-up, spruced-up tots and kids up to the age of 12 strutting their stuff. Decorated carriages, strollers, wagons and bicycles, and bands and floats add to the fun. The Baby Parade extends as far back as the turn of the century and has been a summer tradition in Ocean City ever since. It's the oldest baby parade on the Jersey Shore and undoubtedly the best. The parade is usually held in August; check with the information center for a specific date.

Night in Venice is a carnival of seacraft and just as popular as the Baby Parade. Held in July, nearly everyone turns out for the annual dazzling display of Ocean City's pleasure boats, most of which are lavishly decorated with the hope of landing the grand prize for best looking boat. The Night in Venice festivities take place on the bay side of Ocean City. Bleachers are set up along the bay's edge. Most every homeowner on this side of town throws a party or invites friends over. Many homes are also decorated for the occasion. It's a special night in Ocean City, and if the town ever lets loose, it's during this celebration.

CORSON'S INLET STATE PARK

If you drive south through Ocean City and remain on Scenic Drive, you'll come upon a short stretch of highway with marshland on both sides. Though there's no visitor's center or even a sign to tell you you're on state property, the area is part of Corson's Inlet State Park. Just up ahead is Corson's Inlet, a picturesque, though tricky waterway due to its many shoals. There's a small boat launch here, a bathing area, fishing, bird-watching, hiking and lots of poison ivy. It's also a great place to go windsurfing. During a particularly breezy day in spring, summer or fall, you're apt to see dozens of colorful sails and sleek boards on the water.

A pleasant half-day's outing would be to bicycle down to Corson's Inlet State Park from Ocean City, explore some of the park, perhaps enjoy a picnic and then bike back home. You can do the same if you ride north from Strathmere or Sea Isle City. If you're a fisherman or boater, you'll probably want to spend the day at the park. For more information, write to the Superintendent of Belleplain State Forest, Box 450, Woodbine 08270, or call (609) 861-2404.

STRATHMERE

Anyone visiting Corson's Inlet State Park who prefers something more to eat than a box lunch or picnic snack, should consider the **Deauville Inn** in neighboring Strathmere. Located on Willard's Road, just off Ocean Drive, the Deauville Inn actually sits on Corson's Inlet. The view is as good as the food. The restored country inn serves sit-down dinners, hot and cold sandwiches dockside and breakfast, to boot. During the evening there's live entertainment, and for sailors, the marina has virtually everything you'd need to stock your boat and head out onto the ocean.

SOMERS POINT

When Ocean City gets thirsty, or when the under-30 crowd needs to be revved up with rock 'n' roll, they drive across the bay to Somers Point. But there's more to Somers Point than Ocean City watering holes.

Somers Mansion, built in 1725, is the oldest house in Atlantic County. It overlooks Great Egg Harbor Bay and was the home of John Somers and family, one of the most important and wealthiest families in colonial South Jersey. Today, Somers Mansion is a New Jersey historical site and open to the public. The mansion, constructed of brick laid in Flemish bond, is three stories high and contains a number of excellent colonial furnishings. When you visit the house, make sure you walk out onto the balcony of the second floor where you're treated to a view of Great Egg Harbor Bay.

Perhaps the most unusual feature of the house is the roof. Get permission to walk up to the third-floor attic. Notice that the framework supporting the roof, thought to be constructed by a shipwright, resembles the hull of a ship. It is said that if the house were somehow ever flipped over and placed in water, it would simply float away. The Somers Mansion is located on Shore Road at the Somers Point Traffic Circle. Admission is free. Open all year. Closed Mondays and Tuesdays.

Around the corner from the Somers Mansion is the **Atlantic County Historical Museum and Library**. Located on the lower floor of the building, the museum is stocked with Victorian household items and furniture; a collection of Lenni Lenape Indian tools, weapons and other artifacts; a number of old shipbuilding implements; and a large model of the ship, the *Intrepid*. Upstairs is the library of the Atlantic County Historical Society. Much of the South Jersey historical research that goes on stems from here. On record are deeds, wills, diaries, letters and ships' logs as well as photographs and family trees.

Finally, there's the **Gateway Playhouse** on Bay and Higbee avenues where the South Jersey Regional Theatre group puts on professional performances of popular plays. Call (609) 653-0553 for further details and this year's schedule of performances.

DID YOU KNOW THAT ... RICHARD SOMERS, A DESCENDANT OF JOHN SOMERS, WAS COMMANDER OF THE *INTREPID*, THE KETCH THAT BLEW UP IN THE TRIPOLI HARBOR WITH ALL HANDS ON BOARD? THIS WAS DURING THE WAR WITH THE BARBARY PIRATES AND WAS ONE OF AMERICA'S FIRST POST-REVOLUTIONARY WAR NAVAL SORTIES ABROAD. FROM THAT DAY ON, THERE HAS ALWAYS BEEN A SHIP NAMED *INTREPID* IN THE U.S. NAVY.

SEA ISLE CITY

Sea Isle City, founded a century ago by Charles Landis, was originally to have been a duplicate of Venice, the Italian city of romance and waterways. Instead, Sea Isle City is somewhat of a scaled down version of Ocean City. Like Ocean City, Sea Isle City advertises itself as a true family resort, even though liquor is sold in town and a lively young crowd plays on the beach each summer. The five-mile stretch of beach is Sea Isle City's biggest attraction. Beach badges are required. They are sold at the Dominic C. Raffa Community Center at 127 John F. Kennedy Boulevard. To cater to the cultural needs of vacationers, the town provides free weekly concerts on the Promenade during July and August. It also sponsors arts and crafts shows, surfing contests and even a baby parade, although it lacks the size and scope of the one held in Ocean City.

Sea Isle City is also known for its fishing. Drive along the Ludlam Bay side of town, and you'll come across a number of party boats that make daily trips offshore. Bluefishing is quite popular here as is fishing and crabbing in the bay; there are places dockside where one can rent a small skiff and fish the day away on the bay. You'll also find commercial fishing boats here as well. Lobster fishing is an important part of the local economy. If you happen to be in the area when a lobster boat is pulling in after a weary couple of days out on the Atlantic, don't hesitate to ask if you might purchase a live lobster or two for dinner that evening. Chances are you'll pay a very fair price for a very tasty treat.

Sea Isle City doesn't possess a boardwalk in the traditional sense, that is, wooden planks to walk on—but it does have a paved walkway that parallels the beach. As for an amusement area, **Fun City** is located on Landis Avenue, between 32nd and 33rd streets. It's fine for the kids, but if you're bent on a full night of amusement thrills, best to head south to Wildwood.

AVALON

Avalon and its neighbor, Stone Harbor, share a skinny stretch of barrier island beach known as Seven Mile Beach. Townsend's Inlet to the north and Hereford Inlet to the south keep these two beautiful beach towns away from the more commercial trappings of Ocean City and Sea Isle City and the Wildwoods. This and the fact that both towns possess a deep interest in preserving the ecological balance of Seven Mile Beach make them the two most attractive towns on the South Jersey Shore.

Avalon has not succumbed to the lure of developers, at least not yet. True, there are condominiums in town, and Avalon has surely experienced a growth spurt in recent years. But any large-scale development is impossible on Avalon's coveted marshlands, because it is the property of the World Wildlife Fund. The organization owns nearly one thousand acres of wetlands and intends to keep it in its natural state—forever.

Avalon, however, is most noted for its sand dunes and its beach, which rates with the very best found on the Jersey Shore. Its white, extra-fine sand, gentle water (thanks to offshore sandbars, which placate much of the ocean's power) and, of course, its beautiful sand dunes make a day at the beach in Avalon a most enjoyable one.

Residents of Avalon are most proud, needless to say, of their sand dunes and beach. But they also enjoy a low-key, mild-mannered approach to tourism and the influx of summer visitors. That's not to say that Avalon doesn't have its share of restaurants and nightspots; it does. And a boardwalk runs from 20th to 32nd Street, not to mention the social and recreational programs available, such as dances, concerts, roller-skating, and tournaments in tennis, bocce ball, basketball and softball, which originate out of the Avalon Community Center at 29th Street and Avalon Avenue. An Information Center on 30th Street provides the details and dates of such activities plus information on lodging in Avalon.

But Avalon never seems to forget the individual who comes to town in search of simple peace and relaxation. For the full enjoyment of those two precious elements, few places on the South Jersey shoreline cultivate them like Avalon does.

Sand Dunes: The Hows and Whys of Preservation

Question: Why are sand dunes not only aesthetically pleasing but also critical to the survival of a barrier island?

Answer: Sand dunes offer the best protection from storms, natural beach erosion and large, pounding waves. Without sand dunes, a barrier island could very well disappear over the course of time.

Question: Why aren't people allowed to walk on sand dunes?

Answer: Sand dunes are actually very delicate constructions. People who disregard this fact are sand dunes's worst enemies.

Question: Why is dune grass so important to the preservation of sand dunes?

Answer: The dune grass roots play a most important role in keeping the dunes intact. The roots of a dune grass plant will extend deep into the dune and help control natural dune erosion.

Question: Aren't stone jetties and seawalls more effective protection for a shoreline than sand dunes?

Answer: No. Jetties and seawalls actually encourage the loss of beach sand in some cases. When winter storm waves crash against seawalls and jetties, sand is carried back into the sea as the water retreats. Jetties and seawalls are not effective on barrier islands because a barrier island is in a constantly shifting situation and is made up of nothing but sand. Jetties and seawalls are used in many areas of the Jersey Shore, especially the North Jersey Shore, as a last resort and where sand dunes have already been permanently destroyed via overdevelopment.

Question: How do environmentalists encourage the growth of sand dunes?
Answer: With regular dune grass plantings, regular fertilization, and proper placement of snow fences. These three together promote the growth of sand dunes.

Question: What can I do to help maintain sand dunes on the Jersey Shore?
Answer: Obey signs that restrict access onto sand dunes. Walk only on established paths. Don't allow your dog to run on or dig in sand dunes. Don't litter. Fully appreciate the value and beauty of sand dunes. Pass this information along to a friend.

STONE HARBOR

Stone Harbor seems a mere continuation of Avalon as you drive south from the one town to the next. The attitude toward tourism is pretty much the same: encourage it, but keep it controlled. The commitment to ecology preservation is the same: Stone Harbor's nationally known bird sanctuary and Wetlands Institute (see below) are proof of this. The high quality of beaches is the same, although Stone Harbor does not possess the sand dunes that Avalon does. The lovely lagoons on the bay side of both towns are quite similar. About the only thing that Stone Harbor has that Avalon doesn't is a completely renovated downtown center, filled with interesting shops and eateries.

You can spend the better part of a cloudy morning or afternoon browsing through the Stone Harbor shops. In addition to the usual items found in beach town stores—beachwear, rafts, umbrellas, mats and boogie boards—you'll also find stores such as the **Irish Pavilion** (9825 Ocean Drive), which carries authentic Irish imports, and the **Sandpiper Galerie** (109th Street and Third Avenue), which sells paintings, duck decoys, antiques and unusual nautical crafts. Most of the shops are on 96th Street or Third Avenue, or at least in the vicinity of them.

For some reason, Stone Harbor has more than its share of top-notch ice cream parlors. The **Strawberry Patch** (270 96th Street) features imaginative ice cream concoctions, Belgian waffles and homemade brownies. **Springer's** (9420 Third Avenue) is well known for its deliciously rich homemade ice cream. And you'll find wonderfully tempting sundaes at **Le Grand Dipper** (299 97th Street) as well as chocolate-covered strawberries.

Stone Harbor's beaches are wide and clean. Beach badges are mandatory and can be purchased at the Borough Hall ((609) 368-5102). Expect to pay around $7 for a full-season badge, which will get you on not only Stone Harbor beaches, but Avalon beaches, too. There is good surfing, bodysurfing and raft-riding in Stone Harbor as well as windsurfing and wavejumping.

While in Stone Harbor, be sure to spend some time visiting its noted bird sanctuary, located at the southern end of town on Third Avenue, between 111th and 117th streets. You don't have to be an experienced bird-watcher to enjoy the egrets, herons and ibises—all long-legged wading birds—fly to and from the 21-acre sanctuary in search of food and a mating partner. You don't even need binoculars. At a small parking lot on Third Avenue you'll find pay binoculars and information pertaining to the birds.

The best time to visit is just after the break of dawn in late July and early August. It is the busiest time of the year for the birds as the nesting season is drawing to a close. At this time, environmentalists estimate there are over 10,000 birds in the sanctuary, including seven species of herons.

> DID YOU KNOW THAT ... THE STONE HARBOR BIRD SANCTU-
> ARY IS THE ONLY HERONRY IN AMERICA SPONSORED BY A
> MUNICIPALITY? ITS ONLY COUNTERPART IN THE REST OF THE
> WORLD IS A SMALL JAPANESE TOWN OUTSIDE OF TOKYO.

No visitor to Stone Harbor should miss a trip to the **Wetlands Institute** on Stone Harbor Boulevard. A nonprofit organization "dedicated to promoting public understanding of, and concern for, the coastal and wetlands ecosystem," the Wetlands Institute is an excellent educational experience for young and old alike.

The Institute is situated on a 6000-acre tract of coastal marshlands. Inside the cedar-shake building with a balconied, built-in observation deck are laboratories, an auditorium, a gift shop and a small, yet thoroughly delightful, hands-on museum for children. The institute sponsors year-round lectures—"Beach Erosion at Stone Harbor," "Birds of Beach and Bay," and "Do Yourself A Favor: Eat Seafood," among numerous others—conducts guided explorations into salt marches, and sponsors an annual and very popular Wings 'N' Water Festival (decorative bird carving shows, wildlife paintings and seascapes, guided beach and marsh walks) each September. In addition, there are a number of fine programs for children, including a most educational five-day, summer ecology class.

When visiting the Wetlands Institute, don't forget to take the self-guided tour along the salt marsh trail (get a copy of the guide pamphlet from the front desk) and climb the observation tower for an inspiring view of the institute's marshland. Anyone the least bit interested in wetland ecology will find the Wetlands Institute quite fascinating. Open year-round. Summer: Tuesday through Saturday 10 a.m.–4:30 p.m. Winter: Tuesday, Thursday, Saturday 10 a.m.–4:30 p.m. Admission is free, but a donation is encouraged. One might even want to become a full-time member of the Wetlands Institute. Your membership fee is tax deductible. Write to the Wetlands Institute, Stone Harbor Boulevard, Stone Harbor 08247, or call (609) 368-1211.

THE WILDWOODS

Located just below Seven Mile Beach is Five Mile Beach, another South Jersey barrier island. The three towns on it—North Wildwood, Wildwood and Wildwood Crest—are famous for their beaches. For one thing, they're free; that means no beach badges, a definite rarity on the Jersey Shore. For another, they're incredibly wide and possess extra-fine, seemingly filtered white sand.

If the beaches of the Wildwoods are spectacular, then so is the boardwalk there, with its six amusement piers, all of them stocked with some of the most thrilling, spine-tingling rides in the world. One could spend perhaps an entire week full of exciting nights on the Wildwood boardwalk and still not experience every ride. The Wildwoods also have dozens of restaurants and small-scale eateries featuring a broad range of cuisines, and the best nightlife south of Atlantic City. To ride along Ocean Avenue is to ride through a gamut of neon lights that blaze the names of bars and dance clubs along with the Top 40 bands, trios and solo piano players, which perform in them until early morning.

To fully enjoy what the Wildwoods have to offer, one has to be a day *and* night person. Vacationing here often means spending the day soaking up the sun's rays on the beach and at night, club hopping or boardwalk walking. The next day the routine is repeated. And repeated the day after that. It's a fast, even hectic pace, and a far cry from what's found in Stone Harbor and Avalon, but for those who spend their vacations in Wildwood, anything less or more staid would be downright disappointing.

The Wildwoods are saturated with hotels and motels, and bungalows and guesthouses of every price and fancy. Yet, it is a very good idea to select one before arriving in Wildwood and make the necessary reservations, because availability can be a problem during the summer. To do this, write or call The Greater Wildwood Hotel and Motel Association for a copy of its Visitor's Guide, a 200 plus page volume that lists and describes all of the accommodations in the Wildwoods. It is a valuable source for making Wildwood vacation plans. Write The Greater Wildwood Hotel and Motel Association, P.O. Box 184, Wildwood By-the-Sea 08260. The Greater Wildwood Chamber of Commerce (Box 823, Wildwood, 08260) sends out an Accommodation Directory upon request. It's filled with information on lodging, of course, but it also contains information on restaurants and entertainment. If you plan to stay primarily in North Wildwood, you can send for a free Summer Vacation Kit, which will provide you with specific information pertaining to North Wildwood. Write to Summer Vacation Kit, Office of the Mayor, Box 499, North Wildwood 08260.

The Hereford Inlet Lighthouse on First and Central avenues acts as a tourist information outlet and is a good place to pick up brochures and such on the area for those just passing through or spending only the day. Other Wildwood area information centers are Wildwood Information Bureau, Boardwalk and Schellenger Avenue; Wildwood Information Center in Convention Hall at Burk Avenue and Boardwalk; the Wildwood Crest Pier Information Center, Wildwood Crest; and the Wildwood Crest Visitor's Center at the end of Rambler Road. Most are seasonal, which means they're open from Memorial Day through Labor Day Weekend, and depending on the weather, on weekends through September.

Camping Near the South Jersey Shore Resorts

Camping is an excellent alternative means of lodging near the South Jersey Shore, because so many campgrounds are close to the beaches and other areas of interest. A campsite is also cheaper than a hotel or motel room. Most of the South Jersey campgrounds are suited for the vacationing family, and provide water, electric and sewer hookups, plus other basic amenities. Some even have fishing and swimming facilities, children's playgrounds, game rooms and a camp store.

Here's a list of private and state-owned campgrounds that are close to the South Jersey Shore area. For more information on camping here, write to the Cape May County Campgrounds Association, Box 608, Ocean View 08230.

Private Campgrounds

Oak Ridge Campground
518 South Shore Road
P.O. Box 598
Marmora 08223
(609) 390-0916
(609) 399-0807

Whippoorwill Campground
810 South Shore Road
Marmora 08223
(609) 390-3458

Frontier Campground
90 Newbridge Road
Ocean View 08230
(609) 390-3649

Shady Oaks Campground
62 State Highway 50
Ocean View 08230
(609) 390-0431

Seaville Campground
98 Corson Tavern Road
Ocean View 08230
(609) 624-0564

Green Holly Campground
Box 193
Goshen 08218
(609) 465-9602

Big Timber Lake Camping Resort
Box 366
Cape May Courthouse 08210
(609) 465-4456

Blue Dolphin Campground
P.O. Box 71
Cape May Courthouse 08210
(609) 465-4518

North Wildwood Campground
527 Shellbay Avenue
Cape May Courthouse 08210
(609) 465-4440

Shellbay Campground
527 North Shellbay Avenue
Cape May Courthouse 08210
(609)465-4770

Sea Grove Campground
(P.O. Box 603) 164 Shore Road
Ocean View 08230
(609) 624-3529

**Yogi Bear's Jellystone Park
   Resort**
Box 107, Route 9
Ocean View 08230
(609) 624-3666

Ocean View Campground
(Box 607C) 134 Shore Road
Ocean View 08230
(609) 624-1675

Pine Haven Campground
(Box 606) 432 Shore Road
Ocean View 08230
(609) 624-3437

Tamerlane Campground
Box 510
Ocean View 08230
(609) 624-0767

Hidden Acres Campground
Box 354C, R.D. #1
Cape May Courthouse 08210
(609) 624-9015

Driftwood Campground
478 Shore Road (Route 9)
Cape May Courthouse 08210
(609) 624-1899

Avalon Campground
492 Shore Road
Clermont 08210
(609) 624-0075

Fort Apache Campground
Route 47 at Fulling Mill Road
Rio Grande 08242
(609) 886-1076

Beachcomber Campground
462 Seashore Road
Cape May 08204
(609) 886-6035

**Holly Shores Best Holiday
   Travel Park**
491 Route 9
Cape May 08204
(609) 886-1234

Lake Laurie Campground
669 Route 9
Cape May 08204
(609) 884-3567

Seashore Campsites
720 Seashore Road
Cape May 08204
(609) 884-4010

Cape Island Campground
709 Route 9
Cape May 08204
(609) 884-5777

Cold Spring Campground
541 New England Road
Cape May 08204
(609) 884-8717

Belleplain State Forest
Box 450
Woodbine 08270
(609) 861-2404

State Owned Campgrounds

Bass River State Forest
Box 118
New Gretna 08224
(609) 296-1114

North Wildwood

North Wildwood is situated at the northern end of Five Mile Beach
and is the first of the Wildwoods you'll visit if driving south on Scenic
Drive or getting off the Parkway at Exit 6. Lighthouse enthusiasts will

want to stop at the Hereford Inlet Lighthouse, located near the entrance to Hereford Inlet before heading to the beach or boardwalk.

It is an interesting lighthouse to tour because, unlike other lighthouses on the Jersey coast, the Hereford Inlet is principally Victorian in design. Built in 1874, the lighthouse was meant to serve as a landmark for those fishermen who fished the waters off Five Mile Beach and returned to shore through the treacherous channel in the inlet. Exceptionally strong tidal currents and everchanging shoals made navigation difficult even in good weather.

Because the original settlement on Five Mile Beach—a village called Anglesea—grew to be a large fishing center, which, at times, rivaled Gloucester, Massachusetts, as the East Coast's fishing capital in the late nineteenth century, the lighthouse and its beacon were especially important to commercial fishermen.

It has been only a few years since the Hereford Inlet Lighthouse was decommissioned (a more modern light tower now stands on the property and sends its beam out to sea). Thus, restoration continues on the structure; even so, the lighthouse is open to the public during the summer. Admission is free. Future plans call for the creation of a park, museum and cultural center on the lighthouse grounds.

WILDWOOD

When in Wildwood think beach and boardwalk. A big beach and a big boardwalk. In the north part of town, near Hunt's Pier, the beach is over one thousand feet wide. That's a fifth of a mile. Elsewhere in Wildwood the beach isn't quite that wide, but it comes close. Because it's such a long trip from the boardwalk to the water's edge, be sure to wear something on your feet as the sand can get awfully hot, especially at midday.

The boardwalk owns impressive figures, too. It's more than two miles long, stretching the entire length of Wildwood. To get a good overview of the boardwalk, catch one of Wildwood's Boardwalk Tramcars, which will take you from one end of the boardwalk to the next if you wish. Those visiting Wildwood for only the day or evening will find the Tramcar a perfect way to see and do as much as time permits. You can flag down a Tramcar at any point on the boardwalk, and you can get off wherever you want.

There are so many amusement rides, concession stands, games of chance, T-shirt outlets, fast food joints, saltwater taffy and fudge shops, pizza and cheesesteak walk-ins, ice cream stalls and hot dog/hamburger palaces that for a boardwalk junkie, Wildwood must surely be the closest thing to paradise. Where else can one find a boardwalk chapel, a boardwalk McDonald's and pony rides, of all things, on the beach. Wildwood has got it all—and more.

You'll quickly notice that most of those strolling the boards are young. Wildwood, as already mentioned, lures a young crowd. Still,

adults and families come and enjoy Wildwood, too. But the bulk of
activities on the boardwalk are most assuredly aimed at teens and those
in their twenties.

Some things to do on the boardwalk: Pick a shady spot, put on your
sunglasses and treat yourself to an afternoon's worth of people watching.
You'll see all sizes and shapes and some of the skimpiest bathing suits
around. Play bingo; it's fun and it's cool in the arcade, and you just
might win a prize. For 99¢ you can get four hot dogs at the **Wildwood
Candy and Ice Cream Company.** For 50¢ you get a half quart of Coke.
Try a slice of **Angelo's New York Style Pizza** or **Mack's Pizza**; both
are delicious. Buy a Belgian waffle at **Snarky's Ice Cream Factory.** Or
have **Mrs. Ann** analyze your handwriting.

As for amusement rides, here's a brief rundown on the piers and
the best rides. **Midway Pier:** The Katapault (great for future astronauts),
Castle Dracula and the Dungeon Boat Ride (not for those with heart
problems), the Matterhorn (a true amusement ride classic). **Hunt's
Pier:** Log Flume (wear your bathing suit), the Flyer roller coaster (good,
but the old Screem Machine was better). **Mariner's Landing:** Sea
Serpent (only for the daring and brave and don't eat before you go),
Great Wheel (a huge ferris wheel with a super view at the top), Ripley's
Believe It or Not (weird and funny things to look at).

Other boardwalk-related things to do: Teen dances ("Dancetime
U.S.A.") are held throughout the summer at the Wildwood Convention
Hall for the under-21 generation. There's no alchohol and a dress code
is enforced, and the show is often televised on cable TV a la *American
Bandstand.* For older music fans, Convention Hall frequently hosts big
name performers in concert. Melissa Manchester, Laura Branigan,
Maynard Ferguson and other pop and jazz greats play there in the
summer. Stop by the box office for a calendar of events and ticket
information.

Finally, Wildwood has a team in the fledgling, but shaky, United
States Basketball League called the Wildwood Aces. Games are played
at Convention Hall during June, July and August. For a schedule of
home games, write to Wildwood Aces, 4519 Ocean Avenue, Wildwood
08260.

Ocean Avenue and those Wildwood streets that run adjacent to it
are action-packed until late at night during the summer. Clubs such as
Martinique (Oak Avenue), the **Rainbow** (Spicer and Pacific avenues),
Sundance (Oak and New Jersey avenues), **Pier Top Lounge** (Atlantic
Avenue at the beach), **Club Cheers** (Cedar and Pacific avenues), **Club
Casba** (Spicer and Atlantic avenues), the **Playpen** (Atlantic Avenue
at Diamond Beach) and, oh, so many others make the Wildwoods *the*
place for club hopping. Some clubs have dress codes; some don't. Most
have a cover charge. All have either live entertainment or a fast spinning
disc jockey. To best decide what club or clubs to go to, and also to find
out who's playing where, what clubs have all-male revues or go-go girls,
or a wet T-shirt contest, or even a quiet table for two where couples

go to sip pina coladas and listen to soft rock and pop, consult the free,
weekly entertainment newspaper, *Shout*. It's readily available in Wildwood, Wildwood Crest and North Wildwood nightspots.

Wildwood has other things to do besides go to the beach, ride the
Sea Serpent and dance the night away. Cloudy days can be spent at
the **George Boyer Historical Museum** on the second floor of City
Hall (Montgomery and New Jersey avenues). Admission is free. It's a
decent museum as far as municipal museums go, and you'll learn quite
a bit about Wildwood's past. Open Monday through Friday, 1–3 p.m.

Diamond Beach offers pretty fair surfing when a swell is running.
And for fishermen, a number of party and charter boats make daily
trips to offshore fishing grounds from the Wildwood area. Most boats
depart at 8 a.m. and return at 4 p.m. Check what they're catching at
Otten's Harbor (Davis and Park Boulevard), the **Wildwood Yacht
Basin** (Rio Grande and Susquehana avenues), and the **Shawcrest Yacht
Basin** (Shawcrest Road).

Boaters should know that there are public boat ramps between 4th
and 6th avenues on New York Avenue, and small boats for rent at
Dad's Place (North Wildwood Boulevard) in North Wildwood and
Lake View Docks in Wildwood Crest (Rambler Road and Park
Boulevard).

WILDWOOD CREST

Wildwood Crest is the most quiet—if such a word could be used to
describe any of the Wildwoods—and certainly the most family-oriented.
It's perfectly situated at the southern end of Five Mile Beach. When
Wildwood Crest vacationers want the flash and excitement of the
boardwalk, Wildwood is mere minutes away. Yet, it's in Wildwood Crest
where one can escape all the action when one wants—or needs—to
and still enjoy the gorgeous beaches and warm summer sun.

Wildwood Crest boasts more well-kept, family-owned cottages and
summer homes, and more higher priced hotels and motels than the

---

DID YOU KNOW THAT ... WILDWOOD'S BEACHES ARE SOME
OF THE PRECIOUS FEW BEACHES ON THE EAST COAST OF THE
UNITED STATES THAT ARE *GROWING* INSTEAD OF DIMINISH-
ING? IN SOME CASES, THE SHORELINE HAS GAINED AN INCRED-
IBLE 100 FEET IN JUST ONE YEAR.

---

other two Wildwoods. It also more resembles a beach community with
regular summer residents returning each year than Wildwood, where
the average vacation is more apt to be a week rather than a month.

Another difference between Wildwood Crest and Wildwood is the
former's lakeside where one can catch splendid sunsets in late August
and early September. Sunset Lake and the park nearby often provide
a nice alternative to the ocean and beach. Here you'll find windsurfers,

water-skiers, and jet skiers enjoying the water, and picnickers and children enjoying the park.

Other beach alternatives in Wildwood Crest include a possible visit to the **Wildwood Crest Museum** on Seaview Avenue, a concert at the **Gazebo** on Rambler Road, or participation in any of a number of athletic programs or social events sponsored by the town.

Some Recommended Restaurants on the South Jersey Shore

Busch's
87th Street
Townsend's Inlet
(609) 263-8626
Price Code: Moderate
Menu: Seafood

Famous for its she-crab soup. Popular restaurant for years with many returning customers.

The Chatterbox
500 9th Avenue
Ocean City
(609) 399-0113
Price Code: Inexpensive
Menu: Beef, chops, seafood

This is where many of the year-round locals eat. Breakfast, lunch and supper, open 24 hours. Good salad bar.

Culinary Garden and Inn
841 Central Avenue
Ocean City
(609) 399-3713
Price Code: Moderate
Menu: Seafood, Italian

Fast becoming an Ocean City favorite as word gets round that there are no disappointing dishes on the menu.

Deauville Inn
Willard Road and Bay Drive
Strathmere
(609) 263-2080
Price Code: Inexpensive/Moderate
Menu: Seafood

Very good seafood sandwiches, great view of Corson's Inlet.

Dragon House
3616 Pacific Avenue
Wildwood
(609) 522-2320
Price Code: Inexpensive/Moderate
Menu: Chinese

The house specialty is Peking duck and any of its soups. Routinely rated the best Chinese restaurant on the South Jersey Shore.

Johnson's Seafood Restaurant
4601 Pacific Avenue
Wildwood
(609) 522-1976
Price Code: Moderate
Menu: Seafood

Johnson's has been a reputable Wildwood restaurant since 1946. It must be good.

Mildred's Strathmere Inn
Ocean Drive and Prescott Road
Strathmere
(609) 263-8209
Price Code: Moderate
Menu: Mostly seafood

Nicely prepared seafood dishes. Be sure to leave room for a piece of homemade cake or pie.

Neil's Steak and Oyster House
222 E. Schellenger Avenue
Wildwood
(609) 522-6060
Price Code: Moderate
Menu: Steaks and seafood

If you enjoy oysters, especially oyster chowder, Neil's is the place for you. Very good prime ribs and steaks, too.

Point Pub
Somers Point Shopping Center
Somers Point
(609) 927-1522
Price Code: Moderate
Menu: Beef, seafood

The Point Pub could very well be the best unheralded restaurant in the area. Whether you order a hamburger or a juicy steak, you won't be disappointed.

Ravioli House
102 E. Bennett Avenue
Wildwood
(609) 522-7894
Price Code: Inexpensive/Moderate
Menu: Italian

If the Ravioli House had atmosphere, it would be known state-wide for its superb pasta dishes.

Restaurant Renault Atop The Winery
Renault Winery/Bremen Avenue
Egg Harbor City

(609) 965-2111
Price Code: Expensive
Menu: Gourmet
Multicourse meals, wine-tasting, superbly prepared dishes.

Spadafora's Clam Bar
9th Street and Atlantic Avenue
Ocean City
(609) 398-6154
Price Code: Inexpensive
Menu: Seafood
Everything is good, but frittered clams is the big favorite.

Urie's Fish Fry
448 W. Rio Grande Avenue
Wildwood
(609) 522-4947
Price Code: Moderate
Menu: Seafood
One of the most popular restaurants in Wildwood with tourists.

Urie's Reef and Beef
338 W. Rio Grande Avenue
Wildwood
(609) 552-7761
Price Code: Moderate
Menu: Seafood and beef
Good prime ribs, cousin of Urie's Fish Fry.

Watson's
901 Ocean Avenue
Ocean City
(609) 399-1065
Price Code: Moderate
Menu: Standard American
A fine family restaurant. Those who summer in Ocean City year in and year out eat at Watson's.

Zaberer's
Spruce and Maryland avenues
North Wildwood
(609) 522-1423
Price Code: Moderate
Menu: Standard American
Practically a landmark in the Wildwood area; food is generally good; atmosphere borders on the zany.

South Jersey Winery Tours
Most people don't think of New Jersey when the subject of American wines is mentioned. California and New York, yes. But New Jersey? Yet New Jersey is indeed a wine producing state, and a fairly good one at

that. Most of the state's wineries are located in South Jersey and are well worth a visit. Those described below are all well within an hour's drive of most South Jersey Shore resort towns. Touring one or more of them is an excellent way to spend a day away from the beach.

Renault Winery. This is the largest and most popular of New Jersey wineries and the one that offers the most for the visitor to see and do. Located on Bremen Avenue in Egg Harbor City (look for the big Renault bottle at the intersection of Route 30 and Bremen Avenue), Renault conducts regular tours of its winery. You'll sample wines and get an up-close glimpse of the wine-making and bottling process. A good time to visit is in early fall when Renault's Annual Grape Harvest Festival takes place. A big attraction is the grape stomping contest. If you're selected to participate and win the contest, you receive the juice of the grapes you stomped bottled as a souvenir.

Also on the premises is a wine glass museum, an excellent gourmet restaurant, called the Restaurant Atop The Winery, the **Garden Cafe and Ice Cream Parlor**, and a wine and champagne shop where you can purchase spirits. Speaking of champagne, Renault is internationally noted for its champagne; 7 of the 28 varieties of wine made at Renault are champagne. Renault is also the only winery in the country that makes blueberry champagne.

For more information on the Harvest Festival, wine tours, and dinner at the **Restaurant Renault Atop The Winery**, call (609) 965-2111.

Balic Winery. Balic is a small, rather nondescript winery on Route 40 in Mays Landing. Yugoslavian-raised Savo Balic is the proprietor of the family-owned winery, which includes some 30 acres of vineyards and a wine-tasting room. It is the smallest winery in New Jersey and one of the very few wineries that still harvests all grapes by hand.

The public is permitted to tour the vineyards, but arrangements should be made beforehand as there are no regularly scheduled tours like what you'll find at Renault. Call (609) 625-2166 for details. Souvenir wine sets can be purchased in the wine tasting room. Balic sells ten different varieties of wine and champagne.

Tomasello Winery. The Tomasello Winery does not conduct regular tours of the winery and vineyards either, but Charles Tomasello will take groups through if arrangements are made in advance. The wine tasting room, however, is open daily. Those interested in the bottling process of wines should certainly make plans to tour Tomasello, since its setup and Mr. Tomasello's explanation of it is very interesting.

Like Renault, Tomasello is most known for its champagne. There's also a growing demand for its fruity grape wines. Located about halfway between Atlantic City and Camden, Tomasello's is the furthest winery from the South Jersey Shore. It's on Route 30 in Hammonton, just west of the Route 206 intersection. Tomasello Winery has an outlet and small museum at Smithville for those interested in purchasing wine, but not in driving out to the winery.

Bernard D'arcy Wine Cellars. Located in Absecon Highlands, just nine miles from Atlantic City, the Bernard D'arcy Winery was formerly known as the Gross Highland Winery. There are self-guided tours and free samples of the wine produced there. Make sure you walk through the wine cellars and take in the rich bouquet of the fermenting wines. An audiovisual show for visitors explains the complicated wine-making process. A number of their 13 wines and 6 champagnes have won national and international awards in winetasting competitions. For more information, call (609) 652-1187.

DID YOU KNOW THAT ... RENAULT WINERY IS THE OLDEST CONTINUOUSLY OPERATING WINERY IN THE UNITED STATES? IT SECURED A GOVERNMENT PERMIT TO MAKE RENAULT WINE TONIC THROUGHOUT THE 14 YEARS OF PROHIBITION, WHICH WAS SOLD IN DRUGSTORES. IT HAD AN ALCOHOLIC CONTENT OF 22 PERCENT.

9. CAPE MAY

Cape May is not the type of resort you visit just once. There's an irresistible lure, an enchanting touch, to Cape May that pulls you back to it again and again. People come, of course, in the summer. But they also come in the spring, fall and even in the dead of winter. The special warmth and charm of the town, regardless of the season, plus its live-in museum atmosphere, its tree-lined side streets, its quaint shops and eateries, its history and, ultimately, its firm dedication to the spirit and style of the Victorian Age make Cape May a special place indeed. And over the last few years, more and more people have been finding this out. Today, Cape May ranks with Atlantic City as New Jersey's most popular seaside resort.

Cape May claims that it is America's oldest seaside resort. Long Branch, up on the North Jersey Shore, say historians, has just as much a right to the title as Cape May does (see chapter 2). Yet, it's Cape May that is benefiting most from the claim to fame, because it has cultivated a continuous restoration movement and actively seeks to relive its past glories. Long Branch does no such thing, thus perhaps Cape May wins the decision by default.

Another one of Cape May's claims—that it possesses the largest concentration of authentic Victorian structures in the nation—can also be disputed by another North Jersey Shore town, Ocean Grove (see chapter 2 again). Both are literally filled with beautifully restored Victorian homes, so it really doesn't matter who has the slight numerical edge. However, it's Cape May that does more, much more, for the sake of tourists, than Ocean Grove does when it comes to marketing its Victorian gems. It centers such popular activities as Victorian Week, Victorian house tours, Victorian candlelight tours, Victorian this and Victorian that around its Victorian heritage. Cape May encourages tourism on the grandest level; Ocean Grove encourages it too, but not nearly with the enthusiasm that Cape May does. Thus, once again, Cape May wins the title by default.

A visit to Cape May is a visit to an era long gone. The Victorian Age was an age when fancy gingerbread lace adorned verandas with rocking chairs on them; when the rest of the house was painted in bright, bold colors; when flower gardens hugged white picket fences; when the soft, dreamy light of gas lamps lit up the streets each evening; when gracious ladies and gentlemen socialized in rooms filled with ornate furnishings, or strolled walkways and paths and talked of Admiral Dewey's Great White Fleet and Teddy Roosevelt and his daring

DID YOU KNOW THAT... HENRY FORD AND LOUIS CHEVROLET
STAGED AUTOMOBILE RACES ON CAPE MAY'S BEACH IN 1905?
LATER, FORD OFFERED TO BUILD THE FIRST FORD AUTOMO-
TIVE PLANT IN CAPE MAY, BUT CITY OFFICIALS TURNED HIM
DOWN.

charge up San Juan Hill. The Victorian Age seemed inundated with
niceties and a delectable romanticism that's difficult to find these days,
except, of course, in Cape May.

And that's why people enjoy Cape May so much. The town and its
year-round residents live and breathe Victoriana. But unlike other
noted historical towns like Williamsburg, Virginia, for instance, Cape
May conducts the transformation from present to past without too
much spectacle. Although one can easily spend a weekend or week
soaking up as much Victorian grandeur as possible, never is what's
offered overly contrived or artificial. Cape May holds a strong commitment to authenticity, and the town has just enough restraint not to
make it a Victorian circus.

Cape May was named for Cornelius Jacobsen Mey, a Dutch sea
captain who explored the Delaware Bay area in 1620. Gradually the
vicinity began to be settled by New England and Long Island whalers
and their families who found Cape May's closeness to whaling routes
particularly profitable. The first settlement, called Town Bank or Cape
May Town, was a whaling village. Unfortunately, the ground where
the village was established has been lost to erosion and the sea.

Whaling in Cape May flourished until the early 1700s, and those
who mastered the art of killing and beaching whales and the business
associated with whaling grew considerably wealthy. However, sightings
of whales became less and less frequent, due most, say historians, to
the indiscriminate slaughter of them. Eventually, this led many settlers
to abandon whaling and turn to farming to make a living.

Cape May's economy took on still another direction when physicians
from Philadelphia began advising their patients to spend a part of the
summer in Cape May. It was felt the salt air and water would have a
soothing, even curing effect on their ills. Word of Cape May's appeal
spread, and soon healthy Philadelphians began visiting Cape May in
the mid-1700s to escape the inland summer heat. Thus, the seeds were
sown for Cape May's real destiny, namely, that of a resort town.

It wasn't, however, until the 1800s that Cape May really began to
take the shape of a summer resort. The first hotel, the Atlantic Hotel,
soon had much competition. By the middle of the 1800s, several dozen
hotels and inns had been built to accommodate those who came to
summer in Cape May. The Mount Vernon, built in 1853, was at the
time, the largest hotel in the world. Unfortunately, it burned down
three years later. Visitors such as Abraham Lincoln, Henry Clay and
U. S. Grant signed their names in Cape May guestbooks. Later on,

notables such as P. T. Barnum, John Philip Sousa and Henry Ford would also summer in Cape May.

Cape May's progress as a grand resort was stunted by a fire, the Great Fire of 1878. The blaze practically destroyed half the town. Hotels, homes, businesses all fell to the flames. The disaster couldn't have occurred at a worse time. Up north, Long Branch was capturing the attention of the wealthy as well as famous politicians, and its gambling halls were internationally known. But to make matters worse for Cape May, Atlantic City, which was considerably closer, was quickly becoming a major resort, too. That would leave Cape May practically out of the resort picture if it didn't rebuild, and rebuild fast.

Cape May did, in fact, rebuild, and quickly regained most of her reputation as a premier summer resort. This was the Victorian Age, and many of the Victorian structures that grace Cape May's streets today were built in the 1880s and 1890s after the Great Fire. Cape May's resurrection was furthered considerably by President Benjamin Harrison who spent much of the summer of 1890 and 1891 residing in Cape May Point. He set up the Summer White House in Cape May's Congress Hall.

Cape May enjoyed its rebirth through the early part of the twentieth century. Then came the Great Depression and World War II. People don't spend much money in summer resorts in times of crisis, money that Cape May desperately needed to survive. Add to this a major problem with beach erosion coupled with angry Atlantic storms, especially the one that hit the Jersey coast in March 1962 and inflicted over a million dollars worth of damage in Cape May, and Cape May was all but forgotten by summer visitors.

It was, however, Cape May's glorious past that rescued her present and guaranteed her future. As more and more residents began restoring their Victorian homes and the town began witnessing an influx of new blood, Cape May began yet another comeback. The town received National Historic Landmark status, which fostered an aggressive campaign of continued restoration. Soon visitors were coming back to Cape May. As interest in Victoriana spread, Cape May became more and more popular. Today it is perhaps the most popular Victorian town in America.

It is imperative to plan your visit to Cape May in advance for four important reasons. Cape May is a popular resort, and unless you're coming only for the day, you'll need to make lodging reservations in advance of your stay there. In some of the more well-known bed and breakfasts like the Mainstay and Abbey, reservations six or eight months in advance is not a bad idea.

Second, there is so much to see and do in Cape May, you'll want to make the best of your time there. Sit down and decide beforehand what interests you most and make a point of doing and seeing those things first. The following lists of tours, festivals and activities will help you in your advance planning.

Third, organizations like the Cape May Chamber of Commerce and the Mid-Atlantic Center for the Arts sponsor an amazingly full range of activities, special programs, festivals, shows and concerts for the Cape May visitor. You'll want to make sure you coincide your visit to Cape May when the programs and activities you find most appealing are run. You can contact the above mentioned organizations by writing to The Chamber of Commerce of Greater Cape May, P.O. Box 109, Cape May 08204, and The Mid-Atlantic Center For The Arts, P.O. Box 164, Cape May 08204; they will gladly supply you with dates and up-to-the-minute information of current goings-on in Cape May.

And fourth, Cape May is quite a different place in the fall or spring than it is in the summer or winter. Decide what season appeals to you most. Autumn is when Victoriana reaches its zenith. In the summer, Cape May becomes a seaside resort complete with swimming, sunning, surfing and strolling the boardwalk. Then in the winter Cape May's famous Christmas parade and house tour make it a splendid place to visit during the holiday season. And finally in the spring there's the tulip festival when the entire town is brightened by the colorful flowers, and when tours of the city are less crowded.

Those who come only for the day, or at the spur of the moment, can stop at the Welcome Center on Lafayette Street for information on special events and activities. The hostess there will also assist you in finding a room, if you wish, and if none is available, suggest alternative accommodations in the area.

If you approach Cape May from Route 9 or the Garden State Parkway (as opposed to the Cape May–Lewes, Delaware Ferry), the first thing you'll notice as you pass over the Cape May Canal is not the town's wonderful Victorian architecture, but its surprisingly large harbor area and commercial fishing fleet. Cape May is a prime boating area and many pleasure craft call its marinas home. Its commercial fishing fleet is one of the largest on the East Coast. Numerous party and charter boats are available for full- or half-day fishing excursions. Thus, a Cape May vacation need not be exclusively shorebound.

Antique Shops Along Route 9
from Cape May Courthouse to Cape May

The Cape May area of Route 9 is well-known for its antique shops. Heading south on the highway enroute to Cape May where there are also a number of antique shops and a large, annual antique show at Congress Hall during Victorian Week, you'll find a number of quaint shops selling area treasures. Here's a list of the more popular ones.

Little Teacher Antiques	**Pine Tree Antiques**
Mayville	Erma
(609) 465-7552	(609) 884-3223

Mayville Art & Antiques	**House of Old**
Mayville	Erma
(609) 465-5723	(609) 884-1458

Cuckoo's Nest Antiques
Burleigh
(609) 465-7685

Find It Shop Antiques
Erma
(609) 884-8186

Chippendale Upholstery
Burleigh
(609) 465-3552

Country House Antiques
Erma
(609) 884-2381

Antique Shops in Cape May Proper

Antiques et al
1149 Lafayette Street
(609) 884-2206

Village Woodcrafter
678 Washington Street
(609) 884-4046

Travis Cove Antiques
621 Lafayette Street
(609) 884-5959

Nostalgia Shop
408 Washington Mall
(609) 884-7071

Aunt Lorey's
Physick Estate
1048 Washington Street
(609) 884-7249

Midsummer Night's Dream
668 Washington Street
(609) 884-1380

The Pink House
33 Perry Street
(609) 884-2525

Victorian Look
1159 Washington Street
(609) 884-5360

After passing Cape May harbor, you'll be on Lafayette Street, which will take you to Cape May's historic district and mall. Parking spaces are hard to come by in Cape May, especially in the summer; you should first try the municipal lots adjacent to **Washington Street Victorian Mall**, Cape May's main shopping area, before venturing onto the town's tiny side streets. Once you've found your parking space, you probably won't have to move your car again until you're ready to depart Cape May. Virtually everything in town is within walking distance, and the very best way to see Cape May is to walk through it at your own pace.

At the beginning of the mall, you'll see an information booth. Here is where nearly all the walking tours, both guided and self-guided, begin (see below). It's also here where you can take a trolley or horse and carriage tour of the town.

The Washington Street Victorian Mall contains a collection of boutiques, bookstores, cafes, candy shops, art galleries and other business establishments designed to attract the attention and pocketbook of the Cape May visitor. During Cape May's early 1970s renovation, it was decided to close this section of Washington Street to traffic and make it into a pedestrian mall. Washington Street was Cape May's original downtown shopping district; a number of the buildings there date back to the turn of the century. Most of them got an extensive facelift, and trees, shrubs and flower beds were planted next to benches, which further spruced up the area.

For those who come to Cape May to shop first and take in the sights later, **McDowell's Gallery** (526 Washington) offers a fine selection of arts and crafts and interesting gifts. **La Patisserie** (524 Washington) is a great place to get a sticky bun and fresh-baked bread. The **Pinebrook** (510 Washington) sells smartly designed Cape May T-shirts and sweatshirts as does **It's A Breeze** (319 Washington). If it's prints or posters you're looking for, try the **Washington Street Gallery** (313 Washington). Christmas ornaments can be purchased at **Elaine's** (304 Washington), and the **Baileywicke** (318 Washington) stocks hand-crafted leather items and jewelry. The **Old Shire Tavern** (315 Washington) is a good choice for lunch or an afternoon drink. It also has live jazz every night during the summer and on weekends in the winter.

During the summer, the beaches of Cape May are as popular as the Washington Street Victorian Mall and the historic sites around town. Despite their popularity, Cape May's beaches are lacking in size and sand quality. The reason is simple: erosion. In some places, like in front of the Christian Admiral Hotel, there's no beach left at all. A seawall now holds back the Atlantic Ocean.

It's no secret that as Cape May's beaches shrink, the beaches of the neighboring Wildwoods grow. Currents in the Atlantic are constantly stealing sand from Cape May and depositing it in the Wildwoods. So, for those who truly require fine bathing beaches, Wildwood is much preferred over Cape May.

Cape May's two-mile-long Beach Drive runs the length of the town's waterfront. On one side of the thoroughfare is the beach, boardwalk and seawall; on the other, restaurants, hotels, motels, guesthouses, inns and bed and breakfasts. The east section contains mostly private homes along with the huge, almost overwhelming Christian Admiral Hotel. It is the least crowded part of Beach Drive because there's little or no beach there. The midsection of Beach Drive is where much of the beach and boardwalk activity occur. Convention Hall is located here and is where many beach-related activities sponsored by the Chamber of Commerce are held. Also found here are concession stands, fudge shops and a few other shops which sell beach items like towels, umbrellas and suntan lotion. Further along, the beach gets a bit wider than it is in the Convention Hall area and is not usually congested. Near the end of Beach Drive is a view of the Cape May Point Lighthouse and Cape May Point State Park.

In between Beach Drive and Washington Street is the bulk of Cape May's Victorian homes and guesthouses. It's here that you'll see the fairy-talelike gingerbread houses painted in the most cheerful of colors and draped with bargeboard and wooden lace. You'll see cupolas and captain's walks, fretwork and featherboarding, magnificent porches and beautiful stained-glass windows that come alive the moment the sun shines on them. Add to this the pretty gardens and meticulously maintained lawns and shrubbery, all on shady, quiet streets. If, somehow, the cars parked there could suddenly disappear, you'd swear the year was 1895.

Walk past the **Mainstay Inn** (635 Columbia Avenue) and the **Abbey** (Columbia and Gurney streets), two of the most exquisite Victorian mansions turned bed and breakfasts in America. Both have been photographed and written up in the world's best travel magazines. In the late nineteenth century the Mainstay was a men's gambling house. Known as Jackson's Clubhouse, it has been painstakingly restored and now is the pride of Cape May's bed and breakfasts (see below for information on tours of the Mainstay and other inns). The **Abbey**, located across the street from the Mainstay, is a Gothic revival structure, originally owned by John B. McCreary, a rich businessman who made his money in coal. Built in 1869, it retains much of its original splendor, both inside and out.

Nearby, the **Balt House** (26 Gurney Street) is one of eight identical cottages designed by the noted local architect, Stephen D. Button, in 1871. The **Dr. Henry L. Hunt House** (209 Congress Place) was built in 1881 and possesses a wide range of Victorian designs and architectural styles and is really one of the more unusual homes in Cape May. It has a mansard roof, a beautiful balcony, Gothic gables and an assortment of fancy details that some might think a bit too much. But during the Victorian era there was no such thing as "too much" when it came to architectural decoration.

Finally, one should also walk past **Congress Hall** (Beach and Congress streets). A most prestigious hotel during the Victorian years, American presidents, foreign dignitaries and celebrities of all types stayed in rooms here. And, as already mentioned, President Benjamin Harrison used it as his summer White House. The **Chalfonte Hotel** (307 Howard Street) is also a grand old hotel. Built in 1876, it was one of the few large structures in Cape May to escape the flames of the Great Fire of 1878. It is the oldest hotel in Cape May.

Virtually all of the houses on Hughes Street are interesting. Most people who visit Cape May consider it the prettiest street in the town. The **Hall House** (645 Hughes Street) and the **Manor House** (612 Hughes Street) are especially attractive. The former was built in 1868, another structure to survive the Great Fire; the latter was built in 1906 and is presently a bed and breakfast inn.

There are many more houses to see in Cape May, some of which are open to the public during specially scheduled tours. It is recommended that you take at least one of these. The guides are quite knowledgeable, and the anecdotes and background history they provide will make your visit to Cape May that much more rewarding.

Cape May's Bed and Breakfasts

Although Cape May boasts many fine hotels and guesthouses, the town is quite known for its bed and breakfasts. Cape May has far more of these alternative lodgings than anywhere else on the Jersey Shore, and almost all of them will provide the visitor with a truly memorable stay.

Cape May bed and breakfasts are meticulously restored Victorian mansions that have been decorated with Victorian furniture and graced with a Victorian hospitality. They offer all the comforts of home—a cozy fireplace, a library, snacks and small talk in the parlor—with the exception of a private bathroom, although many now offer rooms with private baths at an increased rate.

Breakfasts vary. You're not apt to run into many bacon and egg dishes; the Continental tradition of Danish and beverages is much more common. However, more and more bed and breakfasts are offering gourmet breakfasts. You might be served, for instance, an unusually appetizing egg soufflé, fruit-filled crepes smothered with cream, home-made waffles and jams, or quiche.

Since the Cape May bed and breakfast experience is so popular, it is highly recommended that you make your reservations well in advance of your visit. Rates are not included because they vary with the season and often change without notice. Expect to pay, however, somewhere in the neighborhood of $65 a night during the peak summer and fall months.

The Abbey
Columbia Avenue and Gurney Street
Cape May 08204
(609) 884-4506
Victorian opulence and splendor in a setting that makes this one of Cape May's most popular bed and breakfasts. Three- to four-night minimum stays are required between June 15 and September 30. Rooms with private baths are available. Open April through November.

Abigail Adams
12 Jackson Street
Cape May 08204
(609) 884-1371
Very close to beach, three of the six guest rooms face the ocean. Open April through November. Rates include breakfast, afternoon tea, beach badges and free parking.

Albert G. Stevens Inn
127 Myrtle Avenue
Cape May 08204
(609) 884-4717
Beautiful wrap-around veranda complete with white wicker furniture. Three of five guest rooms have private baths. Two-night minimum on weekends. Open year-round.

Barnard-Good House
238 Perry Street
Cape May 08204
(609) 884-5381
Sumptuous breakfast, so good and filling, you won't have to eat lunch. Nan Hawkins is a vivacious, charming hostess. Bicycles are available for guests' use. Open April through November.

Brass Bed
719 Columbia Avenue
Cape May 08204
(609) 884-8075
A classic Gothic Victorian mansion, nicely decorated with antique furnishings. Open all year. Weekly and off-season discounts available.

Captain Mey's Inn
202 Ocean Street
Cape May 08204
(609) 884-7793
Named after Cape May's founder. Located a mere half block from the Washington Street Victorian Mall. Open all year. Beautifully decorated. Good, hearty breakfasts.

Duke of Windsor
817 Washington Street
Cape May 08204
(609) 884-1355
Centrally located, large, airy rooms. Bicycles are provided for guests' use. The 45-foot Queen Anne Tower makes the Duke of Windsor an easy landmark. Open year-round.

Gingerbread House
28 Gurney Street
Cape May 08204
(609) 884-0211
Built in 1869, the Gingerbread House survived the Great Fire of 1878. Many impressive Victorian antiques found throughout the house. Continental breakfast.

Mainstay
635 Columbia Avenue
Cape May 08204
(609) 884-8690
A real gem of a bed and breakfast. Extremely popular, reservations are recommended well in advance. Lavishly restored, museum quality antiques. Innkeepers Tom and Sue Carroll are friendly and are experts in Victoriana. Open April through October.

Manor House
612 Hughes Street
Cape May 08204
(609) 884-4710
Located on the nicest street in all Cape May. Excellent breakfast, impressively decorated. Open year-round.

Manse House
510 Hughes Street
Cape May 08204
(609) 884-0116
Another one that is situated on beautiful Hughes Street. Comfortable, warm atmosphere accented by twin fireplaces. Full breakfast served. Open March through December.

Queen Victoria
102 Ocean Street

Cape May 08204
(609) 884-8702
Queen Victoria rates with Abbey and Mainstay as top-notch. A good
time to visit is during Christmas season. There's tree decoration,
carolling, Dickens read by the fireplace. Full country breakfast. Minimum stay of two nights required on weekdays; three or four on holidays,
during the summer, and for rooms with private bath. Open
year-round.

Tours of Cape May

Virtually all of the tours, activities and special events in Cape May
are conducted by one of three groups: the Mid-Atlantic Center for
the Arts (MAC), the Cape May Chamber of Commerce, or the city
of Cape May. Two free publications—*Victorian Cape May*, published
by the Chamber of Commerce, and *This Week in Cape May*, published
by MAC—list the various activities and goings-on in Cape May. *This
Week in Cape May* is particularly useful because it is published weekly
during the summer in addition to three fall issues, a winter issue and
two spring issues. It lists the times and places for all events in Cape
May in the week or season in question and is readily available throughout town.

Trolley Tours. Run by MAC, these half-hour guided tours are
intended to give a basic overview of Cape May's history and architectural importance. Tours begin in the spring and fall on Ocean Street,
across from the information booth at the Washington Street Victorian
Mall, and during the summer at the Trolley Station on Beach Drive
and Gurney Street. The tours run many times throughout the day
during these three seasons. Choose from three different trolley tours.
One takes in the east end of town, the second does the west end and
the third deals with Beach Drive and the oceanfront. In the winter,
tours combining all three areas are conducted, but on a less frequent
basis. They originate from the Emlen Physick Estate (1048 Washington
Street). Contact MAC for tour schedule.

Walking Tours. The trolley tours are sufficient for those strapped
for time, visiting Cape May only for the day or unable to walk any
distance. Far more comprehensive are the walking tours, also sponsored
by MAC, which usually last for 90 minutes. They also begin in front
of the information booth and take in sections of both east and west
ends of town. Much more of an emphasis is put on architectural detail
as well as spicy gossip concerning the people who once lived in the
houses pointed out on the tour. Offered daily during the summer and
on weekends the rest of the year.

Horse and Carriage Tours. Privately run by the Cape May Carriage
Company, this tour combines parts of all three trolley tours. You ride
in a horse-drawn carriage, which is much more romantic and personal
than a trolley. It too is a half-hour long and begins across the street
opposite the information booth at the Washington Street Victorian
Mall.

Mansions By Gaslight Tour. Beginning at the **Emlen Physick Estate**, home of the Mid-Atlantic Arts Center, this once-a-week tour (Wednesday evenings in the summer; weekend evenings in the spring, fall and holiday season) includes interior tours of the Emlen Physick House, Cape May's most noted Victorian gem; the **Mainstay** and **Abbey**; and the **Wilbraham Mansion**, which contains some of the finest Victorian furnishings in Cape May. Visitors are shuttled via bus from one mansion to the next. Since this is a popular tour, one should get tickets at the Emlen Physick Estate as early as possible. Call MAC at (609) 884-5404 for more information.

Cottages At Twilight Tour. Similar in focus to the Mansions By Gaslight Tour, this one includes interior visits to the **Dr. Henry L. Hunt House**, the **Joseph Q. Williams House**, the **Joseph Hall House, the White Dove Cottage**, and the **Windward House.** The Windward House is quite interesting with its fabulous stained and beveled leaded glass and fine examples of Victorian clothing. Tickets may be purchased at the Dr. Henry L. Hunt House, 209 Congress Place. Sponsored by MAC. Note: Other homes are occasionally substituted for the above mentioned.

Christmas Candlelight Tour. The Christmas Candlelight Tour is a popular holiday tour of a dozen Cape May houses and two or three churches, all of which have been handsomely decorated for Christmas. It is a rather long tour; it often runs four hours. A trolley is used to shuttle people from house to house. Order your tickets well in advance from MAC. The tour is usually conducted the Saturday after Christmas.

Christmas Lights Trolley Tour. Many of the same houses are covered on this tour as on the Candlelight Tour except here, visitors get to see only the exterior of the houses. Sponsored by MAC.

Physick Estate Tours. Built by the renowned architect, Frank Furness, for Dr. Emlen Physick, the 16-room mansion is the main focus of the tour. The estate is located at 1048 Washington Street, six blocks from the mall. You'll marvel at the elegant natural wood paneling, Furness-designed mantle pieces, luxurious furnishings and much more. Behind the mansion is the estate's **Carriage House.** Open year-round, it is the home of the Cape May County Art League and contains an art gallery and museum. The work of Cape May County artists is exhibited, and during monthly wine and cheese receptions, the public can meet the artists whose work is on exhibit. The Art League also sponsors a county-wide house tour of its own the last weekend in June, plus a boardwalk art show, lectures, art classes and other special programs. For further information, write to the Cape May County Art League, P.O. Box 596, 1050 Washington Street, Cape May 08204, or call (609) 884-8628.

Children's Tours of the Physick Estate and Trolley Tours. During the summer, tours of the Physick Estate are held for children between the ages of 6 and 12. The guides are usually retired schoolteachers.

Trolley tours of Cape May are also conducted for children; contact the MAC for time and departure information.

Romantic Moonlight Trolley Ride. This is more of a drive than a tour. Couples take the trolley ride and absorb the evening's ambiance as the trolley winds its way slowly through Cape May's gas-lighted streets. Sponsored by MAC; contact its office for details.

Cape May Festivals

The **Cape May Tulip Festival** occurs each spring on the last weekend in April; it's a carnival of color as more than 50,000 tulip bulbs are planted to celebrate Cape May's Dutch heritage. The two-day fest includes special MAC–sponsored Tulip Garden trolley tours, Dutch folkdancing and food, garden walks, and a juried crafts show held in historic Congress Hall that attracts some seventy master craftsmen.

Each Memorial Day weekend MAC sponsors two notable events: the annual **Quilt and Decoy Show and Sale**, held on Saturday and Sunday in Cape May's Convention Hall, and an **Historic House Tour.** During this tour, ten Victorian homes are opened to the public. Victoriana buffs should consider this tour a must.

The **Victorian Fair** is usually held on the third Saturday in June on the Emlen Physick Estate. Everything from antique handicraft items to doll's clothing and glassware is sold at the fair. To keep the children occupied while mom and dad shop, Victorian games and contests are held throughout the day and include a dunking booth, bean-bag toss and hoop rollings.

During the summer MAC sponsors a **Vintage Film Festival.** The films shown are Hollywood classics such as *The Jolson Story, State Fair, A Star is Born* and *Cheaper By The Dozen.* Movies are shown once a week in the auditorium of the Victorian Towers (Washington and Ocean streets). Contact MAC for this year's selection of films and the dates when they'll be shown.

One can also take in a professionally produced play offered by the Mid Atlantic Stage. Produced outdoors behind the Emlen Physick Mansion, the theater company stages three productions in revolving repertory (usually musicals, murder mysteries and Victorian period pieces). Contact MAC for this year's schedule and information on purchasing tickets.

On the second weekend in June, the **Cape May Seafood Festival** is highlighted by a fabulous seafood smorgasbord and the Blessing of the Fleet.

September is the month when **Founder's Day** is held. Concerts, a five-mile road race and an arts and crafts show help celebrate the discovery of Cape May by Captain Mey and its eventual settlement by New England whalers.

The biggest festival, **Victorian Week,** occurs in October. Here's a sampling of what one can expect: guided tours of private homes, square

DID YOU KNOW THAT ... CAPE MAY IS KNOWN AS A "LOST COLONY" OF *MAYFLOWER* DESCENDANTS? GENEALOGISTS BELIEVE THERE ARE AS MANY *MAYFLOWER* DESCENDANTS RESIDING IN AND AROUND CAPE MAY TODAY AS THERE ARE IN PLYMOUTH, MASSACHUSETTS, THE PLACE WHERE THE *MAYFLOWER* SETTLERS STARTED THEIR FIRST COLONY IN AMERICA.

dancing contests, antique and crafts shows, Victorian vaudeville, stained glass tours, walking and trolley tours, and a restoration workshop in which Victorian house restoration experts lead seminars and discussion groups on such themes as "A Victorian Parlor," "Victorian Furnishings," and "Victorian Lighting Devices and Wallcoverings."

In December, there's **Christmas in Cape May**. It's impossible not to get in the holiday spirit as Cape May is decorated with lavish Christmas displays. Carollers stroll the streets, Old Saint Nick visits with the kids, candlelight walks and tours are conducted nightly, merchants and innkeepers have open houses. There's even an annual Christmas Ball.

Things to Do in Cape May and Cape May Area

Go Deep-sea Fishing. Several charter and party boats make daily trips out onto the ocean and Delaware Bay for bluefish, tuna and flounder. Cape May waters are also a good place to fish for weakfish and drumfish. Also, there are good opportunities for white marlin. The **Miss Chriss Fishing Center** is the home port for *Little Chris, Christine, Nada Jane,* and *Bet Bill.* The *Miss Chriss II* specializes in jumbo Cape May weakfish. The *Delta Lady,* an authentic oyster schooner, offers three-hour and full-day sailing cruises for those not interested in fishing. Over at the South Jersey Fishing Center, the *Fiesta* makes nightly runs in search of blues.

Take a Bicycle Tour of Cape May. There are no guided bike tours of Cape May. At least not yet, anyway. But bicycling through the streets of town at your own pace is a wonderful way to spend an afternoon. You can cover more ground than you can walking, and you're not confined to a trolley; you can also stop when and for how long you please. Once you've ridden through the town's Victorian district, bike down to **Cape May Point State Park**. Simply take Lafayette Street to Sunset Boulevard and watch for signs to the lighthouse. The distance is not more than six miles round trip. The grade is flat and the scenery is that of the **Cape May Bird Sanctuary**. Bicycle riders with more ambition should then ride to **Higbee Beach** through picturesque farmland and Cape May countryside. Get back on Sunset Boulevard, make a left onto Bayshore Road, and then a left onto New England Road, and follow it to the end.

You can rent bikes from **Buckingham Bikes** (1111 Beach Drive), **La Mer Bicycle Rentals** (Beach Drive and Pittsburgh Avenue), and

Village Bicycle Shop (Victorian Village Plaza). All three shops are seasonal, however. All open early in the morning, so you can get a full day's worth of bicycle touring in if you want to. Serious bicyclists should consider riding their own bikes.

Visit the U.S. Coast Guard Training Center. If you ride to the north end of Beach Drive, turn left onto Pittsburgh Avenue, where you'll find the entrance to the U.S. Coast Guard Training Center. It is here where fresh recruits come to complete an eight-week training session. After graduation, sailors are then assigned to various Coast Guard units around the globe. The public is invited to attend recruit graduation parades every Friday morning on Parade Field. Advance permission, however, is necessary to visit the base. Call (609) 884-8451, extension 206, for more information.

Go Horseback Riding. Saddle horses for hire are available at the **Hidden Valley Ranch** (4070 Bayshore Road, (609) 884-8205). The ranch specializes in family trail rides. Hayrides are also available. A good time to ride is in the morning when a 1½-hour Breakfast Ride to Delaware Bay culminates with pancakes, eggs, sausage and coffee. Reservations necessary.

Take a Ferry Ride. The Cape May–Lewes, Delaware Ferry cuts across the entrance to the Delaware Bay. There's not much to see enroute except whitecaps and blue water; nor is there anything of significance in Lewes. Why go? To relax, soak up the sun, and simply enjoy the boat ride. The trip is approximately 70 minutes long and is usually a smooth voyage. There are four ferries in the fleet. They leave from the Cape May Terminal at the end of Ferry Road. The service is seven days a week, but the times and the number of runs differ from season to season. Call (609) 886-2718 for details.

Visit the Cape May County Museum. You'll find no better museum in the Cape May area than the Cape May County Museum on Route 9 in Cape May Courthouse. Run by the Cape May County Historical and Genealogical Society, the **John Holmes House** was built prior to the Revolutionary War and is the museum complex's main attraction. Guides take you through the rooms of the house where there are collections of fine china, furniture and excellent examples of eighteenth- and nineteenth-century household items. The eighteenth-century antiques are especially interesting as is the display in the basement of the Holmes House, which includes guns, swords and uniforms, plus the flag off the Civil War ironclad, the *Merrimac*.

Outside in the barn, you'll find maritime artifacts, whaling implements and shipbuilding tools from Cape May's golden era of shipbuilding, plus Indian weapons and arrowheads and a lens from the Cape May Point Lighthouse. The museum also sponsors a lecture series and special theme open-houses. If you live in Cape May County, you might even want to spend time in the museum's library where you can trace your family tree. Many in the county have done so and have found out that their ancestors came to this country aboard the *Mayflower*.

The museum is open April to December 10 a.m.–4 p.m. Tuesdays through Saturdays. Small admission fee.

Take the Kids to the Cape May County Park and Zoo. Up the road on Route 9, north of the Cape May County Museum, is the Cape May County Park and Zoo. The park is good size—150 acres—and contains a variety of things to do. Hiking, biking, picnicking and jogging are popular activities. So is shuffleboard, badminton, horseshoes and softball, and the facilities for these are well-maintained. Wedding ceremonies are often held at the Gazebo, and kids are permitted to fish in the pond there. But the biggest attraction is the zoo. It's a small one, but it has monkeys, deer, raccoon, Arctic fox, pheasant, turkeys and a lion. Great for children and free. Open year-round. For more information call (609) 464-5271.

Spend an Afternoon at Leaming's Run Botanical Gardens. Those seeking respite from the bustling activity of Cape May, with its many tours, busy streets and rich Victoriana, will find Leaming's Run Botanical Gardens a sheer delight. Carved out of a lower reach of the Pine Barrens, the Gardens consists of 25 separate gardens, each immaculately kept and cared for by the Aprill family.

All the gardens have themes. The Bridal Garden, for instance, has white flowers against a backdrop of green. The Yellow Garden consists of some 50 varieties of domestic and wild yellow flowers. The Blue Garden is noted for its morning glories. The Houseplant Garden is filled with only houseplants, all of which require special attention. There are also lawns, ferneries and lily ponds in the Gardens.

Those familiar with botanical gardens and standard English gardens will find Leaming's Run quite different simply because it's not manicured "prim and proper." Aprill calls Leaming's Run an "American garden," meaning "it's a place to be in and enjoy and feel a part of, rather than to merely walk through and look." Unlike most botanical gardens, which bloom in spring, Leaming's Run is a summer garden. That means if you visit in the height of summer, you'll be sure to see a dizzying display of colorful flowers.

Leaming's Run is also considered an important hummingbird center on the East Coast. When you come to the garden's Gazebo, sit quietly and look around you. In five minutes or so, you're quite certain to see your share of these remarkably tiny birds feeding on the flowers nearby.

In the middle of the gardens is a re-creation of an old South Jersey farm from the time when Thomas Leaming first settled the area in the late 1600s. The main cabin was constructed from logs cut from the pasture area. There's also an herb and kitchen garden to see. At the end of the main path in the gardens is the Cooperage, a barn built in 1730 that has been transformed into a gift shop. Inside, you'll find all sorts of dried flowers hanging from the rafters as well as baskets and candles for sale. The barn was used by Christopher Leaming, a prominent South Jersey whaler in the 1700s, to make barrels for whale oil. The white house next door is where the Aprill family resides. It was

Christopher Leaming's house and is the oldest whaler's house in Cape May County.

The 30 acres that comprise Leaming's Run are open daily from May through October, weather permitting. The best time to visit the Gardens is in the first week of October, says Jack Aprill. Admission is charged, but once you're in the gardens, you can stay as long as you like. Leaming's Run is located on the west side of Route 9 in Swainton. For more information, call (609) 465-5871.

Visit Cold Spring Village. Cold Spring Village is a re-creation of a nineteenth-century South Jersey farm village made up of old buildings from Cape May County that were originally earmarked for destruction. Instead, they were moved to Cold Spring Village and have been turned into minimuseums, shops and places where craftspeople perform traditional trades (candlemaking, spinning, weaving).

Presently there are 15 buildings to visit with more slated to be moved to Cold Spring Village and restored in the near future. You can visit the Spicer-Leaming House, for example, a structure thought to be the second oldest house in Cape May County, and which is now an antique shop; two old railroad stations, one from the nearby town of Rio Grande, and the other from Woodbine; the old Cape May Point jailhouse; and the Heislerville schoolhouse, among others. In all of these are crafts, food and souvenirs for sale, the profits of which help in restoration and upkeep.

Cold Spring Village sponsors a full slate of activities throughout the summer. Antique shows, fife and drums parades, square dancing competition, antique auto shows, and banjo and fiddle concerts highlight the Cold Spring Village calendar. Call (609) 884-1811 for this year's schedule of events. There is a one-time admission charge to the village. Save your pass and you'll be admitted free for the rest of the season. Cold Spring Village is located just outside the town of Cape May on Seashore Road.

Spend the Day at Cape May Point State Park. Cape May Point State Park is well-known for its outstanding bird-watching and its picturesque lighthouse. It's located about two miles southwest of Cape May proper and sits adjacent to the Cape May Migratory Bird Refuge. Before the area became a state park, it was part of the U.S. Coastal Defense network, and during World War II, a huge concrete bunker and gun stood guarding the entrance to Delaware Bay. Today, if you walk along the beach, preferably at low tide, you can view and even climb on the remains of the bunker and gun emplacement. Built in 1942, the bunker was 900 feet from the water's edge. Today it's in the water, a victim of Cape May's erosion problem.

DID YOU KNOW THAT . . . BOTTLE-NOSED DOLPHINS CALVE IN LOWER DELAWARE BAY DURING JUNE EACH YEAR AND CAN BE SEEN FROM THE SHORES OF CAPE MAY POINT STATE PARK?

Most people have been somewhat disappointed to find out they can't climb or enter the Cape May Point Lighthouse. Things are about to change, however. The lighthouse has been leased recently to MAC, which plans to open a ground floor museum and permit visitors to climb the lighthouse tower in the near future. The lighthouse isn't the original, which was built in 1823. That's long gone; so is a second lighthouse, which remained in serivce until 1859 when the present lighthouse was built.

Lighthouse buffs might be disappointed, but bird-watchers are downright thrilled with what they see through their binoculars at Cape May Point State Park. The area is one of the more popular bird-watching sites in South Jersey, because it, like so many other Shore sites, is located on the Atlantic Flyway. Both spring and fall are good times to view birds, although veteran bird-watchers say the best time to view birds of prey, such as hawks, is September and October. Regular hawk sightings occur at the Cape May Point Hawkwatch Observation Deck in the park. You'll also see shorebirds and songbirds, peregrine and other falcons, bald and golden eagles, and meet members of the New Jersey Aubudon Society who come to the park to conduct their annual hawk count.

Before you begin your day of bird-watching, stop first at the Visitor's Center where you can pick up pamphlets pertaining to the birds you might see and the general ecology of the area. Also, you can pick up trail guides so you can spend part of your day hiking over the more than three miles of trails and boardwalks through the Natural Area. Here you'll find photography blinds and more bird-watching platforms. Do stay on the trails, though. The area is well stocked with poison ivy. A half-mile-long nature trail has been built exclusively for use by the handicapped.

Cape May Point State Park doesn't have lifeguarded beaches, but visitors are permitted to swim at their own risk. Fast moving currents can, however, make swimming somewhat dangerous, so be careful, use common sense, and don't venture out too far if you decide to go into the water. If you want a beach-oriented activity, try fishing. Surf fishing is permitted in the park, and weakfish, blues and flounder are common catches.

Visit Cape May Point. The quiet, cozy town of Cape May Point is often ignored by visitors to Cape May, even though they must pass through it to get to Cape May Point State Park. It is a small town; in the winter its population barely rises above 200, and in the summer it goes to 2000. There are no hotels or tourist facilities, just summer bungalows and cottages that are rented out by the month or season. But that shouldn't prevent a visitor to Cape May from spending a couple of hours in the town and taking in some of its charm and history.

Along with Avalon and Stone Harbor, Cape May Point's beaches rank with the prettiest of the South Jersey Shore, due mainly to the preservation of the sand dunes there, and their clean, scrubbed sand. But like its neighbor, Cape May, Cape May Point is suffering badly from erosion as any local will sadly point out. If you walk along Cape May Point's beaches and head northeast, you'll cross into Cape May Point State Park. You'll also pass a large hotellike structure just behind the dunes. That's St. Peter's-by-the-Sea, an old religious retreat. If you walk in the opposite direction, you'll come to Higbee Beach Wildlife Management Area. But before you do, at the end of Sunset Boulevard you'll see what looks like a concrete bunker lying some 200 yards offshore. Actually, it's the hull of a concrete ship called the *Atlantus*. In World War I, the United States government commissioned the experimental construction of concrete ships due to a serious shortage of steel. The *Atlantus* was a 3000-ton freighter built in 1918 and, for a year, was used as a coal steamer. But it was obvious that concrete ships were not the ships of the future. The incredible bulkiness and excessive weight made for very difficult handling in both harbors and the open sea. Decommissioned after the war, the *Atlantus* and two other concrete vessels were purchased by a private company, which planned to use them as ferry docking facilities for a Delaware Bay ferry service. However, during a storm in 1926, the *Atlantus* broke free and went aground off Sunset Boulevard where you see it today. Due to the weight of the ship and the shallow water where it came to rest, salvage efforts were discouraged. Today the ship is a state historic site.

Sunset Boulevard is important for yet another reason. It is the only place left where one can find "Cape May Diamonds," clear, nearly pure quartz crystals that resemble expensive diamonds. The main source of the quartz is the upper part of the Delaware River where the water breaks up the quartz into pebbles. The swift current then takes them down the river to its mouth—the Delaware Bay—a journey which, say some scientists, takes thousands of years. Because of the strong tides in the bay and the positioning of the *Atlantus* offshore, the quartz crystals come ashore today only at Sunset Beach. Before the *Atlantus* went aground, however, they could be found all along Higbee Beach. In fact, Higbee Beach was once known as Diamond Beach.

DID YOU KNOW THAT . . . THE LARGEST CAPE MAY DIAMOND EVER FOUND AT CAPE MAY WAS NEARLY THE SIZE OF A HEN'S EGG AND WEIGHED ALMOST EIGHT OUNCES?

When the quartz crystals are polished, they assume a regal appearance. Gift shops at the edge of Sunset Boulevard sell polished Cape May Diamonds. You can find your own diamonds, though, in the sand in front of the *Atlantus*. Of course, you'll have to polish them for them to resemble diamonds. The best time to search for the quartz crystals is just after a storm. Beachcombers also find, on occasion, Indian arrowheads and fossils.

Visit the Higbee Beach Wildlife Management Area. Higbee Beach is a rich, mostly secluded 600-acre expanse of holly and scrub oak forest, sand dunes blanketed with beachgrass, beach, meadows and ponds. Although it may seem to be facing the ocean, Higbee Beach actually borders Delaware Bay. Higbee Beach is a limited resource area because it's an important stopover for migrating birds, including many endangered species of raptors such as the bald eagle and peregrine falcon.

Nonetheless, Higbee Beach offers a number of things to do to make a visit worthwhile. The sand dunes offer protection from the wind and the area gets a terrific afternoon sun. Thus, Higbee Beach is one of the best places to begin work on an early summer tan. If you walk the beach in early summer, you'll find hundreds of horseshoe crabs on the beach where they deposit their eggs. There's also good fishing at Higbee Beach. Four wheel drive permits are available to fishermen who wish to bring their vehicles on the beach.

As one might expect, Higbee Beach is a good place to bird-watch, especially in the fall. Two of Higbee Beach's southwestern fields have observation blinds. Some birdwatchers actually prefer Higbee Beach over Cape May Point State Park since the former is usually much less crowded.

Higbee Beach also allows hunting; actually, it's one of the best places on the East Coast to hunt woodcock. The Higbee hunting season, however, begins in November due to the area's importance as a rest stop for migrating birds. Hunting licenses are mandatory and can be obtained after passing a hunter's safety course at most New Jersey sporting goods shops. You're also allowed to go horseback riding in the Higbee Beach preserve. You'll need a permit for this activity. You can get an annual permit at the Higbee Beach Field House on the main road as you approach the access to the beach. Expect to pay about $15 for it.

Beach plum preserves spread across a piece of homemade bread is a true Shore treat. The preserves are easy to make and Higbee Beach is *the* place on the South Jersey Shore to pick beach plums. Bring baskets to put the plums in—and bring helpers. Beach plums are tiny, and you need many of them to make a worthwhile batch of preserves.

Two things you can't do at Higbee Beach are go swimming and sunbathe in the nude. The water is shallow, rocky and dangerous, and there are no lifeguards. As for nudity on Higbee Beach, people do sunbathe in the buff, but if they're spotted by a ranger, they're given a summons and can be arrested.

Some Recommended Cape May Restaurants
A & J's Blue Claw
Ocean Drive
(609) 884-5878
Price Code: Moderate
Menu: Seafood

A & J has a retail fish store next to the restaurant. That means you can count on very fresh fish. Try the drumfish, a local specialty.

Alexander's
653 Washington Street
(609) 884-2555
Price Code: Expensive
Menu: A little bit of everything

Great Cape May atmosphere; Alexander's is a restored Victorian mansion where the Sunday brunches are superb and widely known.

Bayberry Inn
Perry Street and Congress Place
(609) 884-8406
Price Code: Moderate
Menu: International

The spicy Hot Thai Chicken Wings in the honey sauce is mouth-watering.

Chalfonte Hotel
307 Howard Street
(609) 884-8409
Price Code: Moderate
Menu: Southern cuisine

If you enjoy Southern cooking, you'll love the Chalfonte. Skip the Southern fried chicken, though, for something more adventurous. Check out the Chalfonte's Candlelight Concert Series, which includes a dinner/concert combination.

Filling Station
Lafayette Street
(609) 884-2111
Price Code: Inexpensive
Menu: American

A good place to bring the kids. Large portions, though little atmosphere. Play "Beat the Clock" and pay as little as $4.30 for your meal.

Louisa's Cafe
104 Jackson Street
(609) 884-5882
Price Code: Inexpensive/Moderate
Menu: Original

Small, crowded cafe, but truly excellent food. One of Cape May's best eateries.

Lobster House
Cape May Harbor
(609) 884-8296
Price Code: Moderate
Menu: Seafood

Seaport setting, traditional seafood dishes. Have a drink on the schooner, *American*, before you eat.

Mad Batter
19 Jackson Street
(609) 884-5970
Price Code: Moderate
Menu: Original

Ranks with Louisa's as Cape May's finest. The Mad Batter menu dares to be different. Everything is excellent. Go for a Cajun or Creole dish if you're in the mood to be adventurous.

Maureen
Beach and Decatur streets
(609) 884-3774
Price Code: Moderate
Menu: Mostly seafood

Eat here and you're bound to return. Regulars say the appetizers are better than the entrees, which is saying something. You be the judge.

Peaches Cafe
Perry and Jackson streets
(609) 884-0202
Price Code: Moderate
Menu: Mostly seafood

A good place to eat lunch, although dinner is also served. Seafood lasagne is a very good choice.

Swallows
400 Broadway
(609) 884-0400
Price Code: Moderate
Menu: Steaks and seafood

Like Alexander's, the Swallows is in a restored Victorian mansion. Romantic atmosphere. Most patrons rave about the desserts.

Top of the Marq
501 Beach Drive
(609) 884-3431
Price Code: Expensive
Menu: Traditional

Located in the Marquis de Lafayette Inn (sixth floor). Filet mignon highlights the menu.

Washington Inn
801 Washington Street
(609) 884-5697
Price Code: Moderate
Menu: Traditional

The Inn is an 1856 plantation house. Good atmosphere, good food. Quite popular as indeed it should be.

Watson's Merion Inn
106 Decatur Avenue
(609) 884-8363
Price Code: Moderate
Menu: Mostly seafood
Been in business since 1885. Go with the stuffed lobster.

Bed & Breakfast Books From The East Woods Press

Quantity	Title	Each	Total
	THE NEW ENGLAND BED & BREAKFAST BOOK, Ross Guide to the finest B & B lodgings in Maine, Connecticut, Massachusetts, New Hampshire, Rhode Island and Vermont.	$8.95	
	THE MID-ATLANTIC BED & BREAKFAST BOOK, Ross Guide to the finest B & B lodgings in New York, Pennsylvania, New Jersey, Delaware, Maryland and West Virginia.	$8.95	
	THE SOUTHERN BED & BREAKFAST BOOK, Ross Guide to the finest B & B lodgings in Alabama, Florida, Georgia, Louisiana, Mississippi, North Carolina, South Carolina, Tennessee, Virginia and the District of Columbia.	$8.95	
	THE CALIFORNIA BED & BREAKFAST BOOK, Strong Sample the diversity of this great state in this comprehensive guide to its varied and delightful B & B accommodations. More than 350 listings!	$8.95	
	THE CARIBBEAN BED & BREAKFAST BOOK, Strong Visits more than 150 charming B & B establishments and includes much information on traveling to these beautiful islands.	$9.95	
	THE BEST BED & BREAKFAST IN THE WORLD, UNITED KINGDOM, 1986-87, Welles & Darbey A fascinating collection of more than 800 lodgings with a special section on B & B in London.		

Prices subject to change.

Subtotal		
Shipping		
Total Enclosed		

Send order to:
THE EAST WOODS PRESS
429 East Boulevard
Charlotte, NC 28203

ALLOW 4 TO 6 WEEKS FOR DELIVERY

Please send my order to:

Name _____

Street _____

City _____ State _____ Zip _____

My check for **$**_____ is enclosed. Or charge my MasterCard or Visa

☐ Please send me your   Account No. _____

   Free book catalog.   Expiration Date _____

For charge orders only, call our toll-free number: (800) 438-1242, ext. 102. In North Carolina (800) 532-0476. We will refund your money, excluding shipping costs, if you are dissatisfied for any reason.

East Woods Press Books

Order from:
The East Woods Press
429 East Boulevard
Charlotte, N.C. 28203